Sing a New Song

Sing a New Song

Recovering Psalm Singing
for the Twenty-First Century

edited by
Joel R. Beeke
and
Anthony T. Selvaggio

Reformation Heritage Books
Grand Rapids, Michigan

Sing a New Song
© 2010 by Joel R. Beeke and Anthony T. Selvaggio

Reformation Heritage Books
3070 29th St. SE
Grand Rapids, MI 49512
616-977-0889
orders@heritagebooks.org
www.heritagebooks.org

Printed in the United States of America
21 22 23 24 25 26/10 9 8 7 6 5 4 3 2

Library of Congress Cataloging-in-Publication Data

Sing a new song : recovering Psalm singing for the twenty-first century
/ edited by Joel R. Beeke and Anthony T. Selvaggio.
    p. cm.
ISBN 978-1-60178-105-5
1. Psalms (Music)—History and criticism. 2. Psalmody. I. Selvaggio,
Anthony T. II. Beeke, Joel R., 1952-
ML3270.S55 2010
264.2—dc22
                                                    2010036783

For additional Reformed literature, both new and used, request a free book list from Reformation Heritage Books at the above regular or e-mail address.

Contents

Foreword

W. Robert Godfrey

For three thousand years the people of God have praised, studied, and cherished the Psalms. The Psalms are received as the inspired Word of God and share, with the rest of the Bible, in the character of the Scriptures taught by Paul: "the holy scriptures, which are able to make thee wise unto salvation through faith which is in Christ Jesus. All Scripture is given by inspiration of God, and is profitable for doctrine, for reproof, for correction, for instruction in righteousness" (2 Tim. 3:15–16).

The Psalms are indeed the Word from God like the Bible as a whole, but in addition they occupy a unique role in the Bible. The Psalms are also words to God from His people. Precisely because they give inspired voice to the deepest spiritual feelings of God's people, they have been treasured and used in both private and public worship, first in the temple and synagogue and then in the church.

The church believed that the Psalms spoke for Christ and for Christians. The ancient church studied and sang the Psalms. In the medieval church parts of Psalms were used liturgically, and the whole Psalter was chanted in the monasteries. In the Reformation the Psalms were given to the people of God as never before through the availability of printed Bibles and the introduction of metrical psalm singing.

For several centuries after the Reformation, especially in the Reformed churches, the psalms fed the piety of Christians. The more they studied the Psalms, the more they found in them. The Psalms deepen a sense of identity with the people of God in every age. They show ways in which

God was the covenant Lord of His people. They express the full range of emotions of those living for God, from grief, repentance, doubt, and struggle to joy, praise, thanksgiving, and assurance.

The poetry of the Psalter connects immediately with readers in the power and beauty of its expressions about God and the condition of Christians before Him. But the careful craftsmanship of the Psalms gives the serious student many layers of literary form to study for increasingly profound insights into the meaning of the Psalms. They are indeed a mine in which gold can continually be found.

In the last fifty years the impact of the Psalms on the church has seriously diminished. Several factors have tended to marginalize the Psalter. First, some modern theologies have stressed the discontinuity of the Old Testament and New Testament in ways that have led Christians not to look as much to the Old Testament for direction in their piety. Second, a diminished place for poetry in our culture and in our education makes the Psalter somewhat less accessible. Third, for the English-speaking world, the loss of the King James Version as the unifying translation of the Psalter has affected familiarity with the language of the Psalms. Fourth, liturgical and musical changes in public worship have not only led to a decline of the use of the Psalms but also introduced forms of worship and song very different from the rich, profound, and carefully crafted psalms of the Bible.

What has been the effect of the diminished influence of the Psalter on the church? Some look at the church of the last fifty years and see great strength and growth. Others, while rejoicing in evidences of numerical growth, see serious decline in Bible knowledge, sound theology, and biblical piety. My fear is that the latter are correct and that the church in our time has been seriously weakened. The diminished role of the Psalter in the church is a symptom and cause of that weakness.

The church today needs renewal in true biblical Christianity. A fresh appreciation of the Psalter is a key element for that renewal. My hope is that this book will be a significant contribution to renewing a love for the Psalms and a commitment to biblical truth and piety.

About the Title

ive psalms in the Psalter are called "new songs" (Pss. 33:3; 40:3; 96:1; 98:1; 149:1). Additionally, while Psalm 144 is not itself a "new song," it includes a promise to sing a "new song" (v. 9) after God grants a longed-for victory. In biblical Hebrew, a new song is not necessarily a song that was recently written. The phrase is an idiom for a certain kind of praise song—the kind of praise one sings loudly for all the nations to hear after God has granted a great victory. Psalm 40 is a good example: "I waited patiently for the LORD; and he inclined unto me, and heard my cry. He brought me up also out of an horrible pit, out of the miry clay, and set my feet upon a rock, and established my goings. And he hath put a *new song* in my mouth, even praise unto our God: many shall see it, and fear, and shall trust in the LORD" (vv. 1–3, emphasis added).

Such a song is sung when the old notes of lament have given way to a new melody of joy and gladness. It bursts forth from the heart because of some momentous deliverance that puts all the old griefs into the distant past.

The whole book of Psalms is called, in Hebrew, the Book of Praises (*Sefer Tehillim*). Not all the Psalms are praise songs. Some are cries of distress. But the book is called the Book of Praises because its many psalms meet us in our present experiences, whatever they are, and invariably point our hearts toward God's victories—realized or promised. Indeed, the whole Psalter reaches its climax with a "new song" (Ps. 149) and a "hallelujah" benediction (Ps. 150). Until that great day comes when all our tears will be wiped away and we will sing only "new song" praises (Rev. 5:9;

14:3), the variety of songs in the Psalter tune our hearts to that joy now. It is for this reason that the Psalter is called the Book of Praises, and this book about singing those ancient songs is called *Sing a New Song*.[1]

> O sing unto the LORD a *new song*: sing unto the LORD, all the earth. Sing unto the LORD, bless his name; shew forth his salvation from day to day. Declare his glory among the heathen, his wonders among all people. For the LORD is great, and greatly to be praised: he is to be feared above all gods (Psalm 96:1–4, emphasis added).

---

1. Richard D. Patterson, "Singing the New Song: An Examination of Psalms 33, 96, 98, and 149," *Bibliotheca Sacra* 164 (2007): 416–34.

Part 1

Psalm Singing in History

Chapter 1

From Cassian to Cranmer:
Singing the Psalms from Ancient Times
until the Dawning of the Reformation

Hughes Oliphant Old and Robert Cathcart

*R*ecovering the singing of psalms in Christian worship remains one of the highest hurdles to reestablishing authentic Protestant worship in the twenty-first century. It has been a keen interest of mine for some time to trace the connection between the patristic period and the Reformation in regards to the reform of worship. My work in this area dates back to the preparation of my dissertation, which I defended in 1971. It is now published in an American edition entitled *The Patristic Roots of Reformed Worship*.[1] This essay, co-authored with my student Robert Cathcart, attempts to uncover another ancient, yet lesser-known contributor to the reformation of worship in the sixteenth century, John Cassian.

It may seem odd that this book, headlined by so many brilliant Reformed scholars, begins with a look at John Cassian. Cassian, a monk born in Scythia Minor (modern-day Romania) around AD 360, may be best known as the leading proponent of Semi-Pelagianism in his day. In addition, he championed an ascetic lifestyle as the means to true piety. Both of these attributes might be enough to make a Reformed reader skip ahead to the next chapter. That, however, would be a grave mistake because Cassian observed, described, and propagated an approach to the singing of psalms that was replicated, with some modifications, during the time of the Reformation and still resonates within the Reformed tradition today.

---

1. Black Mountain, N.C.: Worship Press, 2004.

Around AD 386, John Cassian and his traveling companion, Germa-
nus, set out from Bethlehem for the Desert of Scete in Egypt to observe
the exemplary piety of the Cenobite and Anchorite monks living in that
country. Anchorites are what we might call hermits, isolating themselves
to keep pure from the world and to battle the flesh in solitude. They sought
to emulate Elijah, Elisha, and John the Baptist in their austere, ascetic
lifestyle. The Cenobites, on the other hand, attempted to live like the
apostles in Acts 2:44–45, holding everything in common and experienc-
ing the Christian faith in community. Cassian remained in Egypt for seven
years before returning to Palestine. After returning to Egypt for a second
tour, Cassian reported his findings to Constantinople around AD 400,
and during his time there, John Chrysostom ordained him as a deacon.[2]
Cassian records his observations of and recommendations for monastic
life in his two great works, *The Institutes of the Cenobia* and *The Conferences.* These documents together became "the *Magna Charta* of monastic
life."[3] It has been said that these two works have "no parallel in ancient
Christian literature."[4]

The Institutes, in particular, describe the way in which the Cenobites
celebrated daily prayer. Cassian observes a system of beauty and simplicity
that featured psalmody as it was sung, prayed, and used for meditation.
Although some early monastic practice recommended the chanting of
as many as "twenty or thirty" psalms in one service, Cassian witnessed a
modest and prudent approach in the Egyptian desert. He explains that
"throughout the whole of Egypt and the Thebaid the number of Psalms
is fixed at twelve both at Vespers and in the office of Nocturns, in such a
way that at the close two lessons follow, one from the Old and the other
from the New Testament."[5] Although nocturns are sometimes connected
with night vigils, Cassian has in mind what would later be called matins,[6]

2. *New Catholic Encyclopedia,* 2nd ed., s.v. "John Cassian."

3. Johannes Quaston, *Patrology,* trans. Placid Solari (Allen, Tex.: Christian Classics,
1986), 518.

4. John Cassian, *The Institutes,* trans. Boniface Ramsey (New York: The Newman
Press, 2000), 8.

5. John Cassian, *Nicene and Post-Nicene Fathers,* ed. Edgar C. S. Gibson (Peabody,
Mass.: Hendrickson, 2004), 10:206.

6. Owen Chadwick, *John Cassian* (Cambridge: Cambridge University Press, 1968), 71.

or lauds. Therefore, he has observed a system of morning and evening prayer, each session consisting of twelve psalms and a reading from both testaments. By chanting twelve psalms per service, the monks would then recite the entire Psalter each week.

A key feature of each synaxis, or office of prayer, is that the sung psalms function as an invitation to prayer. In these services, a cantor or a series of cantors leads the monks by chanting the text of the psalms. However, careful attention is paid not to do this in a mechanistic or mindless manner. Cassian unfolds the proper manner for the psalms to be sung:

> They do not even attempt to finish the Psalms, which they sing in the service, by an unbroken and continuous recitation. But they repeat them separately and bit by bit, divided into two or three sections, according to the number of verses in between. For they do not care about the quantity of verses, but about the intelligence of the mind; aiming with all their might at this: "I will sing with the spirit: I will sing also with the understanding." And so they consider it better for ten verses to be sung with understanding and thought than for a whole Psalm to be poured forth with a bewildered mind.[7]

This intermittent singing of the psalms gives rise to opportunities for meditation and for responsorial prayers. Chadwick comments, "In a long psalm the superior stopped the cantor after ten verses to allow silent meditation upon the verses just sung. At the end of the psalms, after standing for some moments in silent prayer, all prostrated themselves in adoration; but the prostration must not be too long lest sleep overcome the prone and resting worshipper, who must rise with the leader to pray with arms outstretched."[8]

The Egyptian monks, therefore, were continuing the practice of the Lord Jesus Christ, who also prayed through the Psalter. We read of His doing so especially surrounding the events of His passion. We think of Him singing through the *Hallel*, the Passover Psalms (113–118), with His disciples after instituting the Lord's Supper (Matt. 26:30; Mark 14:26). Then, in His prayer from the garden of Gethsemane, He alludes to portions of these psalms, particularly Psalm 116:13, "I will take the cup

---

7. John Cassian, *Nicene and Post-Nicene Fathers*, 10:209.
8. Chadwick, *John Cassian*, 71.

of salvation, and call upon the name of the LORD," and when He pleads, "Abba, Father, all things are possible unto thee; take away this cup from me: nevertheless not what I will, but what thou wilt" (Mark 14:36). Also familiar to us is Christ's quoting Psalm 22 from the cross: "My God, my God, why hast thou forsaken me?" (Mark 15:34). We know that Christ alludes to Psalms 69:3 and 22:15 when He cries out, "I thirst" (John 19:28). Cassian's record of Egyptian psalm piety elicits the same type of interaction between the psalms and prayer. Columba Stewart writes,

> Prayer (*oratio*)...happened when the flow of recited or sung text paused and the heart spoke from its own appropriation of the texts. Offered by each monk in silence and then communally in a prayer by the leader, such prayer arises from, and responds to, the biblical words that have been vocalized. For Cassian this interval for prayer was to be of brief duration; the monks would then return to the biblical texts. The Bible and prayer, though not identical, were inseparable.[9]

However, the inducing power of psalms to elicit praise is certainly not restricted to the settings of morning and evening prayer. Instead, the Cenobites were to continue praying and meditating on these psalms as they performed their daily work and as they rested from their labors in the evening.[10] The singing of psalms twice daily in community stands as the central act of piety for these ancient Christians. Quaston illuminates this idea by suggesting the following:

> The monk must always be ruminating on some part of the sacred text, e.g., a passage from the Psalter, in order to succeed in penetrating its profundity, i.e., the spiritual meaning, in purity of heart. This is particularly true with regard to the Psalms. "The task of the monk is to appropriate the biblical prayer to such an extent that it becomes his own sacred reading," says Abba Nestor, "so that this continual meditation may at last impregnate your soul and form it, so to speak, to its own image" (Cassian's *Conferences* 14.10). The monk then no

---

9. Columba Stewart, *Cassian the Monk* (New York: Oxford University Press, 1998), 101.
10. Ibid.

longer recites it as the work of the prophet but as though he were himself the author, and as his personal prayer.[11]

Not only do psalms transform the prayers of the monk into the prayers of the Holy Spirit,[12] they also transform daily tasks, however menial, "into God's work,"[13] as they are consecrated by the scriptural prayers that rise in the midst of them. This sense of work being holy would be further developed during the Reformation era as the doctrine of vocation was worked out carefully by the Reformers. However, from Cassian's observations, it is clear to see the power that a psalm-based piety, filled with singing, meditation, and prayer, has to remove any sense of a sacred/secular dichotomy in the life and work of a faithful Christian, regardless of occupation.

One may rightfully wonder what happened to the Egyptians' simple approach to daily prayer as the Middle Ages dawned. It should be noted that Cassian himself saw a place for more frequent prayer throughout the day. In particular, he mentions that in the monasteries of Palestine, Mesopotamia, and throughout the Orient, the hours of terce (9:00 a.m.), sext (noon), and none (3:00 p.m.) were observed. Each service contained the chanting of three psalms.[14] Cassian gives ample biblical precedent for the observance of these hours, beginning with Daniel's praying three times daily with his windows open in the face of King Darius' decree (Dan. 6:10). He then describes the setting apart of terce as the exact timing of the Pentecost event. The sixth hour (sext) was given special consideration because in this hour, "the spotless victim, our Lord and Savior, was offered to the Father, and mounting the cross for the salvation of the whole world he destroyed the sins of the human race."[15] Additionally, Cassian, with some colorful and creative exegesis, reminds us that Peter received his food vision at noon, the sixth hour of the day. In summarizing the significance of the ninth hour, Cassian recalls how Christ "penetrated hell and extinguished the inextricable darkness of Tartarus by his shimmering brilliance. He broke open its gates of bronze."[16] Cassian mentions the ninth

---

11. Quaston, *Patrology*, 519.
12. Ibid.
13. Ibid., 520.
14. John Cassian, *The Institutes*, trans. Boniface Ramsey, 59.
15. Ibid., 60.
16. Ibid., 61.

hour as the time Cornelius received the good news of Gentile acceptance from Peter. Finally, the ninth hour is also when Peter and John went to the temple to pray in Acts 3:1.

Cassian summarizes his biblical findings by stating, "It is perfectly clear that we too should observe these times, which holy and apostolic men not without reason consecrated by religious rites."[17] Additionally, Cassian argues for three psalms to be chanted at the break of day, presumably at 6:00 a.m, or prime, along with a bedtime prayer at the eleventh hour, which later would be called compline.[18] When we add these five hours of prime, terce, sext, none, and compline to the two set hours that the Egyptians practiced, Cassian explains that they "correspond very clearly in a literal way to that number of which blessed David speaks (although it has a spiritual meaning): 'Seven times a day I have praised you for the judgments of your righteousness.'"[19] Does Cassian's quoting Psalm 119:164 mean that he implicitly denigrates the Egyptians' simpler observance of twice-daily prayer? Absolutely not! In fact, he actually prefers their understanding and their observance. He explains:

> The offices that we are obliged to render to the Lord at different hours and at intervals of time, at the call of a summoner, are celebrated continuously and spontaneously throughout the course of the whole day, in tandem with their work. For they are constantly doing manual labor alone in their cells in such a way that they almost never omit meditating on the psalms and on other parts of Scriptures, and to this they add entreaties and prayers at every moment, taking up the whole day in offices that we celebrate at fixed times. Hence, apart from the evening and nighttime gatherings, they celebrate no public service during the day except on Saturday and Sunday, when they gather at the third hour for Holy Communion. For what is unceasingly offered is greater than what is rendered at particular moments, and a voluntary service is more pleasing than functions that are carried out by canonical obligation. This is why David himself rejoices somewhat boastfully when he says: 'Willingly shall I sacrifice to you.' And: 'May the free offerings of my mouth be pleasing to you, Lord.'[20]

---

17. Ibid., 61.
18. Ibid., 62.
19. Ibid., 63.
20. Ibid., 59.

Certainly, the Egyptians sought to maintain the most ancient and, in their minds, apostolic tradition. It has been noted that this type of morning and evening prayer "probably came about by the end of the 2nd Century,"[21] and stands quite close to the apostolic model.

For Cassian, prayer that springs from the heart in the midst of daily duties is even more precious than that which arises from a strict observance of the seven daily offices. On the other hand, it should be noted that the spontaneous prayers of the Egyptians were rooted and grounded in singing psalms and hearing the Scriptures. Therefore, there was a glorious balance between freedom and fixed forms that so often marks the most mature and edifying prayers of the Christian church.

After Cassian's death around AD 430, another would take up the cause of reforming the spiritual life of the monastery. Benedict of Nursia (c. 480–547) became frustrated with Roman decadence and sought a purer and more Christlike existence. After purportedly performing miracles in Enfide and flirting with the subsequent fame, Benedict, along with his friend Romanus, secluded himself in a cave near Subiaco, Italy. While there, the two friends "consumed and prayed Scripture."[22] After founding thirteen monasteries in Subiaco, Benedict left, wearied from conflict and intrigue. It was in Monte Cassino where Benedict would make his long-lasting mark. He began working on his *Rule*, a directory for the monastic life, to help monks of varied backgrounds live together in peace.[23] There is no question that Benedict builds upon Cassian's observations in *The Institutes* and *The Conferences*. In fact, Benedict thought so highly of Cassian's works that he recommends their communal reading, along with other notable works, after supper in the monasteries. He encourages monks who desire perfection and virtue to consider Cassian's observations.[24] Laura Swan states, "Benedict's gentle genius was to take what was useful from these rules (Pachomius in Egypt, Basil in the Eastern Empire, the Rule of the Fathers, Caesarius in Gaul, the unidentified author of the Rule

---

21. Francis Proctor and Walter Howard Frere, *A New History of the Book of Common Prayer* (London: Macmillan and Company, 1932), 315.

22. Patrick Barry, *St. Benedict's Rule: A New Translation for Today* (Mahwah, N.J.: Hidden Spring, 2004), 1.

23. Ibid.

24. John Cassian, *Nicene and Post-Nicene Fathers*, 10:194.

of the Master) as well as from the writings of John Cassian, add some of his thoughts, and create his 'modest Rule for beginners.'"[25]

Although St. Benedict borrows from Cassian's depository of wisdom, there are obvious departures. In particular, Benedict further emphasizes the seven hours of daily prayer and actually adds an eighth. Therefore, his system includes vigils (midnight), lauds (3:00 a.m.), prime (6:00 a.m.), terce (9:00 a.m.), sext (noon), none (3:00 p.m.), vespers (6:00 p.m.), and compline (9:00 p.m.). Hence, a twenty-four-hour day is divided equally into eight opportunities for prayer. It seems, though, that the primary hours remain lauds and vespers, which correspond to Cassian's Egyptian model of morning and evening prayer. For instance, at lauds, six psalms are to be chanted. At vespers, the monks are encouraged to chant four psalms. The number of psalms sung at lauds and vespers exceeds the number intoned at the so-called "little hours" of prime, terce, sext, and none. In addition, there is a great emphasis on the night vigils, when twelve psalms were chanted. It seems, though, that throughout the Middle Ages, the service of vigils became increasingly attached to lauds. However, Benedict expressly sets apart the hours of lauds and vespers by attaching the Lord's Prayer as a high point in the celebration of daily prayer.[26]

Another element Benedict inserts into the Daily Office is the use of Ambrosian hymns.[27] These compositions, written by Ambrose and those who followed him, have a decidedly doctrinal and Christ-centered focus. When worshipers placed these hymns alongside the regular psalmody and Scripture reading, they achieved a rich experience of daily prayer. Benedict's use of the Ambrosian hymns also helped to propagate and preserve Christian hymnody throughout the medieval period.[28]

---

25. Laura Swan, *The Benedictine Tradition: Spirituality in History* (Collegeville, Minn.: Order of St. Benedict, 2007), xiv.

26. St. Benedict, *The Rule of St. Benedict in English*, ed. Timothy Fry (New York: Vintage Books, 1998), 21–28.

27. Ibid., 26.

28. Some later Latin hymn writers who were influenced by Ambrose's anti-Arian and pro-Trinitarian hymns include Prudentius, Theodulph of Orleans, Bernard of Clairvaux, St. Francis of Assisi, and Peter Abelard. Information found in J. R. Watson, *An Annotated Anthology of Hymns* (Oxford: Oxford University Press, 2002), 10.

Another glaring difference between Cassian's approach and that of St. Benedict is the manner in which psalms are organized for daily prayer. Chadwick explains,

> There were two modes of ordering psalmody which were combined to make the later system of monastic hours. One mode took the psalms in the order of the Bible. The other mode selected psalms appropriate to the time of day—psalms with morning texts for the morning and evening texts for the evening. Of these two modes Cassian stood much nearer to the former.... The only special psalms were those set for Lauds and Prime...the penitential and morning psalms appropriate to the morning office.[29]

We could safely say that Cassian utilized a *lectio continua* approach, while Benedict and those who followed him selected psalms that best fit the time of day. The goal of both approaches, however, is the same: chanting the entire Psalter each week. It must be said that there are benefits to both systems. For instance, when considering Benedict's set psalms for lauds, there is no better way to start one's morning than by coming before the Almighty God of creation, redemption, and providence, pleading the words of Psalm 67:1:"God be merciful unto us, and bless us; and cause his face to shine upon us." The same can be said for the Benedictine psalms for compline. At the onset of sleep, the devout soul finds peace and comfort in the words of Psalms 4, 91, and 134. It should be noted too that, especially at vigils, something similar to a *lectio continua* singing of psalms is practiced.

The weakness of Benedict's ordering of the Daily Office, at least to a twenty-first century Protestant, is that it is fairly complicated and tedious. On the other hand, Cassian's simpler system of praying twelve psalms at lauds and vespers, with some modifications, became the model for Daily Prayer in the later Reformed churches, as we will see. To be fair, it should be noted that Benedict did not expect the monasteries to follow his suggestions slavishly. Showing keen practical and pastoral insight, he writes, "Above all else we urge that if anyone finds this distribution of the psalms unsatisfactory, he should arrange whatever he judges better, provided that the full complement of one hundred and fifty psalms is by all means care-

---

29. Chadwick, *John Cassian*, 77.

fully maintained every week, and that the series begins anew each Sunday at vigils."[30] As Swan asserts, "The point is not how monastic communities gather for the Divine Office, but that the community gathers daily with forethought and prayerful consideration.... Like water slowly dropping on rock until that rock's shape has changed, the daily mundane task of chanting the Divine Office slowly works on an individual's heart, shaping the person into the image of Christ."[31] Surely this noble goal of sanctification stands at the heart of what Benedict, and Cassian before him, sought to accomplish through the singing of psalms. However, that noble purpose would largely be veiled from the majority of Christians until the time of the Reformation.

It would be an overstatement to say that psalm-based Benedictine spirituality had no impact on laypeople in the West. Throughout Western Europe, the hours for prayer were observed in the great cathedrals as well as in the cloistered monasteries. It should be noted, though, that the strict observance of the Benedictine hours began to wane toward the end of the Middle Ages. "At the threshold of the Reformation…many had lost sight of the beauty of this discipline of daily prayer. It was regarded as a heavy burden, barely held up by endowed choirs and a secularized clergy which had lost its spiritual fire."[32]

A movement toward simplicity had also begun in the eleventh century through the ministry of the preaching orders, the Franciscans and the Dominicans. Because they found it difficult to keep the elaborate hours of prayer while functioning in their itinerate ministries, "the Portifory ('to be carried around') or Breviary ('shortened version')" was developed. It included "the seven daily offices…in a simplified form…so that…the daily offices could be recited individually or by several people together, all with their own book."[33] Over time, through the influence of the Breviary and through a lay version of it called the *Book of Hours* or *The Primer*,

---

30. St. Benedict, *The Rule of St. Benedict in English*, 28.

31. Swan, *The Benedictine Tradition*, xviii.

32. Hughes Oliphant Old, "Daily Prayer in the Reformed Church of Strasbourg, 1525–1530," *Worship* 52, 2 (March 1978): 121–38.

33. Kenneth Stevenson, "Worship by the Book," in *The Oxford Guide to the Book of Common Prayer: A Worldwide Survey*, ed. C. Hefling and C. Shattuck (Oxford: Oxford University Press, 2006), 14.

daily prayer simplified even further. Hence, the most significant development "at the eve of the Reformation" is that "the practice had grown up of reciting the daily offices into two main 'blocks,' one in the morning and the other in the evening."[34] In other words, Christians were rediscovering what John Cassian had uncovered almost eleven hundred years earlier—a simple, apostolic, and practical way to sing and pray through the Psalms.

This conflating of daily prayer into two offices is most strikingly seen in England. Thomas Cranmer began to take notice of Spanish Cardinal Francisco de Quinones who had begun reforming daily prayer according to the principles of Christian humanism. John Gibaut records, "Quinones produced a Breviary in 1535 that drastically simplified its predecessor.... The result was a simplified sevenfold office with a large amount of scripture. It remained, however, in Latin and for the use of individual clergy rather than communities."[35] Cranmer, in concert with Martin Luther and Martin Bucer on the continent, desired to liberate the Daily Office for the laity. He aimed to create truly *common* prayer, no longer just for the clergy and written in the vernacular, so that all could participate with understanding. By combining elements of the medieval services with the Christian humanist and Reformation zeal to return to the sources, Cranmer propagated a well-balanced system of morning and evening prayer that resonated well with ancient, apostolic disciplines. Essentially, he returned to the type of service that Cassian observed in the Egyptian desert. "Morning Prayer includes elements of Matins (Vigils), Lauds, and Prime, while Evening Prayer is a combination of Vespers and Compline."[36]

Cassian's system, along with those of Benedict and even Quinones, assumes the chanting/praying through the entire Psalter in one week. Cranmer's Book of Common Prayer slows down the pace considerably, dividing the Psalms evenly between morning and evening prayer so that they are completed in thirty days. Obviously, this moderate speed is much more suited to a parish setting. It also coincides well with a comprehensive Scripture-reading program that encompasses the whole counsel of God. Cranmer set his daily lectionary so that two lessons are read, one from each

---

34. Ibid.

35. John Gibaut, "The Daily Office," in *The Oxford Guide to the* Book of Common Prayer: *A Worldwide Survey*, 453.

36. Ibid.

testament, at morning and evening prayer. If the parish priest is faithful to keep these instructions, then he reads the entire Old Testament in one year, while he reads the New Testament three times per annum.[37] When we factor in that the entire Psalter would be read or chanted twelve times, we realize the staggering amount of Scripture that would pass through the ears and, hopefully, penetrate the hearts of England's worshipers.

It is well known that Quinones, as well as continental Reformers like Martin Bucer, Heinrich Bullinger, Philipp Melanchthon, and Peter Martyr Vermigli, influenced Cranmer, but as important as these resources were, it seems that Cranmer's reforms stand very close to the observations of John Cassian. Is this a mere coincidence, or is there a direct connection? There is evidence to suggest that Cranmer's Christian humanist zeal to go back to the ancient sources led him to Cassian's works. For instance, the British Museum holds an edition of Dionysius Carthusian's paraphrase of Cassian's *Institutes* and *Conferences* that belonged to Cranmer. In fact, Cranmer's autograph graces the copy.[38] Additionally, in his earliest attempts at drafting a revised church calendar, Cranmer included a saint's day for John Cassian, which in itself is remarkable because Cassian was not afforded the honor of sainthood by the Western church.[39] We present these evidences to show the far-reaching impact that Cassian's observations of the Egyptian Cenobites continue to have on the practice of daily prayer. It is indeed remarkable that Anglicans continue to utilize the Book of Common Prayer on six continents today.

It should also be noted that in the city of Strasbourg, under the leadership of Martin Bucer, a similar reform of daily prayer was accomplished, one that also emphasized Cassian's hallmark of morning and evening prayer. A major difference between the Anglican prayer book and the *Strasbourg Psalter* is that the singing of metrical psalms, rather than the chanting of psalms, takes center stage.[40] There is no question, too, that Bucer and the *Strasbourg Psalter* had a profound effect on John

---

37. Hughes Oliphant Old, *The Reading and Preaching of the Scriptures in the Worship of the Christian Church* (Grand Rapids: Eerdmans, 2002), 4:154–55.

38. John Cassian, *Nicene and Post-Nicene Fathers*, 10:194.

39. Proctor and Frere, *A New History of the Book of Common Prayer*, 336.

40. See Hughes Oliphant Old, "Daily Prayer in the Reformed Church of Strasbourg, 1525–1530."

Calvin during his time there after his exile from Geneva (1538–1541). Surely Bucer's insistence on singing psalms in the vernacular helped fuel the creation of the *Genevan Psalter*, which remains the gold standard for all collections of psalms for singing. The *Genevan Psalter* also spawned similar works in England and Scotland as the Marian exiles returned with influences from the continent. Therefore, Cassian's psalm-centric vision for Christian public worship and piety is at the heart of Reformed faith and practice as it developed in the sixteenth century.

As this chapter closes, it may be appropriate to ask if there is anything specific in Cassian's observations that could be applied to the church today. In other words, how do we recover the singing and praying of the Psalms in our day? It would seem that this could be applied in three ways. The first layer would be to reestablish regular parish or congregational morning and evening prayer services during the week. Obviously, metropolitan churches with larger memberships could institute this system of daily prayer more easily. The idea would be to set up services like we find in the Book of Common Prayer where a chapter from each testament would be read and where the singing of metrical psalms takes center stage. Both the reading and the singing could be accomplished using the *lectio continua*. The number of psalms to be sung could be varied, based upon each local context (and attention span). Three at each service would give enough depth without overwhelming the participants. Obtaining a good psalter with a complete set of the Psalms would be a necessary tool in carrying out these sorts of services.[41] Of course there should be time for corporate prayer, whether led by a minister, lay leader, or allowing members of the congregation to lift up their praises, thanksgivings, confessions, and supplications to the Lord. The idea would be for the prayers to flow from the psalmody, just as they did for our Savior and within the ancient church. The goal would simply be to allow the Psalms, along with the

---

41. A few suggestions include *The Psalter* (Grand Rapids: Reformation Heritage Books, 1999), *Trinity Psalter* (Pittsburgh: Crown and Covenant Publications, 1994), *The Book of Psalms for Singing* (Pittsburgh: Crown and Covenant Publications, 1998), the *Psalter Hymnal* (Grand Rapids: CRC Publications, 1987), and *Sing Psalms* (Free Church of Scotland, 2003). The *Trinity Hymnal* (Suwanee, GA: Great Commission Publications, 1990) also includes most of the Psalms written for responsive reading. An option would be to alternate between reading and singing psalms.

Bible readings, to develop a rich, full, mature prayer life for the congregation. Above all, imagine the showers of blessings that the Lord would rain down upon His people if they began praying back His Word to Him on a regular basis!

Another layer of application is singing psalms within corporate Lord's Day worship. Surely other sections of this book will take up this topic in greater detail, but ministers would do well to expose their congregations systematically to the Psalms. If psalm singing has not been a regular part of the church's worship, then the congregation could commit to singing one metrical psalm per week. This could be accomplished by singing them through in a *lectio continua* manner, starting with Psalm 1 and finishing with Psalm 150. Because there may be unfamiliarity with certain tunes, it may be wise to repeat a psalm for a couple of weeks. Another idea would be to follow Benedict's system by selecting morning psalms (exs. 3, 5, 67, 108, 130) for morning worship and evening psalms (exs. 4, 91, 134) for evening worship. Additionally, it would be meaningful to sing the penitential psalms (exs. 6, 32, 51) before or after a corporate prayer of confession. Also, how often do pastors struggle with finding the right hymn to fit the central point of their sermon? Whether their text emphasizes prayer, praise, lament, devotion, or any response or emotion, there is no better place to find the perfect matching song than in the Psalter. As Athanasius famously said, "It is my view that in the words of this book the whole human life, its basic spiritual conduct and as well its occasional movements and thoughts, is comprehended and contained. Nothing to be found in human life is omitted."[42]

The final application for applying the ancient principles of psalm piety in the twenty-first century is a reestablishment of family prayer. One of the primary emphases of the English and American Puritans, there is growing interest in reviving the practice of family prayer today. Some excellent resources exist to aid fathers and mothers in leading their children before the throne of grace each day.[43] A simple way to approach the

---

42. Athanasius, *Ad Marcellinum*; quoted in James Luther Mays, *Psalms* (Louisville: John Knox Press, 1994), 1.

43. Probably the finest resource is Terry Johnson's *Family Worship Book* (Geanies House, Fearn, Ross-Shire, Scotland: Christian Focus Publications, 2003), which contains a large selection of psalms taken from the *Trinity Psalter*, as well as the most well-known

practice is to obtain a good psalter or hymnal, along with a copy of God's Word. Ambitious families could attempt Cranmer's system of morning and evening prayer, reading two chapters, one from each testament, and then dividing up the Psalms so that they are completed within one month. It would seem that most families would adopt a more moderate pace, possibly reading one chapter (or a portion of it) at each setting, and then singing one or two psalms (or portions of them) so that they would sing through the entire Psalter quarterly.

Surely not all of what we find in the theology and practice of the monastic movement, founded by John Cassian and Benedict of Nursia, stands within biblical norms. However, as we move forward with the reformation of Christian worship in our day, we can look back with confidence and see how the Lord preserved the singing of the Psalms from ancient, apostolic times during the Middle Ages. More than this, we can determine how the Reformers recovered the singing of psalms in the sixteenth century for the entire congregation and how the Lord's song can be sung anew in today's liturgical context.

---

and doctrinally rich Christian hymns. He also provides the texts for the Children's Catechism and the Shorter Catechism, along with a Scripture reading guide. For assistance in how to conduct family worship, see Joel R. Beeke, *Family Worship* (Grand Rapids: Reformation Heritage Books, 2008).

Chapter 2

Psalm Singing in Calvin and the Puritans

Joel R. Beeke

ollowing Jewish synagogue practices, the ancient church preferred liturgical music based on psalmody. Hymns were appreciated for personal devotion, but were not judged appropriate for worship. By the fourth century, psalm singing had acquired an authority nearly on par with Scripture. The Synod of Laodicea (AD 350) and the Council of Bracara (AD 563) forbade the singing of non-scriptural hymns. In the early Middle Ages, other sacred music in addition to psalm singing was tolerated. By the ninth century, the Gregorian chant of choirs trumped congregational singing. For centuries, church choirs sang mostly hymns, usually in Latin, with difficult tunes; congregational psalm singing dissipated, though most monks still knew the psalms by heart and sang them in accord with pre-scribed patterns of Gregorian tradition.[1]

The Reformation revolutionized congregational singing, particu-larly through the efforts of Martin Luther (1483–1546) and John Calvin (1509–1564). Calvin and the Puritans felt convicted to sing psalms in public worship and loved doing so. In this chapter, after showing how Calvin developed psalm singing, we will look at the Puritan view of psalm singing, following the outline of John Cotton's representative book on the topic: (1) the duty of psalm singing, (2) the content of the singing, (3) the

---

1. Ross J. Miller, "Calvin's Understanding of Psalm-Singing as a Means of Grace," in *Calvin Studies VI*, ed. John H. Leith (Davidson, N.C.: Davidson College, 1992), 42; Ger-ald R. Procee, "Calvin on Singing Psalms," *The Messenger* 56, 7 (July/Aug. 2009): 10.

singers, and (4) the manner of singing. The chapter will conclude by presenting some spiritual benefits of psalm singing for believers today.

Calvin on Psalm Singing

John Calvin loved the Book of Psalms. For twenty-five years, Calvin immersed himself in the Psalms as a commentator, preacher, biblical scholar, and worship leader.[2] For Calvin, the psalmists' words were always relevant for the New Testament church. The major psalmist, David, reflected an important stage in the history of salvation. In David and the other psalmists, believers still today can see "the living image of Christ."[3] The Psalms, then, were not just biblically safe for the church to use in singing, but they also helped the church worship God faithfully and prevented her tendency to backslide and pervert worship.

Most of Calvin's sermons preached on the Lord's Day from the Old Testament were based on the Psalms. His New Testament commentaries abound with references to the Psalms.[4] Calvin tells us in an autobiographical note prefaced to his *Commentary on Psalms* that the Psalter had comforted him in a major way during years of trial (1549–1554).[5]

The Canonical Manual of Piety

More than anything else, Calvin viewed the book of Psalms as the canonical manual of piety. In the preface to his five-volume commentary on Psalms—his largest exposition of any Bible book—Calvin writes, "There

---

2. John Walchenbach, "The Influence of David and the Psalms on the Life and Thought of John Calvin" (Th.M. thesis, Pittsburgh Theological Seminary, 1969). Part of the first section of this chapter is adapted from my "Calvin on Piety," *The Cambridge Companion to John Calvin*, ed. Donald K. McKim (Cambridge: Cambridge University Press, 2004), 137–39.

3. John Calvin, *Institutes of the Christian Religion*, ed. John T. McNeill, trans. Ford Lewis Battles (Philadelphia: Westminster Press, 1960), 2.6.2.

4. E.g., John Calvin, *Commentary on Romans*, ed. David W. and Thomas F. Torrance, trans. Ross MacKenzie (Grand Rapids: Eerdmans), Rom. 3:4. Cf. Calvin's *Commentary* on Matt. 21:42 and 27:35, which show his Christological hermeneutic of the Psalms; Miller, "Calvin's Understanding of Psalm-Singing as a Means of Grace," 40, 47.

5. *Opera quae supersunt omnia*, ed. Guilielmus Baum, Eduardus Cunitz, and Eduardus Reuss, in *Corpus Reformatorum*, vols. 29–87 (Brunsvigae: C. A. Schwetschke et filium, 1863–1900), 31:19 (hereafter, CO 31:19).

is no other book in which we are more perfectly taught the right manner of praising God, or in which we are more powerfully stirred up to the performance of this exercise of piety."[6] Calvin's preoccupation with this book was motivated by his belief that the Psalms teach and inspire genuine piety in the following ways:

- As revelation from God, the Psalms teach us about God. Because they are theological as well as doxological, they are our sung creed.[7]

- Psalms clearly teach our need for God. They tell us who we are and why we need God's help.[8]

- Psalms are a model for our prayer. They show us how to intercede for the church.[9]

- Psalms offer the divine remedy for our needs. They present Christ in His person, offices, sufferings, death, resurrection, and ascension. They announce the way of salvation, proclaiming the blessedness of justification by faith alone and the necessity of sanctification thorough the Spirit in the Word.[10]

- Psalms demonstrate God's amazing goodness and invite us to meditate on His grace and mercy. They lead us to repentance. They teach us to fear God, trust His Word, and hope in His mercy.

- Psalms teach us to flee to the God of salvation through prayer and show us how to bring our requests to Him.[11] They teach us how to pray confidently in the midst of adversity.[12]

6. CO 31:19; translation taken from Barbara Pitkin, "Imitation of David: David as a Paradigm for Faith in Calvin's Exegesis of the Psalms," *Sixteenth Century Journal* 24, 4 (1993): 847.

7. James Denney, *The Letters of Principal James Denney to His Family and Friends* (London: Hodder & Stoughton, n.d.), 9.

8. See James Luther Mays, "Calvin's Commentary on the Psalms: The Preface as Introduction," in *John Calvin and the Church: A Prism of Reform*, ed. Timothy George (Louisville: Westminster/John Knox Press, 1990), 201–204.

9. *Commentary* on 1 Cor. 14:15.

10. Allan M. Harman, "The Psalms and Reformed Spirituality," *Reformed Theological Review* 53, 2 (1994): 58.

11. John Calvin, *Commentary on the Book of Psalms*, trans. James Anderson (Grand Rapids: Eerdmans, 1949), 1:xxxvi–xxxxix.

12. Ibid., Ps. 5:11; 118:5.

• Psalms show us the depth of communion we may enjoy with our covenant-keeping God. They show how the living church is God's bride, God's children, and God's flock.

• Psalms provide a vehicle for communal worship. Many of the psalms use first-person plural pronouns (we, our) to indicate this communal aspect, but even those with first-person singular pronouns include all who love the Lord and are committed to Him. They motivate us to trust and praise God and to love our neighbors. They prompt reliance on God's promises, promote zeal for Him and His house, and advocate compassion for the suffering.

• Psalms cover the full range of spiritual experience, including faith, unbelief, joy in God, sorrow over sin, trust in divine presence, and grief over divine desertion. As Calvin says, they are "an anatomy of all parts of the soul."[13] We see our affections and spiritual maladies in the psalmists' words. Their experiences draw us to self-examination and faith by the Spirit's grace. David's psalms, especially, lead us to praise God and find rest in His sovereign purposes.[14]

Historical Development of the Genevan Psalter

Early in his ministry, Calvin began working on metrical versions of psalms for use in public worship. On January 16, 1537, shortly after his arrival in Geneva, Calvin, together with Guillaume Farel (1489–1565), asked the Geneva city council to introduce psalm singing into church worship. They wrote to the council: "It is a thing very expedient for the edification of the church to sing some psalms in the form of public prayers through which one may pray to God or sing his praise so that the hearts of all might be moved and incited to form like prayers and to render like praises and thanks to God with similar affection."[15] The council rejected Calvin and

---

13. Ibid., 1:xxxix. See James A. De Jong, "'An Anatomy of All Parts of the Soul': Insights into Calvin's Spirituality from His Psalms Commentary," in *Calvinus Sacrae Scripturae Professor: Calvin as Confessor of Holy Scripture*, ed. Wilhelm H. Neuser, Papers of the International Congress on Calvin Research (Grand Rapids: Eerdmans, 1994), 1–14.

14. *Commentary on Psalms*, 1:xxxix.

15. CO 10:6.

Farel's request; in fact, the issue of psalm singing was one of the reasons the council asked Calvin and Farel to leave Geneva the following year.[16]

Soon after moving to Strasbourg where he became pastor of a French-speaking church, Calvin began work on a Psalter. Since there was no French psalter available, he recruited the talents of men such as Clement Marot (1495–1544), Louis Bourgeois (c. 1510–1560), and Theodore Beza (1519–1605) to produce the *Genevan Psalter*. The first collection (1539) contained eighteen psalms, six of which Calvin put into verse. The French poet Marot, forced to flee to Geneva for political asylum in the early 1540s, arranged the rest. Calvin was eager to enlist Marot's talents, despite his worldly ambitions and anti-Reformed convictions.[17] Interestingly, the eighteen psalms selected for the first edition were of a far different balance from most hymnbooks today: six were psalms of repentance, six were about judgment, three dealt with the law and righteousness, while only three were psalms of praise.[18]

The first Genevan Psalter was printed in 1542, a year after Calvin's return to Geneva. This expanded version contained thirty-five psalms (Marot arranged thirty, Calvin five); it was followed in 1543 by an edition with forty-nine psalms.[19] Calvin wrote the preface to both of those psalters, commending the practice of congregational singing. His second preface in the 1543 edition contains his fullest statement about liturgical music.[20]

After Marot's death in 1544, by which time he had set about fifty psalms to meter, Calvin encouraged Beza to put the rest of the psalms into verse after he happened to find a beautifully rhymed version of Psalm 16 on Beza's desk. Though Marot was a more careful student of the French

---

16. CO 10:6, 192.

17. In contrast to the decadent life at the French royal court which he called a paradise, Marot thought life in Geneva far too strict, even calling it "a hell" (Procee, "Calvin on Singing Psalms," 11). Cf. Joseph Waddell Clokey, *David's Harp in Song and Story* (Pittsburgh: United Presbyterian Board of Publications, 1896), 146.

18. Michael LeFebvre, *Singing the Songs of Jesus: Revisiting the Psalms* (Fearn, Ross-shire: Christian Focus, forthcoming 2010), 17–18. The collection also included Calvin's versified form of the Song of Simeon, the Ten Commandments, and the Apostles' Creed.

19. Cf. Louis F. Benson, "John Calvin and the Psalmody of the Reformed Churches," *Journal of the Presbyterian Historical Society* 5, 1 (March 1909): 1–21; 5, 2 (June 1909): 55–87; 55, 3 (Sept. 1909): 107–118.

20. Miller, "Calvin's Understanding of Psalm-Singing as a Means of Grace," 36.

text than Beza, Beza's Hebrew and theology were better. By the early 1560s, Beza completed his work; two years before his death and after working on it for nearly twenty-five years, Calvin rejoiced to see the first complete edition of the *Genevan Psalter*.[21]

Qualities of the Genevan Psalter

The *Genevan Psalter* offers a remarkable collection of 130 distinct meters and 110 different melodies written specifically for the psalms, plus two biblical canticles that remained in use: the Song of Simeon and the Decalogue. Ross J. Miller writes: "Most of the Psalms, therefore, could only be sung to a particular melody, a melody that was created for that particular psalm. These melodies, furthermore, because they were newly composed, did not refer the hearer to any other text, secular or sacred, except its own psalm. The psalm tunes as well as their texts came to have considerable authority in Reformed circles. Composers of elaborate settings of these melodies for voice or instrument would assure their readers that the melodies had not been changed."[22]

The best known of the outstanding musicians of the *Genevan Psalter* is Louis Bourgeois — chosen by Calvin himself.[23] Arriving from Paris in 1545, Bourgeois became a music teacher in Geneva. He did most of his work on the *Genevan Psalter* in 1549 and 1550, arranging 80 of the 125 melodies, thus becoming one of the three main composers of the *Genevan Psalter*.[24]

The Genevan tunes are melodic, distinctive, and reverent.[25] Sung in half and whole length notes, they clearly express Calvin's convictions that

---

21. Published as *Les pseaumes mis en rime françoise par Clément Marot et Théodore Bèze*.

22. Miller, "Calvin's Understanding of Psalm-Singing as a Means of Grace," 40–41.

23. Elsie Anne McKee, ed. and trans., *John Calvin: Writings in Pastoral Piety* (Mahwah, N.J.: Paulist Press, 2001), 85.

24. http://en.wikipedia.org/wiki/Louis_Bourgeois_(composer) (accessed April 3, 2010). Other significant contributors include Guillaume Franc, cantor at Lausanne; Mattheus Greitner of Strasbourg; Maitre Pierre, a precentor in the Genevan church; and Claude Goudimel, who was mainly responsible for harmonies.

25. Unlike Martin Luther, Calvin tried to avoid mixing secular tunes with sacred singing. He believed that all psalm singing must be in the vernacular, asserting that the evidence of Scripture and the practices of the ancient church were grounds for liturgical psalm singing (VanderWilt, "John Calvin's Theology of Liturgical Song," 72, 74).

the psalms deserve their own music and that piety is best promoted when text takes priority over tune. Since music should help us receive the Word, Calvin says, it should be "weighty, dignified, majestic, and modest"— fitting attitudes for sinful creatures in the presence of God.[26] This type of music promotes the sovereignty of God in worship, properly conforming a believer's inward disposition to his outward confession. It enables a believer to sing under the impulse and direction of the Holy Spirit.[27] As Miller notes, "Psalm-singing in public worship, Calvin believed, enhanced the work of the Holy Spirit in a general way, freeing earthbound human minds and hearts so that they could be lifted heavenward for divine fellowship."[28]

Psalm Singing and Worship

Psalm singing is one of the four principle acts of church worship, Calvin believed. It is an extension of prayer and congregants' most significant vocal contribution. He thus urged his people to sing psalms in Sunday morning and afternoon services. Beginning in 1546, a printed table indicated which psalms would be sung on each occasion. Sermon texts dictated the psalms for worship. By 1562, three psalms were sung at each service.[29]

Calvin felt so strongly about psalm singing that early on he introduced it into his Geneva school. Students were required at the Academy of Geneva to "exercise themselves in singing psalms" every day after the noon meal.[30] Calvin's goal was to enable children to sing psalms at school, church, and home so that they could help their parents learn to sing them also.[31] Calvin wrote, "If some children, whom someone has practiced

---

26. Preface to *The Genevan Psalter* (1562), cited in Charles Garside, Jr., *The Origins of Calvin's Theology of Music: 1536–1543* (Philadelphia: The American Philosophical Society, 1979), 32–33.

27. *Institutes*, 3.20.32. Cf. John Alexander Lamb, *The Psalms in Christian Worship* (London: Faith Press, 1962), 141; Ross J. Miller, "Music and the Spirit: Psalm-Singing in Calvin's Liturgy," in *Calvin Studies VI*, ed. John H. Leith (Davidson, N.C.: Davidson College, 1992), 49–58.

28. Miller, "Calvin's Understanding of Psalm-Singing as a Means of Grace," 41.

29. McKee, *John Calvin: Writings on Pastoral Piety*, 85–86.

30. Theodore Gerold, *Les plus anciennes melodies de l' Eglise protestante de Strasbourg et leurs auteurs* (Paris: Librairie Felix Alcan, 1928), 15.

31. LeFebvre, *Singing the Songs of Jesus*, 13.

beforehand in some modest church song, sing in a loud and distinct voice, the people listening with complete attention and following in their hearts what is sung by mouth, little by little each one will become accustomed to sing with the others."[32]

The Lord's Day was a special time for psalm singing. Before each service, the churches would post on their doors what psalms would be sung. Devoted families would send a family member to check the numbers posted and the entire family would practice singing those psalms before each service. Also, between the Lord's Day services, people were encouraged to sing psalms.[33]

Calvin believed that there was something unique about the Psalms. He observes, "The other parts of Scripture contain the commandments which God enjoined his servants to announce to us. But here [in the Psalms] the prophets themselves, seeing they are exhibited to us as speaking to God, and laying open all their inmost thoughts and affections, call, or rather draw, each of us to [participate]...."[34] Calvin also believed that corporate singing subdued the fallen heart and restrained wayward affections in the way of piety. Like preaching and the sacraments, psalm singing disciplines the heart's affections in the school of faith, lifting the believer to God. It also amplifies the effect of the Word on the heart, multiplying the church's spiritual energy. "The Psalms can stimulate us to raise our hearts to God and arouse us to an ardor in invoking as well as in exalting with praises the glory of his name," Calvin writes.[35] In short, with the Spirit's guidance, psalm singing tunes believers' hearts for glory.

Remarkable Success of the Genevan Psalter

The *Genevan Psalter* was an instantaneous success. Twenty-five editions were printed in the first year, and sixty-two editions within four years of publication. By the nineteenth century, there were fourteen hundred

32. CO 10:12.
33. Miller, "Calvin's Understanding of Psalm-Singing as a Means of Grace," 37.
34. *Commentary on Psalms*, 1:xxxvii.
35. CO 10:12; cited in Garside, *The Origins of Calvin's Theology of Music*, 10.

editions in dozens of languages. The Netherlands alone produced thirty editions in less than two centuries.[36]

Remaining an integral part of Reformed worship for centuries, the *Genevan Psalter* set the standard for successive psalm books in French, English, Dutch, German, and Hungarian. As a devotional book, it warmed the hearts of thousands, but the people who sang from it also understood that its power was not in the book or its words, but in the Spirit who impressed those words on their hearts.

The *Genevan Psalter* promoted piety by stimulating a spirituality of the Word. That spirituality was corporate and liturgical, breaking down the distinction between liturgy and life. The Calvinists freely sang the Psalms not only in their churches, but also in their homes and workplaces, on the streets and in the fields.[37] Miller notes, "According to sixteenth century accounts, Huguenot soldiers and sailors were known for their psalm-singing as they carried out their duties, and French Protestant martyrs faced death singing a favorite, or most appropriate, psalm. A seventeenth-century Catholic bishop, Godeau, noted that 'to know them [the Psalms] by heart is among them a mark of their communion.'"[38]

In short, psalm singing became a "means of Huguenot self-identification."[39] It also became a cultural emblem. As T. Hartley Hall writes, "In

---

36. Michael Bushell, *The Songs of Zion: A Contemporary Case for Exclusive Psalmody* (Pittsburgh: Crown and Covenant, 1980), 175. More than thirty thousand copies of the first complete five-hundred-page *Genevan Psalter* were printed by more than fifty French and Swiss publishers in the first year, and at least 27,400 copies were published in Geneva in the first few months (Jeffry T. VanderWilt, "John Calvin's Theology of Liturgical Song," *Christian Scholar's Review* 25 [1996]: 67). Cf. *Le Psautier de Genève, 1562–1685: Images, commentées et essai de bibliographie*, intro. J. D. Candaus (Geneva: Bibliothèque publique et universitaire, 1986), 1:16–18; John Witvliet, "The Spirituality of the Psalter: Metrical Psalms in Liturgy and Life in Calvin's Geneva," in *Calvin Study Society Papers, 1995–1997*, ed. David Foxgrover (Grand Rapids: CRC, 1998), 93–117.

37. Witvliet, "The Spirituality of the Psalter," 117.

38. Miller, "Calvin's Understanding of Psalm-Singing as a Means of Grace," 42. Cf. Charles W. Baird, *History of the Huguenot Emigration to America* (New York: Dodd, Mead, and Co., 1885), 81, 103, 206.

39. W. Stanford Reid, "The Battle Hymns of the Lord: Calvinist Psalmody of the Sixteenth Century," in *Sixteenth Century Essays and Studies*, ed. C. S. Meyer (St. Louis: Foundation for Reformation Research, 1971), 2:47; cf. Benson, "John Calvin and the Psalmody of the Reformed Churches," *Journal of the Presbyterian Historical Society* 5, 2 (June 1909): 57–67.

scriptural or metrical versions, the Psalms, together with the stately tunes to which they were early set, are clearly the heart and soul of Reformed piety."[40] No wonder, then, that in many parts of Europe, the term *psalm singer* became nearly synonymous with the title *Protestant*.[41]

The Puritans on Psalm Singing

Like Calvin, the Puritans practiced psalm singing. Percy A. Scholes, a Puritan music scholar, explains: "The English Puritans, being Calvinist and not Lutheran, held to the view that the only proper worship song was that provided of God once for all in the Book of Psalms (and Biblical canticles). This was Calvin's conviction and a metrical psalm before and after the sermon was the usual practice at Geneva."[42]

When approximately eight hundred Protestants went into exile under Bloody Mary's reign, their churches in exile commonly used metrical psalmody in their liturgy.[43] Beth Quitslund concludes,

For the English communities in exile, metrical psalms helped define a Protestant identity that could respond to the trauma of the Marian accession. As writings that offered great scope for penitence, consolation, and oppositional self-presentation, they were well suited for the task, and the paraphrases that Whittingham composed at Frankfurt show the language of these biblical songs framed to the times. Congregational singing itself, both psalms and in the hymns composed by the English Protestants in Germany, answered a need for communal expression that the exiles felt more keenly than they had in the religious climate of Edwardian England. This attachment to psalm-singing as a way to unite the people in godly affection did not abate, however, when Elizabeth's accession restored England's

---

40. "The Shape of Reformed Piety," in Robin Maas and Gabriel O'Donnell, *Spiritual Traditions for the Contemporary Church* (Nashville: Abingdon Press, 1990), 215. Cf. Reid, "The Battle Hymns of the Lord," 2:36–54.

41. LeFebvre, *Singing the Songs of Jesus*, 13.

42. Perry A. Scholes, *The Puritans and Music in England and New England: A Contribution to the Cultural History of Two Nations* (London: Oxford University Press, 1934), 253. I wish to thank Brian Najapfour for his research assistance on this section of the chapter.

43. Beth Quitslund, *The Reformation in Rhyme: Sternhold, Hopkins and the English Metrical Psalter, 1547–1603* (Aldershot, U.K.: Ashgate, 2008), 114–53.

national Church to Protestantism. Many of the texts and tunes that had supported the English abroad became staple songs of the Elizabethan Church, importing the confessional ideology they nourished and the anti-Marian militancy they articulated with them.[44]

When the exiles who had settled in Geneva returned to England, they took the *Genevan Psalter* with them. By 1562, they published the first complete English metrical version of the Psalms, *The Whole Booke of Psalmes*, which contained 150 numbers with 64 tunes in 462 pages.[45] This version became known as the *Sternhold and Hopkins Psalter*, named after its two major contributors, Thomas Sternhold and John Hopkins.[46] Other contributors included William Kethe, John Marckant, John Pullain, Thomas Norton, William Whittingham, and Robert Wisdom.[47]

The Whole Booke of Psalmes continued to play a major role in the life of the Elizabethan church from 1562 to 1603. Quitslund writes, "Counting only those printed in England and containing the whole text of at least the psalms, 14 editions survive from 1562 to 1572; from 1573 to 1582, 37 editions; from 1583 to 1592, 42 editions; and from 1593 to 1603, 53 editions."[48] Quitslund goes on to address the question, "Why did the largely anti-puritan Elizabethan authorities support metrical psalmody, overlook the Genevan associations of Day's book, and allow such a confessionally strident volume to become so important to English worship?" Her answers include (1) that the "basic theology of the English Church as a whole during the sixteenth century was very like that of Calvin's Geneva," (2) that the make-up of the Bishop's bench and the Privy Council was

---

44. Ibid., 152–53.

45. For the development of the Anglo-Genevan metrical psalter from 1556 to 1562, see ibid., 156–238.

46. Sternhold (d. 1549), who served as Groom of the Royal Wardrobe, metricized psalms for young Edward VI (1537–1553) and for the Court's edification (ibid., 19–58, esp. 27–31, 55–57). Sternhold's work generated "the production of an extraordinary number of works of scriptural texts in meter" from 1549 to 1553 (ibid., 72–93), including those by his most important imitator, John Hopkins (ibid., 93–103).

47. Ibid., 283.

48. Ibid., 241. The only other large collection of metrical psalms printed in the Elizabethan period was Matthew Parker's *Whole Psalter translated into English metre*. Quitslund notes that "Parker had written the versifications of the psalms themselves, and perhaps the liturgical hymns that accompany them, in his retirement during Mary's reign, completing them in 1557" (ibid., 251).

largely conservative in the first part of Elizabeth's reign, (3) that most congregants felt some enthusiasm for the Reformed faith and viewed psalm singing as welcome "propaganda" for the still tenuous religious settlement, and (4) that most people "thoroughly enjoyed singing psalms."[49]

"The singing of these psalms became a signature of Puritanism,"[50] says W. Stanford Reid. Yet since many Christian churches already engaged in considerable psalm singing, Scholes was reluctant to regard psalmody as "a special mark of Puritanism" since psalter use was nearly universal.[51] People sang psalms at city banquets, soldiers hummed them on the march, farmers whistled them in the fields, and pilgrims sang them as they sailed for new continents. Nevertheless, while psalm singing was not a uniquely Puritan practice, the Puritans developed the theology of psalmody and emphasized its lawfulness and necessity beyond other groups of Christians. That is why when Oliver Cromwell (1599–1658), sympathetic to the Puritans, established the Commonwealth, only metrical psalms in their simplest forms were allowed to be sung in churches. The new leadership also abolished the liturgy and prayer book, dismissed choirs, and destroyed or silenced organs.[52]

Let us not misunderstand the Puritans here. Their motivations were rooted in their conviction of what would later be called the regulative principle of worship—anything not expressly commanded in Scripture was forbidden in worship. This varied substantively from the Anglican view, which followed the Lutheran tradition and view of Scripture, asserting that what Scripture did not expressly forbid and tradition sustained was permissible in the church. For the Puritan mind, Anglican cathedral music was too complex, its anthems too obscure, its choirs too professional, and its entire theology of music too divorced from the principles of edification and the priesthood of all believers.[53]

---

49. Ibid., 264–65.
50. Reid, "The Battle Hymns of the Lord," 2:52.
51. Scholes, *The Puritans and Music in England and New England*, 272–74. Scholes admits that Roman Catholics and Quakers did little psalm singing.
52. Edwin Liemohn, *The Organ and Choir in Protestant Worship* (Philadelphia: Fortress Press, 1968), 55.
53. Horton Davies, *Worship and Theology in England* (Princeton: University Press, 1975), 255.

Since the Puritans and their successors, the Nonconformists, taught that every part of worship needed scriptural warrant, uninspired hymns were unacceptable. How could church leaders assume that they were capable of deciding what was appropriate for worship when God had already decided that for them in Scripture by restricting God's praise to the metrical psalms, His own handbook for singing? The Puritans' conservative views on singing in worship services were grounded in what they deemed to be non-negotiable scriptural principles. The issue at stake was not their distaste for music, but their deep conviction that Scripture must be obeyed at all costs.[54]

In Massachusetts Bay Colony, New England, a group of "thirty pious and learned" Puritans, principally Thomas Welde, Richard Mather, and John Eliot, worked together to produce a better psalter. Published in 1640 as the first book printed on the American continent, *The Whole Booke of Psalmes* became known as the *Bay Psalm Book*.[55] Is it not fascinating that the first published book in America was a faithful translation of the Hebrew psalms into English? The *Bay Psalm Book* eventually replaced the *Sternhold and Hopkins Psalter* and included a preface explaining "not onely the lawfullnesse, but also the necessity of the heavenly ordinance of singing Scripture psalmes in the churches of God."[56]

The *Bay Psalm Book* used about forty common tunes in its first edition. By the 1698 edition, that number was only thirteen, indicating how the quality of singing degenerated among the New England Puritans during the last half of the seventeenth century.[57] That degeneration, common to both Old and New England, was one factor that helped open the door to hymn singing in the eighteenth century.

---

54. Ibid., 254. In fact, many Puritans were fine vocal and instrumental performers. Cromwell himself employed an organist for his own organ, thoroughly enjoyed choral music, and hired an orchestra to play at his daughter's wedding.
55. Wilberforce Eames, Introduction to *The Bay Psalm Book: Being a Facsimile Reprint of the First Edition* (Cambridge, Mass.: Printed by Stephen Daye, 1640, reprint; Bedford, Mass.: Applewood Books, 2002), vi.
56. *The Whole Booke of Psalmes* (Cambridge, Mass.: Stephen Daye, 1640), title page.
57. Zoltán Haraszti, *The Enigma of the Bay Psalm Book* (Chicago: University of Chicago Press, 1956), 68–70.

John Cotton (1584–1652), the well-known New England Puritan who may have written the preface to the *Bay Psalm Book*,[58] wrote an important treatise in 1647, typical of Puritan thought: *Singing of Psalmes: A Gospel-Ordinance Or A Treatise, Wherein are handled these foure Particulars. 1. Touching the Duty it selfe. 2. Touching the Matter to be Sung. 3. Touching the Singers. 4. Touching the Manner of Singing.*[59] This was "the first major work by a New Englander on psalmody and worship."[60] It is one of the best sources for the study of Puritan psalmody, as it carefully addresses the main issues in psalm singing. For most of the remainder of this chapter, we will follow Cotton's four-step order.

The Duty of Singing Psalms

On the title page of the *Bay Psalm Book*, Cotton states that psalm singing is a gospel ordinance. His grandson Cotton Mather called psalm singing a "holy, delightfull and profitable Ordinance in the Church or Household."[61] The Westminster Assembly divines said in their "Directory for the Publick Worship of God" that it is the duty of all Christians "to praise God publickly, by singing of psalms together in the congregation, and also privately in the family."[62]

Cotton points out that Christ sang a psalm with His disciples after "the administration of the Lords Supper" (Matt. 26:30).[63] Matthew Henry remarks: "Singing of psalms is a gospel-ordinance. Christ's removing the hymn from the close of the passover to the close of the Lord's Supper, plainly intimates that he intended that ordinance should continue in his

---

58. Ibid., 18. Perry Miller and Thomas Johnson, on the other hand, believe Richard Mather wrote the preface. See their *The Puritans* (New York: American Book, 1938), 669.

59. London: Printed by M. S. for Hannah Allen, at the Crowne in Popes-head-alley: and John Rothwell at the Sunne and fountaine in Pauls-church-yard, 1647. Hereafter, *Singing of Psalmes*.

60. David P. McKay, "Cotton Mather's Unpublished Singing Sermon," *New England Quarterly* 48, 3 (1975): 413.

61. Cotton Mather, "Text of Cotton Mather Singing Sermon April 18, 1721" in ibid., 419.

62. "The Directory for the Publick Worship of God," in *Westminster Confession of Faith* (1646; Glasgow: Free Presbyterian Publications, 1997), 393.

63. *Singing of Psalmes*, 7.

church, that, as it had not its birth with the ceremonial law, so it should not die with it."[64]

When Cotton Mather published *Accomplish'd Singer* in 1721, his father, Increase Mather, wrote an endorsement for the book, remarking that psalm singing was "somewhat lost in many places."[65] The problem was not new. Cotton had already dealt with it in *Singing of Psalmes* (1647). In the first section of this volume, Cotton specifically addresses the issue of vocal psalmody. He says there are "Antipsalmists, who doe not acknowledge any singing at all with the voyce in the New Testament, but onely spirituall songs of joy and comfort of the heart in the word of Christ."[66] In arguing for vocal psalms, Cotton cites two classic texts on singing psalms: Ephesians 5:19 and Colossians 3:16. He says that in these verses Paul exhorts us to sing not only silently in our hearts but also audibly with our voices.

Cotton further argues that lifted voices should be understandable, so that even uneducated hearers "might be edified, and say, Amen, at such giving of thankes" (1 Cor. 14:14–15).[67] Psalm singing should bless not only the singer but also the listener. Yet, edification should not be the chief aim in singing—it should be God's glory. As Cotton Mather declares, "Let a sincere View to the Honour of God (the great End of Psalmody) animate and regulate your Endeavors to attain this worthy Accomplishment. Let all be done after a godly Sort, that even by this common action you may please and glorify God."[68]

Because God's glory is psalmody's supreme goal, the Puritans believed that singing in worship should be robust rather than reserved, as some have caricatured their singing. While the Puritans sang out of duty, they did so with profound joy and delight in their souls. That is why Mather calls psalm singing a "delightful ordinance."

---

64. Matthew Henry, *Commentary* (Peabody, Mass.: Hendrickson Publishers, 1991), 5:318.

65. See "An Attestation from the Very Reverend Dr. Increase Mather," in Cotton Mather, *Accomplish'd Singer* (Boston: Printed by B. Green, for S. Gerrish at his Shop in Cornhill, 1721).

66. *Singing of Psalmes*, 2.

67. Ibid.

68. "Text of Cotton Mather Singing Sermon April 18, 1721," in McKay, "Cotton Mather's Unpublished Singing Sermon," 422.

The Matter to Be Sung
Should singing in public worship be confined to the book of Psalms? Should congregations sing the songs of Moses, Mary, Elizabeth, and other biblical saints? And should the church be allowed to sing hymns composed by spiritually gifted believers? Cotton addresses these questions in the second part of his book.

Cotton says the singing of uninspired hymns should not be allowed in public worship.[69] Quoting Ephesians 5:19 and Colossians 3:16, he says that when Paul exhorts or commands us to sing, he instructs us to sing "psalms and hymns and spiritual songs," which, for Cotton, are "the very Titles of the Songs of David."[70] To stress his point, Cotton says that the word *hymn* in Matthew 26:30 is "the generall title for the whole Book of Psalmes."[71] Therefore, Paul was directing us to sing not hymns or spiritual songs written by any believer, but specifically the psalms of David. In Cotton's mind, the title "Psalms or Songs of David" refers to all 150 psalms, even though David did not write all the psalms.

Other Puritans supported Cotton's interpretation of Ephesians 5:19 and Colossians 3:16. In commenting on Colossians 3:16, Edward Leigh argues: "As the Apostle exhorteth us to singing, so he instructeth what the matter of our Song should be, viz. Psalmes, Hymnes, and spirituall Songs. Those three are the Titles of the Songs of David, as they are delivered to us by the Holy Ghost himself."[72] Similarly, Jonathan Clapham, maintaining the worth of singing David's psalms, says, "The Apostle, Eph. 5 and Col. 3, where he commands singing of Psalmes, doth clearly point us to David's Psalms, by using those, Psalmes, hymnes, and spirituall songs,

69. *Singing of Psalmes*, 32.
70. Ibid., 16.
71. Ibid., 25.
72. Edward Leigh, *Annotations upon all the New Testament philologicall and theologicall wherein the emphasis and elegancie of the Greeke is observed, some imperfections in our translation are discovered, divers Jewish rites and customes tending to illustrate the text are mentioned, many antilogies and seeming contradictions reconciled, severall darke and obscure places opened, sundry passages vindicated from the false glosses of papists and hereticks* (London: Printed by W. W. and E. G. for William Lee, and are to be sold at his shop, 1650), 306.

which answer to the three Hebrew words, *Shorim, Tehillim, Mizmorim,* whereby David's Psalmes were called."[73]

Thomas Ford, a member of the Westminster Assembly of Divines, also affirmed this view. He asserted in his *Singing of Psalmes: the duty of Christians under the New Testament. Or A vindication of that Gospel-ordinance in V. sermons upon Ephesians 5. 19. Wherein are asserted and cleared 1. That 2. What 3. How 4. Why we must sing* (1653):

> I know nothing more probable then this, viz. That Psalmes, and Hymns, and spiritual Songs, do answer to Mizmorim, Tehillim, and Shirim, which are the Hebrew names of David's Psalmes. All the Psalmes together are called Tehillim, i.e. Praises, or songs of praise. Mizmor and Shir are in the Titles of many Psalmes, sometimes one, and sometimes the other, and sometimes both joyn'd together, as they know well who can read the Originall. Now the Apostle calling them by the same names by which the Greek Translation (which the New Testament so much follows) renders the Hebrew, is an argument that he means no other then David's Psalmes.[74]

Ford's statement is important because it indicates that when the Westminster Confession of Faith says that "singing of psalms with grace in the heart" is a part of "the ordinary religious worship of God" (21.5), it means exclusively the book of Psalms.[75]

---

73. Jonathan Clapham, *A short and full vindication of that sweet and comfortable ordinance, of singing of Psalmes. Together with some profitable rules, to direct weak Christians how to sing to edification. And a briefe confutation of some of the most usual cavils made against the same. Published especially for the use of the Christians, in and about the town of Wramplingham in Norf. for the satisfaction of such, as scruple the said ordinance, for the establishment of such as do own it, against all seducers that come amongst them; and for the instruction of all in general, that they may better improve the same to their spiritual comfort and benefit* (London: [s.n.], Printed, anno Dom. 1656), 3.

74. Thomas Ford, *Singing of Psalmes: the duty of Christians under the New Testament. Or A vindication of that Gospel-ordinance in V. sermons upon Ephesians 5. 19. Wherein are asserted and cleared 1. That 2. What 3. How 4. Why we must sing* (London: Printed by A. M. for Christopher Meredith at the Crane in Pauls Church-yard, 1653), 15, 16.

75. *Westminster Confession of Faith*, 92.

Nick Needham, however, suggests that the framers of the confession did not intend the word *psalms* to mean only the psalms of David.[76] Needham argues:

> If only they [the composers of the confession] had written "David's psalms," that would be an end of the matter. But they did not write "David's psalms." From a purely linguistic standpoint, it is therefore wholly possible and legitimate to interpret the unqualified word "psalms" in 21.5 either as David's psalms, or as religious songs in general.[77]

This would thus allow for uninspired hymns.

Matthew Winzer, who understands the term *psalms* in the confession to refer strictly to the book of Psalms, challenges Needham's view. Winzer concludes that Needham "failed to properly represent the view of the Westminster Assembly when he claims that exclusive psalmody is the least probable historical-contextual interpretation of the reference to 'singing of psalms' in Confession 21.5."[78] Winzer's argument seems to hold more weight than Needham's.

Though Cotton made a strong case for the exclusive psalmody interpretation of Ephesians 5:19 and Colossians 3:16, he was not a strict advocate of exclusive psalmody. He stated: "Not onely the Psalms of David, but any other spirituall Songs recorded in Scripture, may lawfully be sung in Christian Churches, as the song of Moses, and Asaph, Heman and Ethan, Solomon and Hezekiah, Habacuck and Zachary, Hannah and Deborah, Mary and Elizabeth, and the like."[79]

As for doctrinally sound uninspired, or extra-scriptural, hymns, Cotton says they should not be sung in public worship, but they may certainly be sung in "private houses."[80] He instructed, "We grant also, that any pri-

---

76. Nick Needham, "Westminster and Worship: Psalms, Hymns, and Musical Instruments?" in *The Westminster Confession into the 21ˢᵗ Century*, ed. J. Ligon Duncan (Fearn, Ross-shire: Mentor, 2003), 2:250–53.

77. Ibid., 253.

78. Matthew Winzer, "Westminster and Worship Examined: A Review of Nick Needham's essay on the Westminster Confession of Faith's teaching concerning the regulative principle, the singing of psalms, and the use of musical instruments in the public worship of God," *The Confessional Presbyterian* 4 (2008): 264.

79. *Singing of Psalmes*, 15.

80. Ibid., 32.

vate Christian, who hath a gift to frame a spirituall Song, may both frame it, and sing it privately, for his own private comfort, and remembrance of some speciall benefit, or deliverance: nor doe we forbid the private use of an Instrument of Musick therewithal; So that attention to the instrument, doe not divert the heart from attention to the matter of the Song."[81]

Cotton does not deny "that in the publique thankesgivings of the Church, if the Lord should furnish any of the members of the Church with a spirituall gift to compose a Psalme upon any speciall occasion, he may lawfully be allowed to sing it before the Church, and the rest hearing it, and approving it, may goe along with him in Spirit, and say Amen to it."[82]

In a word, Cotton sanctioned singing newly composed religious songs, but only in special gatherings. He was concerned that only David's psalms and other Scripture songs be sung in worship services.[83]

The Singers

Who must sing these divinely inspired songs? Should an individual be allowed to sing for the congregation, or should the entire congregation sing? Should men and women sing, or men only? Should unbelievers be allowed to sing with believers? Should people who are not church members be allowed to sing? Cotton addresses these kinds of questions in the third section of his book.

While solos might be appropriate in other settings, Cotton says that in public worship God wants the entire congregation to sing together. Intriguingly, Cotton explains that after partaking of the Lord's Supper, Jesus and His disciples—a sort of congregation—sang a psalm. Likewise, in the Old Testament, "Moses and the children of Israel [who were a body of people] sang a Song of Thanksgiving to the Lord" (Ex. 15:1).[84]

Cotton says women may sing along with men in congregational singing, citing Exodus 15:20–21, which says that Miriam and other women sang God's praises along with men. For Cotton, this passage is sufficient

---

81. Ibid., 15.
82. Ibid.
83. For Thomas Manton's similar view, see William Young, *The Puritan Principle of Worship* (Vienna, Va.: Publications Committee of the Presbyterian Reformed Church, n.d.), 27–28.
84. *Singing of Psalmes*, 40.

ground "to justifie the lawfull practice of women in singing together with men."[85]

Cotton spends much time addressing the questions of whether believers who are not members of the local church and unbelievers are allowed to sing with believing church members in public worship. Some people in Cotton's day believed that only professing church members had the right to sing during a worship service. Cotton's response was that since psalm singing is a moral duty of all Christians, every person, whether a church member or not, is "bound to sing to the praise of God."[86] He says psalm singing is a "generall Commandment"; thus, as the psalms themselves make clear, everyone in the world—including unbelievers—is called to lift up his voice to the Lord. Scripture is plain: "O sing unto the LORD a new song: sing unto the LORD, all the earth" (Ps. 96:1); "Make a joyful noise unto the LORD, all ye lands" (Ps. 100:1); "Sing unto God, ye kingdoms of the earth; O sing praises unto the LORD; Selah" (Ps. 68:32).[87]

Not all Puritans agreed with Cotton on granting unbelievers the right to participate in congregational singing. For example, this issue surfaced in John Bunyan's Bedford meeting house. Two years after Bunyan's death, the Bedford church met and "discussed the subject and gravely decided… that Publick Singing of Psalms be practiced by the Church with a caution that none others perform it but such as can sing with grace in their Hearts according to the command of Christ."[88]

The Bedford congregation's conviction was not uncommon among separatist churches, which said a local church should consist only of believers; thus, in public worship, only believers should sing. But Cotton made it clear that on the basis of the general nature of the command to sing to the Lord, none is "exempted from this service."[89] Most Puritans agreed. However, Cotton acknowledged that "the grounds and ends of Singing… peculiarly concerne the Church and people of God and therefore they [the believers] of all others are most bound to abound in this Dutie."[90] While

---

85. Ibid., 43.
86. Ibid., 44.
87. Ibid., 45.
88. Scholes, *The Puritans and Music in England and New England*, 268.
89. *Singing of Psalmes*, 45.
90. Ibid.

the unsaved are commanded to make melody to the Lord, the redeemed
should delight in this command.

The Manner of Singing
In the final segment of *Singing of Psalmes*, Cotton addresses the issue of
whether it is lawful to sing psalms in meter to tunes invented by men.
Using common sense, Cotton reasons that if it is "the holy will of God,
that the Hebrew Scriptures should be translated into English Prose in
order unto reading, then it is like sort his holy will, that the Hebrew
Psalmes, (which are Poems and Verses) should be translated into English
Poems and Verses in order to Singing."[91] Practically speaking, Cotton says
a metrical psalter makes "the verses more easie for memory, and more fit
for melody."[92] Hence, singing David's psalms in meter is not only proper
but also wise.

As for tunes, Cotton says that since the Lord "hath hid from us the
Hebrew Tunes, and the musicall Accents wherewith the Psalmes of David
were wont to be sung, it must needs be that the Lord alloweth us to sing
them in any such grave, and solemne, and plaine Tunes, as doe fitly suite
the gravitie of the matter, the solemnitie of Gods worship, and the capaci-
tie of a plaine People."[93] God gives us freedom to compose reverent tunes
for the Psalms, so long as the rhythm and tunes are pleasing to God and
edifying to His people.[94] We should never use this liberty to satisfy our
selfish desires.

Cotton suggests that a minister read each line of a psalm before asking the congregation to sing it. Though the Bible does not require this
practice, Cotton found it helpful "that the words of the Psalme be openly
read before hand, line after line, or two lines together, that so they who
want [lack] either books or skill to reade, may know what is to be sung,
and joyne with the rest in the dutie of singing…and by Singing be stirred
up to use holy Harmony, both with the Lord and his people."[95]

91. Ibid., 55.
92. Ibid.
93. Ibid., 56.
94. Ibid., 60.
95. Ibid., 62–63. For more on Cotton's view, see Young, *The Puritan Principle of Worship*, 20–27.

The Westminster divines similarly advise:

In singing of psalms, the voice is to be tunably and gravely ordered; but the chief care must be to sing with understanding, and with grace in the heart, making melody unto the Lord.

That the whole congregation may join herein, every one that can read is to have a psalm book; and all others, not disabled by age or otherwise, are to be exhorted to learn to read. But for the present, where many in the congregation cannot read, it is convenient that the minister, or some other fit person appointed by him and the other ruling officers, do read the psalm, line by line, before the singing thereof.[96]

A "Puritan" Baptist Exception

As Puritanism waned at the close of the seventeenth century, a Puritan-minded Baptist preacher named Benjamin Keach (1640–1707) introduced hymns, in addition to psalms and paraphrases, into the English Noncon-formist churches. He began by allowing one hymn after each administration of the Lord's Supper, then moved to one hymn per Sabbath.[97] Eventually he became "a pioneer of congregational hymn singing."[98]

In response to Isaac Marlow's *A Brief Discourse Concerning Singing in the Public Worship of God in the Gospel Church* (1690), which argued that any congregational singing was a distortion of true worship,[99] Keach wrote his first book on the subject: *The Breach Repaired in God's Worship; or Singing of Psalms, Hymns, and Spiritual Songs, Proved to Be an Holy Ordinance of Jesus Christ* (1691). Keach went beyond the Puritans and argued for hymn singing based on examples from David, Solomon, and others, and its "educational value." This book, together with Keach's *Spiritual Melody; containing near Three Hundred Sacred Hymns* (1691), created quite a stir,

---

96. "The Directory for the Publick Worship of God," in *Westminster Confession of Faith*, 393.

97. J. R. Watson, *The English Hymn: A Critical and Historical Study* (Oxford: Clarendon Press, 1997), 110; cf. Horton Davies, *Worship and Theology in England from Andrewes to Baxter and Fox, 1603–1690* (Princeton: Princeton University Press, 1975), 510.

98. Hugh Martin, *Benjamin Keach, Pioneer of Congregational Hymn Singing* (London: Independent Press, 1961).

99. For Isaac Marlow, see Davies, *Worship and Theology in England from Andrewes to Baxter and Fox*, 274–75.

even in Keach's own church, where nine people withdrew their membership. That, however, was the tip of the iceberg. Marlow responded with an appendix to his own book even before Keach's *The Breach Repaired* was available to the public, moving Keach to add an appendix to his own book. That sparked a pamphlet war among a number of pastors, most of whom supported Keach. Despite this, Keach lost an additional twenty members to Robert Steed, who wrote against congregational singing in *An Epistle Written to the Members of a Church in London Concerning Singing* (1691).[100] The following year the issue of singing reached the General Assembly, which censured both sides for their uncharitable reflections against their brethren; with that, the pamphlet war ceased for four years.[101]

In 1696, the pamphlet war began again after Keach published *A Feast of Fat Things; containing several Scripture Songs and Hymns*. In all, Keach himself wrote nearly five hundred hymns and promoted hundreds more by publishing hymnbooks that circulated throughout the United Kingdom and North America. His work paved the way for Isaac Watts (1674–1748), often called "the father of English hymnody," whose renowned *Hymns and Spiritual Songs* (1707) dealt a serious blow to the fading Puritan convictions about psalm singing in public worship.[102] For the first time in church history, manmade hymns replaced psalm singing.[103]

Conclusion: Practical Benefits of Psalm Singing

Albert Bailey rightly concludes that Calvin's theological beliefs about the Psalter helped unite the Reformers and Puritans around the conviction that "only God's own Word was worthy to be used in praising Him."[104] Psalm singing was important to Calvin and the Puritans, however, not

---

100. James Patrick Carnes, "The Famous Mr. Keach: Benjamin Keach and His Influence on Congregational Singing in Seventeenth Century England" (M.A. thesis, North Texas State University, 1984), 59–61.

101. Robert H. Young, "The History of Baptist Hymnody in England from 1612 to 1800" (Ph.D. dissertation, University of Southern California, 1959), 43–44.

102. Carnes, "The Famous Mr. Keach," 94–95. For a succinct study of Watts, see Watson, *The English Hymn: A Critical and Historical Study*, 133–70; cf. Darryl Hart's chapter, "Psalters, Hymnals, Worship Wars, and American Presbyterian Piety," in this volume.

103. LeFebvre, *Singing the Songs of Jesus*, 14.

104. Albert Bailey, *The Gospel in Hymns: Backgrounds and Interpretations* (New York: Charles Scribner's Sons, 1950), 17.

only because it is biblical and historical and is our theological and moral duty to God, but also because of the gracious effects it has upon those who sing. Here are some spiritual and practical benefits of psalm singing:

• Psalm singing comforts the soul. It lifts up the spiritually downcast and provides spiritual riches that are Christ-centered and experiential. Cotton says psalm singing "allayeth the passions of melancholy and choler, yea and scattereth the furious temptations of evill spirits, 1 Sam. 16.23."[105] It "helpeth to ass[u]age enmity, and to restore friendship favour, as in Saul to David."[106] Increase Mather observes "that musick is of great efficacy against melancholy." Mather says, "The sweetness and delightfulness of musick has a natural power to [overcome] melancholy passions."[107]

For Calvin and the Puritans, a psalter is what Robert Sanderson (1587–1662) called "the treasury of Christian comfort."[108] Sanderson, Bishop of Lincoln, ejected from his professorship at Oxford and imprisoned by Parliament, found great comfort through difficult times in the Psalter. Subsequently, he wrote that a psalter is "fitted for all persons and all necessities; able to raise the soul from dejection by the frequent mention of God's mercies to repentant sinners: to stir up holy desire; to increase joy; to moderate sorrow; to nourish hope, and teach us patience, by waiting God's leisure; to beget a trust in the mercy, power, and providence of our Creator; and to cause a resignation of ourselves to his will: and then, and not till then, to believe ourselves happy."[109]

• Psalm singing cultivates piety. Lewis Bayly included a section on psalm singing in *The Practice of Pietie*. He set down five rules for psalm singing:

1. Beware of singing divine Psalmes for an ordinary recreation; as do men of impure Spirits, who sing holy Psalmes, intermingled

---

105. *Singing of Psalmes*, 4.

106. Ibid., 4.

107. Increase Mather, *A History of God's Remarkable Providences in Colonial New England* (1856; reprint, Portland, Ore.: Back Home Industries, 1997), 187.

108. Cited in Rowland E. Prothero, *The Psalms in Human Life* (1903; reprint, Birmingham. Ala.: Solid Ground Christian Books, 2002), 176.

109. Cited in ibid.

with prophane *Ballads*. They are Gods Word, take them not in thy mouth in vaine.

2. Remember to sing Davids Psalmes, with Davids Spirit.

3. Practice Saint Pauls rule: I will sing with the Spirit, but I will sing with the understanding also.

4. As you sing, uncover your heads, and behave your selves in comely reverence, as in the sight of God, singing to God, in Gods owne Words: but bee sure that the matter makes more melody in your hearts, than the Musicke in your Eares: for the singing with a grace in our hearts, is that which the Lord is delighted withal....

5. Thou maist, if thou thinke good, sing all the Psalmes over in order: for all are most divine and comfortable. But if thou wilt chuse some speciall Psalmes, as more fit for some times, and purposes: and such, as by the oft-usage, thy people may the easilier commit to memory.[110]

• Finally, psalm singing helps us glorify God, as the Reformation and post-Reformation divines tell us repeatedly. Calvin wrote, "Truly, we know through experience that [psalm singing] has great force and vigor to move and enflame hearts to invoke and to praise God with a more lively and ardent zeal." Calvin goes on to say, quoting Augustine: "When we sing these psalms…we are certain that God puts the words into our mouths as if he were singing in us to exalt his glory."[111] Wilhelmus à Brakel, a primary Dutch Further Reformation divine of Puritan mind, agrees: "Singing [psalms] is a religious exercise by which, with the appropriate modulation of the voice, we worship, thank, and praise God."[112]

Therefore, let those who sing psalms, sing for the praise of God! "Sing praises to God, sing praises: sing praises unto our King, sing praises. For God is the King of all the earth: sing ye praises with understanding" (Ps. 47:6–7).

---

110. Lewis Bayly, *The Practice of Pietie* (London: Printed by R. Y. for Andrew Crooke, 1638), 233–34.

111. Miller, "Calvin's Understanding of Psalm-Singing as a Means of Grace," 38, 40.

112. Wilhelmus á Brakel, *The Christian's Reasonable Service*, trans. Bartel Elshout, ed. Joel R. Beeke (Morgan, Pa.: Soli Deo Gloria Publications, 1995), 4:31.

Chapter 3

The History of Psalm Singing
in the Christian Church[1]

Terry Johnson

*T*he canonical book of Psalms may be viewed properly as the Bible's own devotional book. Dietrich Bonhoeffer made this point in his brief work *The Psalms: Prayer Book of the Bible.*[2] Indeed, it is the primary source from which all other devotional books have been drawn. "The Psalter is the great school of prayer," said Bonhoeffer elsewhere.[3] Thomas à Kempis (1380–1471), for example, quotes the Psalms more than the Gospels in his *The Imitation of Christ,* "the most popular of all Christian devotional books."[4] The Psalter has provided the people of God with the verbal images, names, and terminology with which to understand God and how we are to relate to Him. They have taught us how to speak to God as we address Him with praise, confession of sin, thanksgiving, and intercession. "There is no one book of Scripture that is more helpful to the devotions of the saints than this," says Matthew Henry, "and it has been so

---

1. Some of this material appeared in T. L. Johnson, "Restoring Psalm Singing to Our Worship," in ed. Philip G. Ryken, et al., *Give Praise to God: A Vision for Reforming Worship* (Phillipsburg, N.J.: P&R Publishing, 2003), 257–86. It will also appear in a forthcoming publication: *The Case for Historic Reformed Worship.*

2. Dietrich Bonhoeffer, *The Psalms: Prayer Book of the Bible* (1940; Oxford: SLG Press, 1982).

3. Dietrich Bonhoeffer, *Life Together,* trans. John W. Doberstein (New York: Harper & Row, 1954), 47.

4. Paul Westermeyer, *Te Deum: The Church and Music* (Minneapolis: Fortress Press, 1998), 24.

in all ages of the church, ever since it was written."[5] But the Psalter is not only our prayer book, it is also and even primarily God's hymnbook, given by the inspiration of the Holy Spirit: "God…by the mouth of thy servant David hast said," as the apostle Peter expressed it (Acts 4:24, 25). "From earliest times the Psalter has been both the hymn-book and the prayer book of the Christian Church," say Derek Kidner and J. G. Thomson.[6]

Apostolic Church

"Psalmody was a part of the synagogue service that naturally passed over into the life of the church," says E. F. Harrison.[7] Morning prayers at the synagogue normally began with the chanting of Psalms 145 to 150. Not surprisingly, we find the early Christians lifting their voices "with one accord" (Acts 4:24), likely indicating singing or reciting psalms in unison. These were not spontaneous free prayers. Luke supplies us with the text of Psalm 146:6, likely indicating that they sang the whole psalm, if not a series of psalms, following the pattern of the synagogue: "And when they heard that, they lifted up their voice to God with one accord, and said, Lord, thou art God, which hast made heaven, and earth, and the sea, and all that in them is" (Acts 4:24).

The believers then sang or read a second psalm, Psalm 2:1–2. The phrasing in this verse may indicate a different mode of communication (i.e. reading) than was indicated for the previous psalm: "Who by the mouth of thy servant David *hast said*, Why did the heathen rage, and the people imagine vain things? The kings of the earth stood up, and the rulers were gathered together against the Lord, and against his Christ" (Acts 4:25–26, emphasis added).

The recitation of the psalm was then followed by a meditation on its meaning in light of these believers' current situation: "For of a truth against thy holy child Jesus, whom thou hast anointed, both Herod, and Pontius Pilate, with the Gentiles, and the people of Israel, were gathered together, for to do whatsoever thy hand and thy counsel determined before

5. Matthew Henry, *An Exposition of the Old and New Testament* (Philadelphia: Tavar & Hogan, 1829), in his introduction to the *Book of Psalms*.

6. Derek Kidner and J. G. Thomson, "Book of Psalms," in J. D. Douglas, et. al., *The New Bible Dictionary* (Leicester: InterVarsity Press, 1962), 1059.

7. Everett F. Harrison, *The Apostolic Church* (Grand Rapids: Eerdmans, 1985), 134.

to be done" (Acts 4:27–28). We do not know exactly how this meditation took place, whether by sermon, prayer, or discussion. But "taken simply," says Hughes Old, what the text "seems to indicate is that an exposition of Scripture is taking place in prayer."[8] The Word was sung, read, and preached in this service of daily prayer.

A prayer follows: "And now, Lord, behold their threatenings: and grant unto thy servants, that with all boldness they may speak thy word, by stretching forth thine hand to heal; and that signs and wonders may be done by the name of thy holy child Jesus. And when they had prayed, the place was shaken" (Acts 4:29–31a). They pray for protection, for help, for boldness, for spiritual power in Jesus' name. All in all, Old reckons, this is "a rather thorough description of a daily prayer service."[9] Again he says, "This prayer service held by the Apostles, like the prayer service of the synagogue, was made up of three elements, the chanting of psalms, a passage of Scripture, and prayers of supplication and intercession."[10] Note as well the instinct to interpret the Psalms christologically and to allow the Psalms to shape the prayer life of the church.

"The Psalms formed the core of the praises of the New Testament church," as Hughes Old has observed.[11] The apostle Paul commanded both the Ephesian and Colossian churches to sing psalms (Eph. 5:19; Col. 3:16) and commented on the Corinthian practice of doing so (1 Cor. 14:15, 26). James instructed his readers ("the twelve tribes which are scattered abroad" [1:1], apparently referring to the whole church) to sing psalms (5:13, ψάλλω). With surprising frequency the New Testament cites the Psalms (e.g. Acts 2:24–26; Heb. 1:5–13; 2:5–10,12,13; 3:7–4:7; 5:1–7), demonstrating as they do a keen awareness of both their christological and devotional importance.[12] "From the earliest times the

---

8. Hughes O. Old, "The Service of Daily Prayer in the Primitive Christian Church: A Study of Acts 4:23–31," unpublished paper, 1979.

9. Hughes O. Old, *Themes and Variations for a Christian Doxology* (Grand Rapids: Eerdmans, 1992), 9.

10. Hughes O. Old, *Worship That Is Reformed According to Scripture* (Atlanta: John Knox Press, 1984), 145.

11. Ibid., 37.

12. According to William L. Holladay, there are fifty-five direct citations of the Psalms in the New Testament. R.E.O. White finds another 150 clear allusions to the Psalter and still another two hundred fainter ones. See William L. Holladay, *The Psalms through Three*

Christian community sang the psalms," summarizes Mary Berry, "following the practice of the synagogue."[13]

The Patristic Church

The church fathers and earliest Christian writings demonstrate a devotion to the Psalms, and particularly to the singing of the Psalms, that is startling.[14] Calvin Stapert speaks of the fathers' "enthusiastic promotion of psalm singing," which, he says, "reached an unprecedented peak in the fourth century."[15] James McKinnon speaks of "an unprecedented wave of enthusiasm" for the Psalms in the second half of the fourth century.[16] The writers of *The Psalms in Christian Worship* and others, including most recently John D. Witvliet, have collected a number of testimonies of psalm singing from the church fathers that survive to this day.[17] For example, Tertullian (c. 155–230), in the second century, testified that psalm singing was not only an essential feature of the worship of his day but also

Thousand Years: Prayerbook of a Cloud of Witnesses (Minneapolis: Fortress Press, 1993), 115; "Psalms," R.E.O. White, in *Evangelical Commentary on the Bible*, ed. Walter A. Elwell (Grand Rapids: Baker Book House, 1989), 373.

13. Mary Berry, "Psalmody" in *The New Westminster Dictionary of Liturgy and Worship*, ed. J. G. Davies (Philadelphia: Westminster Press, 1986), 450; Stapert, citing the work of James McKinnon, "The Question of Psalmody," and J. A. Smith, "The Ancient Synagogue, the Early Church and Singing," argues that the psalms were not sung in the synagogue but the home and came from there into Christian households and finally into formal worship.

14. Holladay, 162–65. He notes that *1 Clement* (c. AD 96) has forty-nine citations from thirty-two psalms; *Epistle of Barnabas* (c. AD 130) has twelve citations from ten psalms; *Didache* (second century AD) has three citations from three psalms; *Ignatius of Antioch* (c. AD 98–117) and Polycarp (fl. c. AD 175– c. 195) make virtually no reference to the Psalms, but Justin Martyr's writings (c. AD 150) are loaded with citations from the Psalms (e.g. *Dialogue with Trypho* has forty-seven references from twenty-four psalms), as are those of Irenaeus (c. AD 70–155/160).

15. Calvin R. Stapert, *A New Song for an Old World: Musical Thought in the Early Church*, The Calvin Institute of Christian Worship Liturgical Studies (Grand Rapids: Eerdmans, 2007), 150.

16. Cited by Paul Bradshaw, "From Word to Action: The Changing Role of Psalmody in Early Christianity," in ed. Martin Dudley, *Like a Two-Edged Sword: The Word of God in Liturgy and History* (Norwich: The Canterbury Press, 1995), 25.

17. John McNaughter, *The Psalms in Christian Worship* (1907; Edmonton: Still Water Revival Books, 1992); John D. Witvliet, *The Biblical Psalms in Christian Worship: A Brief Introduction and Guide to Resources* (Grand Rapids: Eerdmans, 2007), 3–10.

had become an important part of the daily life of the people. Athanasius (300–343) says it was the custom of his day to sing psalms, which he calls "a mirror of the soul,"[18] and even "a book that includes the whole life of man, all conditions of the mind and all movements of thought."[19] Eusebius (c. 260 – c. 340), bishop of Caesarea, left this vivid picture of the psalm singing of his day: "The command to sing Psalms in the name of the Lord was obeyed by everyone in every place: for the command to sing is in force in all churches which exist among nations, not only the Greeks but also throughout the whole world, and in towns, villages and in the fields."[20] Basil the Great (c. 330–379) comments, in his sermons on the Psalms, on the "harmonious Psalm tunes" that mix "sweetness of melody with doctrine" and are sung by the people not only in the churches but "at home" and "in the marketplace" as well.[21] Augustine (343–430), in his *Confessions* (ix.4), says, "[The Psalms] are sung through the whole world, and there is nothing hid from the heat thereof."[22]

Jerome (d. 420) said that he learned the Psalms when he was a child and sang them daily in his old age. He also writes, "The Psalms were continually to be heard in the fields and vineyards of Palestine. The plowman, as he held his plow, chanted the Hallelujah; and the reaper, the vinedresser, and the shepherd sang something from the Psalms of David. Where the meadows were colored with flowers, and the singing birds made their plaints, the Psalms sounded even more sweetly. These Psalms are our love-songs, these the instruments of our agriculture."[23]

Sidonius Apollinaris (c. 431– c. 482) represents boatmen, who, while they worked their heavy barges up the waters of ancient France, "[sing] Psalms till the banks echo with 'Hallelujah.'" Chrysostom (d. 407), the renowned Greek father and patriarch of Constantinople, says,

> All Christians employ themselves in David's Psalms more frequently than in any other part of the Old or New Testament. The grace of the Holy Ghost hath so ordered it that they should be recited and sung

---

18. McNaughter, *The Psalms in Christian Worship*, 550.
19. Berry, "Psalmody," 451.
20. Ibid.
21. Witvliet, *Biblical Psalms*, 4, 5.
22. McNaughter, *The Psalms in Christian Worship*, 550.
23. Ibid., 504.

night and day. In the Church's vigils the first, the middle, and the last are David's Psalms. In the morning David's Psalms are sought for; and David is the first, the midst, and the last of the day. At funeral solemnities, the first, the midst, and the last is David. Many who know not a letter can say David's Psalms by heart. In all the private houses, where women toil—in the monasteries—in the deserts, where men converse with God, the first, the midst, and the last is David."[24]

He says again, "David is always in their mouths, not only in the cities and churches, but in courts, in monasteries, in deserts, and the wilderness. He turned earth into heaven and men into angels, being adapted to all orders and to all capacities" (Sixth Homily on Repentance). [25]

Over against this devotion to singing psalms, there was a growing skepticism about hymns "of human composition" throughout this period because of the use to which they were put by heretics. For this reason the Council of Braga (AD 350) ruled, "Except the Psalms and hymns of the Old and New Testaments, nothing of a poetical nature is to be sung in the church."[26] The important Council of Laodicea, which met about AD 360, forbade "the singing of uninspired hymns in the church, and the reading of uncanonical books of Scripture" (canon 59).[27] While these were not the decisions of ecumenical councils, nearly one hundred years later, the Council of Chalcedon (AD 451), the largest of all the general councils, confirmed the Laodicean canons.

We cite these decisions to underscore the point that the Psalter clearly was the primary songbook of the early church. Worship in the early church was "according to Scripture" and consequently filled with scriptural praise.

Middle Ages

It is certain that during the patristic period all of the people participated in singing psalms.[28] But during the Middle Ages, congregational sing-

---

24. Ibid., 166, 504.
25. Ibid., 170.
26. Ibid., 550; cf. Mary Berry, "Hymns," in *The New Westminster Dictionary of Liturgy and Worship* (Philadelphia: The Westminster Press, 1986), 262.
27. Ibid., 167; cf. Stapert, *A New Song*, 159.
28. Berry, "Psalmody," 451.

ing eroded. "More and more it was the monks who were charged with the praise of the church," notes Hughes Old.[29] The people gave way to the monastic *schola cantorum*. Over time the church's music also became increasingly sophisticated. The tunes were difficult, and the words were in Latin. The common people could neither sing nor understand them.

Still, the use of the Psalms was, if anything, intensified by the medieval monastic orders, which, following the rules of St. Benedict, chanted their way through the entire Psalter each week.[30] "Psalmody is also at the heart of the music of the mass," Mary Berry reminds us.[31] Most of the texts used for the choral propers (the parts of the service that changed according to the calendar) were taken from the Psalms. The Psalms dominated the music of the monastery and the cathedral, even if the music and language proved too remote for the town church or village chapel.[32]

The Reformation

The Reformers were aware of much of this history, as Hughes Old has demonstrated, and sought to restore congregational psalmody.[33] They appealed to the kind of scriptural and patristic evidence that we have already noted. For example, Bucer appealed to Pliny the Younger's report on the worship of the early church. Calvin appealed to the church historians (e.g. Eusebius, Socrates, Sozomen) as well as the church fathers (e.g. Augustine, Basil, Chrysostom). While the Reformers did not advocate the exclusive singing of Psalms, they did express "a partiality for Psalms and hymns drawn from Scripture," says Old.[34] The Reformers did not oppose moderate use of hymns "of human composition" in principle. Rather, congregational psalmody was a preference that grew out of their consistent concern that worship be conducted according to Scripture. For their ideal to be realized, it would be necessary to develop a simpler music as well as vernacular translations. The new psalmody would be designed for congregations rather than trained monastic choirs.

---

29. Old, *Worship*, 40; Westemeyer, *Te Deum*, 106–110.
30. Stapert, *A New Song for an Old World*, 161; Berry, "Psalmody," 451.
31. Ibid.
32. Old, *Worship*, 42.
33. Old, *Patristic Roots*, 253–69.
34. Ibid., 258.

It was Luther who first suggested that congregations should sing the Psalms. Luther specified in his *Formula missae* (1523) the use of German hymns in the still Latin mass. In a letter to Georg Spalatin he described his plan to develop vernacular psalmody. His reason for doing so is typical of the whole program of reform: "so that the Word of God may be among the people also in the form of music."[35] For this Luther can be called both the "father of congregational hymnody" and the "inventor of the vernacular metrical Psalm."[36] The Protestant conviction that people are to sing the Word of God was expressed in these two forms—hymns and psalms. Under Luther's guidance, the first Protestant hymnal was produced in 1524, the *Geistliche Gesangbuchlein*.[37] Within a year a hymnal also had been published in Strasbourg, whose example was followed by other south German and Swiss cities. The Protestant revolution in preaching and praying was paralleled by this other crucial liturgical revolution in church song. "A Mighty Fortress Is Our God," Luther's Psalm 46, is an example of his work. Similarly, Martin Bucer, writing in his seminal defense of Reformed worship, *Grund und Ursach* (1524), explained, "We use neither songs nor prayers which are not based on Holy Scripture."[38]

Moreover, among Reformed Protestants, it was whole psalms and the whole Psalter that were to be sung. Why sung? Because they were written to be sung—and sung in context. The biblical texts the Reformers cited, the same ones mentioned previously in this chapter, demonstrated that the early church sang Psalms and the New Testament commanded them to be sung, an understanding reinforced by testimonies from the early church fathers, also already cited in this chapter. The Psalms are not merely a collection of poems to be recited. They are songs, each one complete in itself and having its own integrity, to be sung. "The Psalms may be

---

35. Bartlett R. Butler, "Hymns," in ed. Hans J. Hillerbrand, *The Oxford Encyclopedia of the Reformation* (New York: Oxford University Press, 1996), 2: 290.

36. Ibid., 2:291; cf. Roland Bainton, *Here I Stand: A Life of Martin Luther* (New York: Abingdon Cokesbury Press, 1950), 344.

37. Jeremy S. Begbie, *Resounding Truth: Christian Wisdom in the World of Music* (Grand Rapids: Baker Academic, 2007), 104.

38. Martin Bucer, *Grund und Ursach*. Text is found in O. F. Cypris, *Basic Principles: Translation and Commentary of Martin Bucer's* Grund und Ursach, 1524 (Dissertation: Union Theological Seminary of New York, 1971), 208.

spoken," says Paul Westermeyer, "but they cry out to be sung."[39] That in itself is worth pondering. "The Psalms are poems," adds C. S. Lewis, "and poems intended to be sung."[40]

Calvin further explains the Reformers' partiality to the Psalms in his *Preface to the Psalter* (1543). The Psalms, he argued, were the songs of the Holy Spirit.

> Moreover, that which St. Augustine has said is true, that no one is able to sing things worthy of God except that which he has received from Him. Therefore, when we have looked thoroughly, and searched here and there, we shall not find better songs nor more fitting of the purpose, than the Psalms of David, which the Holy Spirit spoke and made through him. And moreover, when we sing them, we are certain that God puts in our mouths these, as if He Himself were singing in us to exalt His glory.[41]

John D. Witvliet points out that one of the distinguishing dynamics of Reformation era psalm singing was "the singing of whole or large portions of individual Psalms rather than the versicles used in the medieval Mass."[42] The Reformers would not have been content with the "versicles," or fragments of psalms, that are virtually all that have been available in recent years. This would be true of the partial collections of Psalms (sixty-five to eighty psalm settings) found in the Presbyterian hymnals of the last century (e.g. *The Presbyterian Hymnal* [1933], *The Hymnbook* [1955], *Trinity Hymnal* [1961, 1980], as well as their compilers' "too prissy" (as

---

39. Westermeyer, 25.

40. C. S. Lewis, *Reflections on the Psalms* (London: Geoffrey Bless, 1958), 2. "The Psalms were written to be sung, not just read. To sing them is to honor God's intention in giving them to us" (Lawrence C. Roff, *Let Us Sing,* [Atlanta: Great Commission Publications, 1991], 65).

41. Calvin, *Preface to the Psalter,* 1543. From the facsimile edition of "Les Pseaumes mis en rime francoise par Clément Marot et Théodore de Béze. Mis en musique a quatre parties per Claude Goudimel. Par les héritiers de Francois Jacqui" (1565); published under the auspices of *La Société des Concerts de la Cathédrale de Lausanne* and edited, in French, by Pierre Pidoux and in German by Konrad Ameln (Kassel: Baeroenreiter-Verlag, 1935). http://www.fpcr.org/blue_banner_articles/calvinps.htm (accessed August 3, 2010).

42. John D. Witvliet, "The Spirituality of the Psalter: Metrical Psalms in Liturgy and Life in Calvin's Geneva," *Calvin Theological Journal*, 32 (1997): 296; also available in John D. Witvliet, *Worship Seeking Understanding: Windows into Christian Practice* (Grand Rapids: Baker Academic, 2003), 203–229. See 228.

Hughes Old calls it) editing of those that were included. They "went much too far in trying to clean up the treasury of David."[43] Neither would they have been content with the practice of isolating particular verses of psalms to be sung as "Scripture songs." To sing the Psalms is to sing the Psalter. Each psalm has its own thematic integrity. The book of Psalms as a whole is characterized by theological, christological, and experiential wholeness. The Holy Spirit gave the Psalter as a complete collection whose strength is collective: laments not isolated from praise, imprecations not isolated from confessions of sin, but all together. The whole gospel of the whole Christ is found in the whole Psalter.

Consequently, the Reformers produced collections of psalms for singing as an early part of their liturgical reforms. The *Strasbourg German Service Book* of 1525 (just eight years after Luther's posting of the Ninety-Five Theses) included a collection of metrical psalms. This collection was increased in the *Strasbourg Psalter* of 1526 and subsequent editions (1530, 1537). The *Constance Hymn Book* of 1540, called by Hughes Old "one of the most important monuments in the history of Reformed liturgy," included hymns by Zwingli, Leo Jud, Luther, Wolfgang Capito, and Wolfgang Musculus, among others.[44] But half of the collection was metrical Psalms.

Genevan psalmody began with the *French Evangelical Psalm Book* of 1539 and grew into the *Geneva Psalter* of 1542, and finally the *Geneva Psalter* of 1562, a complete psalter of 150 psalms, metered for singing, most with a distinctive tune.

The singing of psalms became one of the most obvious marks of Reformed Protestantism. The Genevan psalms were translated into Spanish, Dutch, German, and English, among others, twenty-four languages in all. English editions developed and evolved both in the Church of England and the Church of Scotland. The French refugees streaming into Geneva in large numbers immediately embraced psalmody. Louis F. Benson, the leading hymnologist of a previous generation, wrote a series of scholarly articles in 1909 for the *Journal of the Presbyterian Historical Society* entitled

---

43. Hughes O. Old, "The Psalms as Christian Prayer: A Preface to the Liturgical Use of the Psalter," unpublished manuscript, 1978, 18.

44. Old, *Worship*, 44.

"John Calvin and the Psalmody of the Reformed Churches."[45] In these articles he discussed the impact that the *Geneva Psalter* had upon the French
exiles in Geneva as they first encountered psalm singing: "The sight of the
great congregation gathered in St. Peter's, with their little Psalm books in
their own hands, the great volume of voices praising God in the familiar
French, the grave melodies carrying holy words, the fervor of the singing
and the spiritual uplift of the singers,—all of these moved deeply the emotions of the French exiles now first in contact with them."[46]

As these refugees flowed in and out of France, they took with them a
love for the Psalms that they had learned in Geneva. By 1553 the *Genevan
Psalms* were sung in all of the Protestant churches of France.[47] In 1559 it
became the official "hymnal" of the Reformed churches of France. These
psalms played a great part in "spreading the Genevan doctrines in France,"
says Benson.[48] When the first complete edition was published in 1562 it
was immediately consumed, going through twenty-five editions in its first
year of publication.[49] During this time of fervent devotion to the Psalms,
the French church grew with extraordinary speed. In 1555 there were five
underground churches in France. By 1559 the number had jumped to
more than one hundred. By 1562 there were estimated to be more than
2,150 churches established in France with approximately three million
attending.[50] Witvliet maintains that "metrical Psalm singing was a maker
of the Reformation."[51] It popularized Reformed piety, "opening up the

---

45. Louis F. Benson, "John Calvin and the Psalmody of the Reformed Churches,"
Journal of the Presbyterian Historical Society, 5, 1 (March 1909): 1–21; 5, 2 (June 1909):
55–87; 5, 3 (September 1909), 107–118.

46. Ibid., 57.

47. Ibid., 67.

48. Ibid., 69.

49. Ibid., 71. There were fifteen editions in 1563, eleven in 1564, thirteen in 1565,
a total of sixty-four editions in the first four years of publication. Witvliet cites with
approval the description of the rapidly selling psalter as "the most gigantic enterprise ever
undertaken in publishing until then" (274).

50. Frank A. James, III, "Calvin the Evangelist" in *RTS: Reformed Quarterly*, fall 2001,
8; ed. W. Sanford Reid, *John Calvin: His Influence in the Western World* (Grand Rapids:
Zondervan Publishing House, 1982), 77.

51. Witvliet, "Spirituality of the Psalter," 296.

Scriptures to the laity,"[52] says Miriam Chrisman, joining the sermon and catechism, says Witvliet, "as the chief means of spiritual formation."[53]

The completion of the *Genevan Psalms* in 1562 proved to be a providential provision for the French Protestants, as attempts at reconciliation with Rome and the French crown failed, and civil war broke out that year. "They found in it," Benson says, "a well opened in the desert, from which they drew consolation under persecution, strength to resist valiantly the enemies of their faith; with the assured conviction that God was fighting for them, and also (it must be added) would be revenged against their foes."[54] "To know the Psalms," says Benson, "became a primary duty" for the Huguenots, as French Protestants became known.[55] The powerful appeal of the Psalms sung "made Psalmody as much a part of the daily life as of public worship."[56] Families at home, men and women in the workplace or engaged in daily tasks, were recognized as French Protestants because they were overheard singing psalms. "The Psalter became to them the manual of the spiritual life."[57] Moreover, the Psalter "ingrained its own characteristics deep in the Huguenot character, and had a great part in making it what it was," says Benson.[58] For the Huguenot, "called to fight and suffer for his principles, the habit of Psalm singing was a providential preparation."[59] Benson elaborates: "The Psalms were his confidence and strength in quiet and solitude, his refuge from oppression; in the wars of religion they became the songs of the camp and the march, the inspiration of the battle and the consolation in death, whether on the field or at the martyrs' stake. It is not possible to conceive of the history of the Reformation in France in such a way that Psalm singing should not have a great place in it."[60]

A similar story can be told of the Scottish Presbyterians. As John Knox and other Protestant refugees returned to Scotland from exile on the continent in the late 1550s, they came with a zeal for an English-

---

52. Cited in Witvliet, "Spirituality of the Psalter," 297.
53. Witvliet, "Spirituality of the Psalter," 296.
54. Benson, "John Calvin and Psalmody," 77, 78.
55. Ibid., 73.
56. Ibid.
57. Ibid.
58. Ibid.
59. Ibid.
60. Ibid.

language psalter corresponding to the *Genevan Psalter*. The result eventually was the *Scottish Psalter* of 1564, then of 1635, and finally of 1650. The last of these became the standard psalter for the Scots and "passed straight into the affections of the common people," says Millar Patrick, in his *Four Centuries of Scottish Psalmody*.[61] "It was a godsend," he says, published a few years before the enormous suffering of the Killing Time (1668–88), by which time "it had won its place in the people's hearts, and its lines were so deeply imprinted upon their memories that it is always the language thus given them for the expression of their emotions, which in the great hours we find upon their lips."[62] Note what he says: the language that they used to interpret and express their experience was the language of the Psalms, which they sang. Patrick continues: "You can imagine what it would be to them. Books in those days were few. The Bible came first. The Psalm book stood next in honor. It was their constant companion, their book of private devotion, as well as their manual of church worship. In godly households it was the custom to sing through it in family worship."[63]

To their psalms they turned, he says, "to sustain their souls in hours of anxiety and peril," and from them they "drew the language of strength and consolation."[64] He continues, "It was there that they found a voice for faith, the patience, the courage, and the hope that bore them through those dark and cruel years."[65] The Scottish metrical psalms, he says, "are stained with the blood of the martyrs, who counted not their lives dear to them that by suffering and sacrifice they might keep faith with conscience and save their country's liberties from defeat."[66]

The singing of psalms has been an important part of the "strength and consolation" of all the churches of Reformed Protestantism, including their near cousins, the Congregational and Baptist churches, for three hundred years. Early collections of metrical psalms were published among the Dutch in 1540. In 1568 Peter Dathenus (c. 1531–1588) published a

---

61. Millar Patrick, *Four Centuries of Scottish Psalmody* (London: Oxford University Press, 1949), 115.
62. Ibid.
63. Ibid.
64. Ibid.
65. Ibid.
66. Ibid., 116.

Dutch translation of the French psalter "carefully molded after Genevan texts and melodies," as Butler explains, "which became the official Calvinist songbook for the next two centuries" in Protestant Netherlands.[67] Similarly, the German language edition of the *Genevan Psalter*, the work of Ambrosius Lobwasser (1515–1585), was published in 1573. Even today the Genevan psalms form the core of the sung praises of the French, Swiss, and Dutch Reformed churches.

The Reformed and Presbyterian churches in America were exclusively psalm singing for nearly two hundred years, from the Pilgrim fathers to the Jacksonian Era, as were the Congregationalists and Baptists. The first book published in North America was a psalter. The enormously popular *Bay Psalm Book* (1640) was the hymnal of American Puritanism, undergoing seventy printings through 1773.[68] When the *Bay Psalm Book* and the favorite among Scots-Irish immigrants, the *Scottish Psalter* (1650), were eventually superseded, it was by a book that purported to be yet another psalter, Isaac Watts's *The Psalms of David Imitated* (1719).[69] Ironically Watts's hymns and psalm paraphrases were the primary vehicle through which hymns finally were accepted into the public worship of Protestants, yet not without considerable controversy in the eighteenth and early nineteenth centuries. Still, it was not until the middle of the nineteenth century that hymns began to overtake the Psalms in popular use.[70]

In addition to the Presbyterians, Congregationalists, and Baptists, the Anglican and Episcopal churches boast a three-hundred-year history of exclusive psalmody, singing first from the Sternhold and Hopkin's *Old Version* (1547, 1557), then Tate and Brady's *New Version* (1696, 1698). Not until the publishing of *Hymns Ancient and Modern* in 1861 did hymns gain entrance to the Anglican liturgy.

B. R. Butler speaks of "the phenomenal success of Calvinist psalmody," and particularly of its impact on the people: "For the faithful it was God's Word they were privileged to sing, and it spoke to their most pro-

---

67. Butler, "Hymns" in the *Oxford Encyclopedia of the Reformation*, 2: 294.

68. *The Bay Psalm Book: Being a Facsimile Reprint of the First Edition in 1640*, with an introduction by Wilberforce Eames (New York: Dodd, Mead & Company, 1903), ix.

69. Ibid. New England's churches began to vote to change to Watts in the 1750s.

70. Louis F. Benson tells this story in *The English Hymn: Its Development and Use in Worship* (London: Hodder & Stoughton, 1915), 161–218.

found human needs and aspirations. The Psalms became their badge of identity, the banner of the people of God struggling for power or survival in France, the Low Countries, much of Germany, and elsewhere."[71]

Decline

The supplanting of the metrical psalms by hymns was gradual in American Protestantism. From 1620 to 1800, metrical psalmody dominated the American church scene. The Pilgrim fathers arrived with their *Ainsworth Psalter*, which gave way, as we've noted, to the *Bay Psalm Book* (1640), the psalter of American Puritanism. Presbyterians sang from the *Scottish Psalter* of 1650, and Anglicans from either *Steinhold and Hopkins* (1562) or Tate and Brady's *New Version* (1696). In the 1750s the churches of New England and beyond began to vote to adopt Watts's *Paraphrases* (1719), the popularity of which, along with his hymns, could not be suppressed.

By 1800 the battles over the inclusion of hymns in public worship had largely been fought and won or lost according to one's perspective. Subsequent hymnbooks for the next sixty-five years included both psalms and hymns, typically with a large opening section of psalms. For example, both the New School Presbyterian hymnal of 1843, *Church Psalmist*, and the Old School hymnal of 1843, *Psalms and Hymns*, open with multiple versions of all 150 Psalms, making up forty percent of the former hymnal and over fifty percent of the latter.[72] The distinction between psalms and hymns was clearly maintained. As late as 1863, the New School General Assembly voiced its disapproval of hymnals which, "in the arrangement, blot out the distinction between those songs of devotion which are God-inspired and those which are man-inspired."[73] Yet with the publication of the *Hymnal of the Presbyterian Church* (1866), the distinction was gone, and the Psalms had all but disappeared, without even a scriptural index with which to trace them.[74] The 1866 book was soon superseded by the

---

71. Butler, "Hymns," in the *Oxford Encyclopedia of the Reformation*, 2: 297.

72. *Church Psalmist; or Psalms and Hymns for the Public, Social and Private Use of Evangelical Christians*, 5th ed. (New York: Mark H. Newman, 1845); *Psalms and Hymns Adapted to Social, Private, and Public Worship in the Presbyterian Church in the United States of America* (Philadelphia: Presbyterian Board of Publications, 1843).

73. Benson, *English Hymns*, 386, n.69.

74. *Hymnal of the Presbyterian Church Ordered by the General Assembly* (Philadelphia: Board of Education, 1866).

first hymnal after the reunion of New and Old Schools in the north, *The Presbyterian Hymnal* of 1874. Again, psalms are nowhere evident. If one were to hunt carefully, he could find a few, but they are well hidden and nowhere identified.[75] The same is true of the hymnal of 1895 and its revision in 1911, which still lacked a Scripture index by which to hunt down the Psalms.[76] The southern Presbyterians published *The New Psalms and Hymns* in 1901, with a significant selection of psalms, but they too were scattered and unidentified,[77] prompting Benson's observation that it was "Psalms and Hymns in name only."[78] By the time of the southern church's *The Presbyterian Hymnal* of 1927, the Psalms had completely disappeared.[79] It, too, lacked a Scripture index by which to trace the Psalms, and even the obligatory "All People That on Earth Do Dwell" (Psalm 100) was missing. The northern church's *The Hymnal* of 1933 did have Psalm 100 and Psalm 23, but little else, and also lacked a Scripture index.[80] Psalm singing in the mainline had reached its lowest point. It would be left to the smaller Reformed and Presbyterian denominations to keep psalm singing alive in the twentieth century, as the United Presbyterians (UP), Associate Reformed Presbyterians (ARP), Reformed Presbyterian Church of North America (RPCNA), and the Cumberland Presbyterian Church (CPC) maintained their commitment to metrical psalm singing.

A similar story can be told about the Congregationalists and Baptists. The Connecticut Association commissioned Timothy Dwight, president of Yale College, to revise and complete Watts's psalms, to which was added a collection of 263 hymns, published as *The Psalms of David* in 1801. Dwight's work, plus that of Samuel Worcester, *Psalms and Hymns* of 1819 (revised in 1823 and 1834, and frequently reprinted), familiarly known as "Watts and Select," solidified the dominance of Watts's psalm-

---

75. *The Presbyterian Hymnal* (Philadelphia: Presbyterian Board of Publication and Sabbath-School Work, 1874).

76. *The Hymnal* (Philadelphia: The Presbyterian Board of Publications & Sabbath-School Work, 1911).

77. *The New Psalms and Hymns* (Richmond: Presbyterian Committee of Publications, 1901).

78. Benson, *English Hymns*, 256.

79. *The Presbyterian Hymnal* (Richmond: Presbyterian Committee of Publications, 1927).

80. *The Hymnal* (Philadelphia: Presbyterian Board of Education, 1933).

ody and hymnody into the Civil War era.[81] Thereafter the Psalms quickly fell out of congregational hymnals. Indeed, with the advent of the gospel-song tradition in the post-Civil War era, this new hymnody, says Yale's Sydney Ahlstrom, "swept much of Isaac Watts," and "the older Reformed 'Psalms'... into disuse and oblivion."[82]

This eclipse of psalmody in the late nineteenth century is quite unprecedented. The Psalms, as we have seen, had been the dominant form of church song beginning with the church fathers, all through the Middle Ages, during the Reformation and Post-Reformation eras, and into the modern era. By the beginning of the twentieth century, the church had lost the voice through which it had expressed its sung praise for more than eighteen hundred years.

Revival

Can we hope to see psalm singing revived in our day? Metrical psalmody must contend not only with classical hymnody and gospel songs, but it faces ever stiffer competition from Scripture songs and praise bands. There are some hopeful signs. We must first return our attention to the smaller Reformed churches. The United Presbyterians, still an exclusively psalm singing denomination in the nineteenth century, worked to reverse the downward trend with the publication of its *Book of Psalms* in 1871. It marked progress, in my view, in the development of psalm singing in the English-speaking world because it offered much greater metrical variety than before seen. It provided the foundation for *The Psalter* of 1912, largely the 1871 book, but a collaborative work of nine churches of the Presbyterian-Reformed family in the United States and Canada, who, after fifty years of decline, were beginning again to see the value of singing Psalms. Several Reformed denominations, such as the Free Reformed (FRCNA), Heritage Reformed (HRC), Protestant Reformed (PRC), and Netherlands Reformed (NRC), still use *The Psalter* today, as do a number of independent congregations.[83]

---

81. See Benson, *English Hymns*, 161–68; 373–75; 388–89.
82. Sydney Ahlstrom, *A Religious History of the American People* (New Haven and London: Yale University Press, 1972), 846.
83. *The Psalter* (Grand Rapids: Reformation Heritage Books, 1999.)

Multiple texts from *The Psalter*, 1912, found their way into *The Hymnbook*, 1955, a collaborative work of the Presbyterian Church in the United States (PCUS), Presbyterian Church USA (PCUSA), UP, ARP, and Reformed Church in America (RCA). A similar number were to be found in the Orthodox Presbyterian Church's (OPC) *Trinity Hymnal* of 1961.[84] A revival of psalm singing was well under way. Both of these publications clearly identified psalms as psalms and provided helpful indices by which to find them, though they remained scattered throughout the text. The editors of *The Hymnbook* boasted of "the interweaving of the strands from five denominations," resulting in "the inclusion of many of the Psalms in meter," which it describes as "a happy recovery of one of the great sources of strength of both the Genevan and the Scottish tradition."[85] The next generation of hymnals from the CRC, the *Psalter Hymnal* (1987),[86] and the PCUSA (the reunited northern and southern mainline churches), *Hymns, Psalms, and Spiritual Songs* (1990),[87] restored the Psalms to their own distinct sections and offered a complete (CRC) or nearly complete (PCUSA) selection of all 150 psalms. The revised *Trinity Hymnal* (1990)[88] expanded its psalm offerings without placing them in a distinct section. Meanwhile, the RPCNA published its *Book of Psalms for Singing* (1973),[89] which blended together the selections primarily from the Scottish and Genevan traditions and the 1912 *Psalter*. The *Trinity Psalter* (1994) condensed this work into a slender volume for hymnal-using churches.[90] It has sold forty thousand copies since publication. The Canadian and American Reformed churches maintain the Genevan tradition with their *Book of Praise: Anglo-Genevan Psalter*, first published in 1972 and significant because, for the first time, it provided English

84. *The Hymnbook* (Richmond, Philadelphia, New York: PCUSA, UPCUSA, RCA, 1955); *Trinity Hymnal* (Philadelphia: The Committee on Christian Education, Inc., The Orthodox Presbyterian Church, 1961).

85. *The Hymnbook*, 5.

86. *Psalter Hymnal* (Grand Rapids, Michigan: CRC Publications, 1987).

87. *Hymns, Psalms, and Spiritual Songs* (Louisville, Ky.: Westminster/John Knox Press, 1990).

88. *Trinity Hymnal* (Norcross, Ga.: Great Commission Publications, Inc., 1990).

89. *Book of Psalms for Singing* (Pittsburgh, Penn.: The Board of Education and Publication, Reformed Presbyterian Church of North America, 1973).

90. *Trinity Psalter* (Pittsburgh, Penn.: Crown & Covenant Publications, 1994).

metrical versions of the Psalms that can be sung to the sixteenth-century Genevan melodies.[91]

Benefits

The power of persuasion should not be discounted. Advocates of psalm singing have considerable ammunition at their disposal as they explain to the church why the Psalms ought to be sung.

1. Psalm singing is *biblical.* By this we mean that the Holy Spirit gave the canonical Psalms to be sung. Moreover, we are commanded to sing psalms and are given examples of the New Testament churches singing them.

2. Psalm singing is *historical.* It was the practice of the early church (as attested to by the church fathers), of the medieval monastic orders, of the Reformers, and of virtually all Protestants until the middle of the nineteenth century. Calvin R. Stapert is right in concluding, "There can be no doubt that the Psalms have been the most widely used and universally loved texts that Christians have sung."[92] The Psalms are at once catholic as well as the distinctive form of church song for Presbyterian and Reformed Protestants.

3. Psalm singing is emotionally *satisfying.* Its theological, christological, and experiential richness provides God's people with the language with which to understand and express the vicissitudes of life. Nothing touches the hearts of God's people like the Psalms, particularly sung. Calvin called the Psalms "an Anatomy of all Parts of the Soul; for there is not an emotion of which any one can be conscious that it is not represented here as a mirror." Here, he says, "the Holy Spirit has drawn to life all the griefs, sorrows, fears, doubts, hopes, cares, perplexities, in short, all the distracting emotions with which the minds of men are wont to be agitated."[93]

4. Psalm singing is *sanctifying.* The act of singing (not merely reciting as poetry) the whole Psalter (not merely hymns or even

---

91. *Book of Praise: Anglo-Genevan Psalter* (Winnipeg: Premier Printing, Ltd., 1984).
92. Stapert, *New Song for an Old World*, 151.
93. John Calvin, *Commentary on the Book of Psalms*, trans. James Anderson (Edinburgh: The Calvin Translation Society, 1845), xxxvii.

psalm fragments), given the thematic integrity of each psalm and the divinely balanced content of the Psalter as a whole, has a unique capacity to shape and mold a biblical piety. A distinctive contribution to the health and vitality of the body of Christ is made by the singing of psalms.

Again we find that mainline Protestants seem to understand what the evangelicals have forgotten. Hughes Old waxes euphoric regarding the singing of psalms.[94] So also does Ronald P. Byars. He commends their balance: "Psalms portray the majesty of God as well as the neediness of human beings. Psalms don't ignore human strengths, but they're centered on God rather than on us.... The Psalms get the balance between God's trustworthiness and our need right.... Sung psalmody has a certain gravity because it takes God so seriously.... A virtue of psalmody is that the words come from Scripture."[95] Perhaps we can dare to hope that a revival is underway that will restore the Psalms to their rightful preeminence in the life of Christ's church. New psalters have been produced in recent years in Australia (*The Complete Book of Psalms for Singing*, 1991) and, most recently, from the Free Church of Scotland (*Sing Psalms: New Metrical Versions of the Book of Psalms*, 2003).[96] Also, *Psalter*, a compilation of the 1912 *Psalter* and the 1934 and 1957 *Psalter Hymnals* of the Christian Reformed Church, was published in 1997.[97]

New efforts are underway in both the OPC and RPCNA to publish psalters that combine the best of all that has gone before as well as incorporate the benefits of recent Old Testament scholarship. Whether or not the efforts of the enthusiasts bear fruit in the larger Christian community remains to be seen.

---

94. Old, *Worship*, 92ff.

95. Ronald P. Byers, *What Language Shall I Borrow?: The Bible and Christian Worship* (Grand Rapids: Eerdmans, 2008), 28–30.

96. The Free Church of Scotland, *Sing Psalms: New Metrical Versions of the Book of Psalms* (England: Cambridge University Press, 2003).

97. *Psalter* (Grand Rapids: International Discipleship and Evangelization Associates; I.D.E.A. Ministries, 1997).

Chapter 4

Psalters, Hymnals, Worship Wars, and American Presbyterian Piety

D. G. HART

What is the appropriate psalm to sing for a Christmas Eve service? For many Presbyterians in the United States this question is pointless, and the reasons say much about the liturgical sensibilities that pervade assumptions and expectations for congregational singing. On the one hand, many of the Presbyterian and Reformed Protestants who sing only psalms do not observe the church calendar. Hence, the search for an appropriate psalm at Christmas season does not need to take place in those settings where the default congregational song is the Old Testament Psalter. On the other hand, those congregations that do direct services in the month of December to the theme of the incarnation—even if it does not qualify as a full-blown observance of the liturgical calendar—do not need to worry about finding appropriate songs for the Christmas season. Twentieth-century hymnals are fat with carols and hymns written specifically for the Christmas holiday, thus distancing the birth of Christ from the traditional song of Reformed Protestants.

If the lesson of this thought experiment is that a disproportional relationship exists between psalm singing and Christmas services, that moral may also be useful for understanding the rise of hymnody and the fall of exclusive psalmody among those churches that trace their liturgical heritage back through Scotland to Geneva. Reformed worship has traditionally been a tapestry of mutually reinforcing convictions and practices. Exclusive psalmody was not the only characteristic of a Reformed worship service prior to 1740, when hymns became a popular alternative among

Presbyterians. Along with psalm singing came Sabbatarianism, morning and evening services, and a rejection of the church calendar. Consequently, when Presbyterians on both sides of the Atlantic began to experiment with hymns, they did so not merely by substituting one form of song with another, one of human composition with one from Scripture. Presbyterians who sought to introduce hymns into worship also brought with them a different set of expectations and assumptions about the nature of worship and Christian experience.

Whether the introduction of hymnody into Presbyterian worship was the camel's nose under the tent of Reformed convictions about worship is a question the following considerations will not answer. But the reasons for the competition between hymns and psalms haunt the history of Presbyterian worship and piety and suggest that if contemporary Presbyterians hope to recover the reverence and awe of historic Reformed worship, no better place to start is with exclusive psalmody. At the same time, psalm singing is by itself not the magic wand that will fix Presbyterian worship, because it is only one piece in the tapestry of Reformed worship. In other words, psalm singing will be plausible only in those settings where a full set of Reformed practices are in place.

From King David to Isaac Watts

American Presbyterians did not create their first hymnal until 1831, and they were among the first in the Reformed tradition to do so.[1] In other words, after only 125 years of Presbyterian history in the New World, the Reformed branch of the Protestant Reformation officially embraced hymnody. By then, American Presbyterians apparently felt the need to make

---

1. Parts of the following are adapted from "Twentieth-Century American Presbyterian Hymnody," in D. G. Hart, *Recovering Mother Kirk: The Case for Liturgy in the Reformed Tradition* (Grand Rapids: Baker Academic, 2003), chap. 16.

Throughout this essay the Presbyterians in view are those with direct ties to the first presbytery, founded in 1706 in Philadelphia. That body would eventually grow into the Presbyterian Church, U.S.A., the mainstream church that also hatched the Orthodox Presbyterian Church in 1936 and the Presbyterian Church in America in 1972. The Scottish Presbyterian offshoots in the U.S.—all psalm singers for much longer than the mainstream Presbyterians—the Covenanters (e. g. Reformed Presbyterian Church of North America) and the Seceders (e. g. the Associate Reformed Presbyterian Church) are, consequently, not part of the story covered here.

up for lost time, producing nine different hymnals over the rest of the nineteenth century. With the addition of eight more during the twentieth century, American Presbyterians produced seventeen denominationally sponsored hymnals—at a staggering rate of practically one new hymnal every decade.[2]

The reason for the rush to make hymnals may stem from hymnody's poor prospects among Protestants after the Reformation. Especially among the Reformed, the gravity of worship and the fear of blasphemy made Presbyterians cautious about all elements of worship. As a result, two positions emerged, one propounded by the churches in Zurich under the direction of Ulrich Zwingli and Heinrich Bullinger, the other articulated by the churches in Geneva, led by John Calvin. Although Zwingli was likely the best musician among the Reformers, he removed song from worship, in part because of music's destructive power and also because he found no biblical warrant for singing in worship. Zwingli knew that Paul taught Christians to sing (e.g., Col. 3:16) but countered that this instruction did not necessarily address corporate worship. In fact, Paul's meaning was for believers to sing "in their hearts," not necessarily with their mouths. Consequently, aside from removing organs from Zurich's churches, Zwingli went one step further and left song out entirely. Nowhere is this liturgical point more evident than in the Second Helvetic Confession, written by Bullinger, who made congregational singing optional: "If there be any churches which have faithful prayer in good manner, without any singing, they are not therefore to be condemned, for all churches have not the advantage and opportunity of sacred music" (ch. 23).[3]

---

2. On the history of Presbyterian hymnals, see Louis Fitzgerald Benson, *The English Hymn: Its Development and Use* (Philadelphia: Presbyterian Board of Publication, 1915), 177–95, 372–89, which is unsurpassed on practically all Protestant traditions of hymnody. See also James Rawlings Sydnor, "Sing a New Song to the Lord: An Historical Survey of American Presbyterian Hymnals," *American Presbyterians* 68 (1990): 1–13; and Morgan F. Simmons, "Hymnody: Its Place in Twentieth-Century Presbyterianism," in Milton J. Coalter, et al., *The Confessional Mosaic: Presbyterians and Twentieth-Century Theology* (Louisville: Westminster/John Knox, 1990), 162–86.

3. On Reformation developments in hymnody, see Paul Westermeyer, *Te Deum: The Church and Music* (Minneapolis: Fortress Press, 1998), 141–60, and on Zwingli and Zurich specifically, 149–52; Rochelle A. Stackhouse, *The Language of the Psalms in Worship: American Revisions of Watts's Psalter*, Drew Studies in Liturgy, no. 4 (Lanham, Md.: Scare-

In Geneva the liturgical aesthetics were not so austere. Like Zwingli, Calvin did remove organs, not because he despised music but because he understood its attraction and potential for abuse. But Calvin dissented from Zwingli's spiritualizing of the Pauline writings about song. Believers should really sing, both with voice and heart. The question, then, was what to sing. Calvin's answer was simple — the Psalms. He believed this was the pattern of the early church, which picked up the practice of worship in the synagogue. Calvin also thought song's function in worship was a form of prayer. What better words to use in praying to God than the ones He had inspired? Calvin's understanding of song prompted the Geneva churches to commission the production of a psalter from Clement Marot; Theodore Beza, who supplied the verse; and Louis Bourgeois, who wrote the tunes.[4]

For Presbyterians and Reformed Protestants who sided with Calvin over Zwingli, the way to sing in worship was from a psalter. Indeed, the seventeenth century witnessed little deviation from Calvin's norm, whether in the Church of England, the Church of Scotland, or the dissenting Protestant churches. For Anglicans, *Sternhold and Hopkins*, a psalter produced during the reign of Edward VI, or Tate and Brady's version published in 1696, were the only psalters authorized for use in public worship.[5] The Scottish Kirk produced a psalter as early as 1564, before Andro Hart issued another in 1615, which in 1635 was reissued and updated.[6] When Presbyterians in the eighteenth century began to migrate to North America in numbers large enough to merit a denomination, they packed their psalters. In fact, the Old Side-New Side controversy that led to the first rupture of American Presbyterianism in 1741 may have been as much about rival

---

crow Press, 1997), 29 –70; and Erik Routley, *The Music of Christian Hymnody* (London: Independent Press Ltd., 1957), chaps. 2 – 4.

4.Westermeyer, *Te Deum*, 153–58. The *Genevan Psalter* went through seven editions in Calvin's lifetime (1539, 1541, 1543, 1545, 1551, 1554, and 1562), with the final one including all 150 psalms, with 125 tunes and 110 different meters. Westermeyer concedes that Calvin's practice was closer to the early church's, but different in that Geneva's worship was more restrictive lyrically and musically. The early church was not limited to psalms, and they chanted, a practice that Calvin thought unintelligible to Geneva's Christians.

5. Robert Stevenson, *Patterns of Protestant Church Music* (Durham: Duke University Press, 1953), 120.

6. Routley, *Music*, 42.

psalters as it was about George Whitefield's itinerancy, theological education, and creedal subscription. The stodgier Old Side used *The Psalms of
David in English Meter*, prepared in 1643 by Francis Rous, a Presbyterian
turned independent and member of the Westminster Assembly, or that of
another Puritan, William Barton's *Book of Psalms in Metre* (1644). Those
partial to revivals, the New Side, preferred Tate and Brady.[7]

Also contributing to the colonial Presbyterian split was the introduction of a new type of song. The source of this novelty was Benjamin
Franklin's publication in 1729 of the first American edition of Isaac
Watts's *The Psalms of David Imitated*. To be sure, Watts's songs were not
full-blown hymns like the ones he wrote for *Hymns and Spiritual Songs*
(1707), which were compositions based on scriptural thoughts as well as
the New Testament. In his imitations of the psalter, Watts was simply
trying to present psalms in a way "accommodated to modern Gospel worship."[8] Even so, Watts's Christianizing of the Psalms was an explicit break
with the tradition of metrical psalmody that had prevailed among Presbyterians and Reformed since Calvin.[9]

Watts's psalmody slowly gained a foothold among colonial Presbyterians during the revivals with which George Whitefield, among others,
was associated. The initial publication of Watts in 1729 would have to
wait until 1741 for a second edition.[10] The New Side, who supported
Whitefield, tended to be the ones buying Watts's gospel psalms. As early
as 1746, Whitefield's sympathizers in Newburyport began to use Watts,
and soon thereafter did Congregationalists in Boston.[11] Whitefield himself actively promoted and "greatly admired" Watts's *Hymns* and *Psalms*.
Henry Wilder Foote even claimed that Whitefield prompted Jonathan

---

7. On colonial Presbyterian developments, see Westermeyer, *Te Deum*, 179–80,
252–53; and Benson, *English Hymn*, 177–95.

8. Benson, *English Hymn*, 101. Stevenson, *Patterns*, 107, raises questions about
Watts's Christianization of the psalms since the hymn writer's views on the deity of Christ
were "peculiar" and "dangerous."

9. Benson, *Hymnody*, 88, writes of Watts: "In the light of its immediate surroundings
it was so glaringly original.... I think we shall come to feel more and more that to a larger
view, it was hardly more than a dislodgment of the Calvinistic settlement in favor of a reaf-
firmation of Luther's."

10. Westermeyer, *Te Deum*, 204.

11. Benson, *English Hymn*, 180.

Edwards to introduce Watts into public worship at his Northampton church.[12] In the South, Samuel Davies, an itinerant evangelist in Virginia as early as 1752, introduced not only Watts's psalms but also his hymns. When Davies left Virginia to preside over the newly founded College of New Jersey, an institution with New Side roots, his successor, John Todd, petitioned his presbytery to approve the use of Watts's psalms and hymns since the churches "have received great advantage" from the writer's "excellent compositions, especially his sacramental hymns."[13]

During the seventeen years that the Old Side Presbyterian Church ministered separately from the New Side, from 1741 to 1758, Watts's imitations never gained a foothold. Because the Old Side was predominantly Scotch-Irish, its churches were devoted to Rous's version of the Psalms and were fully prepared to resist innovation. So adamant could the Scotch-Irish be in their opposition to new songs that in 1756 New York's "Scotch Church" withdrew from the Synod of New York (a New Side body) to align with the Associate Presbytery, a communion composed of Seceders from the Church of Scotland. By 1765, after the reunion of the Old and New Sides, the issue was hardly settled, even though banning Watts was impossible to enforce. In a dispute over congregational song, the Synod of New York and Philadelphia ruled that "the inspired Psalms in Scripture" were "proper matter to be sung in Divine worship, according to their original design and the practice of the Christian churches." At the same time, the Synod refused to "forbid" those "whose judgment and inclination lead them to use the imitation of psalms.[14]

From 1765 until 1831, then, American Presbyterians were truly conflicted over congregational song. Watts gained in popularity as his work came out in newer and better editions. At the same time, many Presbyterians continued in their attachment to Rous. Although a denominationally approved hymnal would have to wait until 1831, the first General Assembly of the Presbyterian Church, U.S.A. (1789) resolved the tension in the first *Directory for the Worship of God*. Instead of saying that the "duty of Christians was to praise God publiquely by singing Psalms," as the first

12. Henry Wilder Foote, *Three Centuries of American Hymnody* (Cambridge, Mass.: Harvard University Press, 1940), 147, 148.
13. Benson, *English Hymn*, 182.
14. Ibid.

draft put it, the General Assembly determined that public praise included "psalms and hymns."[15] Since for Presbyterians in the new nation the words *hymns* and *Watts* were synonymous, Watts's *Hymns*, as Louis Benson puts it, "may be called the first hymn book of American Presbyterians."[16] Until 1831, Watts and Rous would be the chief texts that Presbyterians used in corporate worship.[17]

The first official Presbyterian hymnal of 1831 reflected this twin commitment. It began with an entire metrical psalter, followed by 531 hymns, 199 of which were by Watts.[18] Although the numbers have changed, subsequent Presbyterian hymnals display a similarly high proportion of psalms and Watts. This is true even after accounting for theological differences among mainline and sideline Presbyterians. No matter whether Presbyterians are sympathetic to J. Gresham Machen or Eugene Carson Blake, their hymnals reflect the musical genes of their Presbyterian great-grandparents. Despite twentieth-century theological conflicts and church divisions, Presbyterians in the United States followed the pattern established by adding Watts's imitations to the metrical versions of King David's real psalms.

From Isaac Watts to Charles Wesley and Beyond

In his book on Protestant church music, Robert Stevenson observes that Isaac Watts is the favorite songwriter of Presbyterians, Charles Wesley of Methodists, and the Anglican high churchman, John Mason Neale, of Episcopalians.[19] Stevenson's sense is accurate, even if his way of stating the matter slightly misrepresents the actual contents of Presbyterian hymnals. Watts is undoubtedly the most frequently included author in Presbyterian hymnals. Of the eight hymnbooks produced in the twentieth century, Watts accounts for 155 titles, and these make up 295 of the grand total

---

15. Ibid., 191.

16. Ibid., 193.

17. On these developments, see also Foote, *Three Centuries*, 152–56. For a good background on American Presbyterian worship in the eighteenth and nineteenth centuries, see Julius Melton, *Presbyterian Worship in America: Changing Patterns Since 1787* (Richmond: John Knox Press, 1967), chaps. 1–3.

18. Sydnor, "Sing a New Song to the Lord," 4.

19. Stevenson, *Patterns*, 139.

of hymns in Presbyterian hymnals (six percent of the 4,871 total hymns). The runners-up to Watts are Charles Wesley, with 137 total hymns in all the hymnbooks; Catherine Winkworth's translations of German hymns showing up 119 times; Neale's translations and hymns 109 times; and the Scottish Free Church minister, Horatius Bonar, being the fifth most popular with eighty hymns in all the hymnals. Another way of putting it is to say that the average twentieth-century Presbyterian hymnal has thirty-seven hymns by Watts, seventeen by Wesley and Neale, fifteen by Winkworth, and ten by Bonar.[20]

These numbers represent for the twentieth century something of a decline in Watts's popularity. For instance, as early as 1834, Watts accounted for one-third of the hymns in the German Reformed Church's *Psalms and Hymns*. At the end of the century, a survey of 750 different hymnals revealed that two-fifths of the hymns printed were written by Watts. And seven years later, a study of the thirty-two most popular English hymns included five by Watts. These statistics may explain the composition of the first two Presbyterian hymnbooks of the twentieth century, the southern Presbyterian Church's *New Psalms and Hymns* (1901) and the northern Presbyterian Church's 1911 revision of *The Hymnal* (1895). Southern Presbyterians printed 127 Watts hymns in contrast to northern Presbyterians' forty-nine. By 1990, when Great Commission Publications revised the *Trinity Hymnal*, the book of choice for most congregations in the PCA and the OPC, Watts was still holding strong with thirty-six hymns, while the mainline Presbyterian Church, U.S.A's hymnal of the same year had only thirteen.

One of the obvious reasons for Watts's decline over the twentieth century has been growing awareness of the variety of Christian hymnody and denominational efforts to reflect an ecumenical posture in congregational singing. Despite the steady decline of Watts's hymns throughout the twentieth century, he continues to receive the most favorable press from Presbyterian authors on worship. According to Hughes Oliphant

---

20. A sampling of other Reformed, Lutheran, and Episcopal hymnbooks backs up Stevenson's contention about Presbyterians' preference for Watts. In other communions' hymnals, Neale is the most popular, accounting, on average, for eighteen per hymnal; next is Wesley, who averaged seventeen, followed by Watts at sixteen, Winkworth at fifteen, and Bonar at seven.

Old, Watts "exemplifies the Reformed doxological tradition at its best." His "hymnody springs from the psalmody" and its "devotional quality" is "unsurpassed."[21] Old's comments are worth highlighting since they come from a book that may well rank as one of the most thoughtful arguments for historic Reformed worship written in the last 150 years. And yet we should not miss the irony. Among liturgical conservatives, what were once considered innovative practices now provide the best place from which to resist the novelties of contemporary worship.

Watts's appeal to worship traditionalists finds additional support in the work of Horton Davies. In his monumental study of Puritan worship, Davies curiously presents Watts as the culmination of Puritan psalmody. By his "brave defense of the right to paraphrase the songs of the Old Dispensation in the interests of the New," Watts "was delivering the Puritans from the Bibliolatry of the literalists." Davies even goes as far as saying that Watts's hymns and paraphrases "are the finest flowers of Puritan piety."[22] Considering how long it took for Watts to gain a following among most Calvinists, Davies's attempt to hitch the father of English hymnody to the wagon of metrical psalmody could arguably be deemed a stretch. But after two centuries of Presbyterian congregational singing, trying to tell the difference between Watts and historic Reformed practices in congregational song has become almost impossible.[23] This may explain Stevenson's biting remark that "in our day Calvin's precepts on church music are more honored in the breach than in the observance."[24] More winsome but equally apt is Louis F. Benson's comment: "That the hymns of this innovator should thus become a badge and symbol of orthodoxy and conservatism

---

21. Hughes O. Old, *Worship That Is Reformed According to Scripture* (Atlanta: John Knox Press, 1984), 55.

22. Horton Davies, *The Worship of the English Puritans* (1948; Clear Spring, Md.: Soli Deo Gloria, 1997), 178, 179.

23. See, for instance, James Rawlings Sydnor, *The Hymn and Congregational Singing* (Richmond, Va.: John Knox Press, 1960), 28–29, 52, who associates Watts with historic Reformed worship. In contrast, James Hastings Nichols, *Corporate Worship in the Reformed Tradition* (Philadelphia: Westminster Press, 1968), 125–26, links Watts to pietism and revivalism.

24. Stevenson, *Patterns*, 13.

in the churches that once disputed his way is an illustration of personal influence not easy to parallel."[25]

Davies and Old's evaluation may reflect a certain bias toward eighteenth-century hymnody, but Benson, arguably the leading student of hymns and a Presbyterian in his own right, provides ample justification for granting Watts's importance to Presbyterians. Benson did not always regard Watts's hymns as the best and, in fact, argued that the English independent's popularity may have retarded the development of Presbyterian hymnody. During the early nineteenth century, for instance, when revivals spawned "fresh" and "new types" of hymns, Presbyterians remained stuck with Watts, which, according to Benson, seemed "like a step backward."[26] Even so, Watts's contribution was "so glaringly original" in its time that Benson ranked him with patristic hymn writers, and even Luther and Calvin. "The fetters, whether of obligation, or of prudence, or of use and wont, that held the Church's songs so close to the letter of Scripture," Benson summarized, "were in the minds and habits of English-speaking Christians finally severed by Dr. Watts."[27] In other words, Watts deserves credit or blame (depending on your perspective) for upending the tradition of exclusive psalmody among Presbyterians. According to Benson, the quality of Watts's hymns may not have been as good as other authors, but by inaugurating a new era of congregational song, especially for communions that sang only metrical psalms, he became the justification for hymns.

The popularity of Watts, however, did not present a barrier to the Wesley brothers' appeal, especially Charles, who became almost as popular as Watts, his hymns appearing frequently in twentieth-century Presbyterian hymnals.[28] Part of the explanation for Wesley's popularity

---

25. Louis F. Benson, *Studies of Familiar Hymns* (1903; Philadelphia: Westminster Press, 1921), 129.

26. Benson, *English Hymn*, 195–96.

27. Benson, *Hymnody*, 88, 93.

28. In fact, of the ten hymns to appear in every Presbyterian hymnal produced over the course of the last century, Charles Wesley wrote twice as many as Watts. The most popular Wesley hymns among Presbyterians have been "Christ, Whose Glory Fills the Skies"; "Hark! The Herald Angels Sing"; "Come, Thou Long Expected Jesus"; "Ye Servants of God, Your Master Proclaim"; "Rejoice, the Lord Is King"; and "Love Divine, All Loves Excelling." The three by Watts to be printed in every hymnal are "O God, Our Help in Ages Past"; "Joy to the World, the Lord Is Come"; and "When I Survey the Wondrous

among lovers of Watts is that hymnal editors had more opportunities to include Wesley rather than Watts. Wesley wrote more than six thousand hymns compared to Watts's total of seven hundred hymns and psalm imitations.[29]

Still, the Presbyterian use of Wesleyan hymnody is a theological and liturgical oddity that has not generated sufficient comment, especially since many of Charles Wesley's hymns fit under the category of the Christian life, a topic that touches on sanctification and therefore on important disagreements between Reformed Protestants and Wesleyans. Benson contends that the reception of Wesley's hymns was gradual over the course of the nineteenth century because of the growth of the Methodist movement itself. While Watts "moved on the social uplands of English Noncomformity," Wesley worked "behind the hedges," and so Methodists were regarded "as schismatics," "ranters," "sentimentalists," and "sensationalists."[30] So great was the isolation of Methodism and its hymnody that, according to Benson, when Wesley's hymns began to appear in the nineteenth century, compilers often printed them anonymously or attributed them to other authors. Even an accomplished student of hymns such as John Mason Neale attributed "Hark! The Herald Angels Sing" to Philip Doddridge instead of Charles Wesley.[31] Benson, perhaps being overly charitable to fellow Calvinists, explained that "[t]here was a common ignorance concerning Charles Wesley and his work." Even so, Benson added, once other Protestants understood the extent of Wesley's

---

Cross." Rounding out the top ten Presbyterian hymns of the twentieth century is Horatius Bonar's "Here, O My Lord, I See Thee Face to Face." In the category of hymns to appear in all but one of the Presbyterian hymnbooks, Watts wrote two—"Alas! And Did My Savior Bleed" and "From All That Dwell below the Skies"—and Wesley wrote one—"O for a Thousand Tongues to Sing." The third most popular group of hymns—the ones to appear in all but two of the hymnals—included Wesley's "Jesus, Lover of My Soul"; "Soldiers of Christ, Arise"; "Jesus Christ Is Risen Today"; and "Lo! He Comes, with Clouds Descending." Watts contributed one to this list, "Jesus Shall Reign," as well as Bonar, "Blessing and Honor and Glory."

29. For estimations about the number of hymns Watts and Wesley wrote, see Benson, *English Hymn*, 114–16, 245.

30. Ibid., 258.

31. Ibid., 259–61.

contribution, they also recognized the "large area of Christian truth and feeling which all the Churches hold in common."[32]

This ecumenical spin, however, could not overcome the tension that Benson himself recognized in the experiential quality of Wesley's hymns. And this tension points to the unstable compound produced when mixing Presbyterian doctrine and Wesleyan piety. For instance, in his discussion of "Jesus, Lover of My Soul," Benson could not help asking whether "a lyric so tender and deeply felt should be used in public worship or reserved for private devotion." He went on to quote an English bishop who thought Wesley's verse "inexpressibly shocking" to put such sentiments "into the mouths of a large and mixed gathering of people." Benson even noted that "actual investigations" discovered this hymn to be one of the three favored by "English tramps." To the defensive response of noting that the apostle John, who lay on the bosom of the Lord, could have penned these lines, Benson replied, "We are not all St. Johns."[33]

This line of criticism dovetailed with Benson's general assessment of Wesley's "hymnody of the Methodist revival." Unlike Watts, who overthrew the psalter's reign, Wesley's chief contribution was twofold. First, he introduced the genre of evangelistic hymn "as we use that term to-day."[34] These hymns were designed "to bring the unchurched and saved within the sound of the gospel" and lead them to conversion. For Benson, this explained why the first section of the original collection of Methodist hymns was entitled "Exhorting and Entreating to Return to God." Second, Wesley turned hymnody in the direction of Christian experience. In fact, Benson thought Wesley conceived of hymnody primarily as a "manual of spiritual discipline." The experience that Wesley charted may often have been his own, and Benson had reservations about the autobiographical nature of the Methodist's hymns. Was the author's experience, Benson wondered, "fitted to be a norm of Christian experience in general," or did singing Wesley's texts render the worshiper guilty of "religious insincerity"? Even so, Benson concluded that Wesley's hymns charted

32. Ibid., 261.

33. Benson, *Studies of Familiar Hymns*, second series (1923; Philadelphia: Westminster Press, 1926), 43.

34. Benson, *English Hymn*, 252, 248.

"with firmness and precision" the entire scope of "the operations of the Spirit in the heart."[35]

Although Benson assessed Wesley more from the perspective of his research of hymnody than from Presbyterian convictions, his reservations may account for the popularity of Wesley among Presbyterians. Ever since colonial division between Old and New Side Presbyterians, Presbyterians in the United States have embraced the revival as a valuable means for reaching new converts and invigorating old ones.[36] In other words, Presbyterians in America had no intrinsic objections of principle to the evangelistic purposes or experiential piety involved in Wesley's hymns. Presbyterians did take a while to include his compositions in their hymnals. But even if their confession and catechisms articulated a piety that was oriented more toward the objective character of Christianity than to the subjective experience of the Christian, Presbyterian history nurtured among Presbyterians a taste for the intimate and soul-penetrating piety often expressed in Wesley's hymns.[37]

At the same time, Watts likely prepared the ground that Wesley tilled. Indeed, Watts's hymns of "divine love" delved into matters of the heart in ways that many of his contemporaries and later commentators would find unprecedented and off putting. For instance, John Wesley, who omitted his brother's "Jesus, Lover of My Soul" from the Methodist collection of hymns, wrote that Watts offended him "in a more gross manner than in

---

35. Ibid., 248, 249, 250, 249.

36. On the importance of revivalism to eighteenth-century American Presbyterianism, see Leonard J. Trinterud, *The Forming of an American Tradition: A Re-examination of Colonial Presbyterianism* (Philadelphia: Westminster, 1949); and Leigh Eric Schmidt, *Holy Fairs: Scottish Communions and American Revivals in the Early Modern Period* (Princeton: Princeton University Press, 1989).

37. For other assessments of Wesley and Watts, see Bernard L. Manning, *The Hymns of Wesley and Watts: Five Informal Papers* (London: Epworth Press, 1942); J. Ernest Rattenbury, *The Evangelical Doctrines of Wesley's Hymns* (London: Epworth Press, 1941); Harry Escott, *Isaac Watts, Hymnographer* (London: Independent Press, 1962); Rochelle A. Stackhouse, "Changing the Language of the Church's Song circa 1785," *Hymn* 45 (July 1994): 16–19; and E. K. Simpson, "Isaac Watts: A Rounded Life," *Evangelical Quarterly* 21 (1949): 190–202. Presbyterian receptivity to the emotionalism of Watts and Wesley could also well account for the way some congregations today have welcomed the genre of praise songs and choruses, even though it also makes less defensible the so-called "traditionalist" position of defending "standard" hymns in the contemporary worship wars.

anything which was before published in the English tongue." He faulted
Watts especially for inserting "coarse expressions" in "spiritual hymns."
"How often," Wesley complained, "in the midst of excellent verse, are lines
inserted which disgrace those that precede and follow."[38] Robert Stevenson noted the amorous quality of the English Dissenter's verse, such as
Watts's references to Christ's "sweet Lips" and "Heavenly Look" that "seek
my kisses and my Love." Stevenson also observed that Watts's use of the
word *die*, used in a comparison of the believer's dissolving in the arms
of Christ to "the Billows [that] after Billow rolls to kiss the Shoar, and
Dye," had unwholesome connotations in the context of eighteen-century
romantic poetry.[39]

The only Presbyterian among the authors of American Presbyterians' favorite hymns, falling well behind Watts and Wesley, was Horatius
Bonar (1808–1889). A minister in the Free Church of Scotland, first in
Kelso and later in Edinburgh, Bonar was, at least by Benson's reckoning,
"the greatest of Scottish hymn writers."[40] He was also, according to Benson, the only answer to the charge that Presbyterians have not written
hymns of lasting value.[41] Just as likely, however, is the emotional character of Bonar's lyrics. According to Benson, one Church of England
bishop thought Bonar's hymns belonged "to the class known as 'subjective hymns' or 'hymns of inward experience.'"[42] Benson himself concluded
that Bonar was more like the "writers of the Evangelical Revival" than any
other group. At the same time, Bonar's premillenialism may account for
the dominant theme of pilgrimage in his hymns. For instance, in his most
popular hymn, "I Heard the Voice of Jesus Say," Christ is a source of com-

38. John Wesley, *The Works of the Rev. John Wesley* (New York, 1856), 2:443, quoted
in Stevenson, *Patterns*, 105.
39. Watts, *Horae Lyricae, Poems Chiefly of the Lyric Kind* (London, 1706), 80, 83,
quoted in Stevenson, *Patterns*, 106.
40. Benson, *Studies of Familiar Hymns*, second series, 209.
41. Ibid., 218. Benson adds the following names to the list of Presbyterian hymn
authors of note: from Scotland, "Bruce, Logan, Morison, J. D. Burns, Norman MacLeod,
Matheson, Miss Borthwick and Mrs Findlater, Brownlie, Mrs Cousin and the Duke of
Argyll"; from Canada, Robert Murray; and from the U.S., "Davies, J. W. Alexander, Duff-
ield, Dunn, Hastings, Mrs. Prentiss, Wolfe, Hopper, March, Mrs. C. L. Smith, and van
Dyke" (219).
42. Ibid., 216.

fort to the weary pilgrim, offering him rest, water, and light. The world, accordingly, offers no delights of its own, nor does God work through His creation to meet the needs of His children. Instead, Bonar's piety is absorbed with the immediate ministry of Christ as an escape from the toil, tedium, and darkness of this life. Benson concluded that Bonar's texts were so escapist that one "High Church lady" attributed his hymns to the Middle Ages.[43]

If the popularity of Watts, Wesley, and Bonar is a good indication, revivalism has played an enormous influence on Presbyterian hymnody. Not only did Watts and Wesley write for the revivals of the First Great Awakening, but the form of devotion that revivals encouraged — a soul-wrenching new birth and a Christian life characterized by zeal for holiness — nurtured a form of congregational singing that exclusive psalmody could not match. To claim that American Presbyterians would still be singing the songs that Calvin prescribed if not for the First and Second Great Awakenings is an overstatement. But the fact that American Presbyterians, both conservative and liberal, mounted serious efforts to recover the Reformed pattern of singing psalms at a time when spirit-filled forms of Christianity became questionable (e. g., Pentecostalism and the charismatic movement) seems more providential than coincidental.[44]

Conclusion: Singing God's Praise in a Praise-Song Age

Although psalm singing communions are not known for being liturgical, an argument could be made that exclusive psalmody as part of the traditional elements and order of Reformed worship is in fact Reformed Christianity's liturgy, with the Psalter functioning as the church's book of prayer. Whatever the reasons for Scottish Presbyterians renouncing prayer

---

43. Ibid., 211. Bonar has not received much attention in the historical literature, but Kenneth R. Ross, "Calvinists in Controversy: John Kennedy, Horatius Bonar and the Moody Mission of 1873–1874," *Scottish Bulletin of Evangelical Theology* 9 (1991–1992): 51–63, is helpful for placing Bonar's views about revivalism and thus adds another link connecting hymns and evangelistic piety.

44. On the twentieth-century recovery of psalm singing, see Bertus Frederick Polman, "Church Music and Liturgy in the Christian Reformed Church of North America" (University of Minnesota: Ph.D. dissertation, 1980); and Emily R. Brink, "Metrical Psalmody in North America: A Story of Survival and Revival," *The Hymn* 44, 4 (Oct. 1993): 21.

books, even though John Knox had not thought to reject them, liturgical worship and exclusive psalmody are not inherently at odds, as the practice of Reformed churches on the Continent makes clear. From John Calvin's 1560 Geneva to the Christian Reformed Church's 1930 Grand Rapids, the use of forms in worship was every bit compatible with singing only psalms. Consequently, even while the Covenanters and Seceders rejected prayer books and liturgy, their practice was not necessary, as if exclusive psalmody precluded liturgy.

This chapter raises enough questions about the origins of hymnody to prompt a reconsideration of the Psalms as both the historic practice of Reformed churches and as the best way for believers to praise their God in corporate worship. Indeed, one of the contemporary obstacles to Reformed worship in the United States is the failure of Presbyterians to be discerning about the common idiom of American culture. According to the English sociologist of religion, David Martin, American culture is inherently Wesleyan: "[T]he difference between America and England is the American insistence on sincerity and openness rather than on form and privacy. The whole American style was, and is, 'Methodist' in its emphases, whereas in England the culturally prestigious style remained Anglican. 'Enthusiasm' of all kinds, religious, cultural and personal, became endemic in America; in England enthusiasm remained intermittent and the object of some mild curiosity."[45]

Of course the low-church style of many Presbyterians in the United States makes it difficult to place Presbyterianism on Martin's formal/ informal spectrum. Still, if Reformed worship is characterized more by reverence and awe than by enthusiastic emotion, American Presbyterians need to be more discerning than they have been about using widely popular American Protestant idioms in their practice of worship.

Part of this greater discernment will also require Presbyterians to be especially attentive to the charismatic traces of Wesleyan piety in Reformed worship. In a foreword to a book on contemporary worship, the Southern Baptist scholar on hymnody, Donald P. Hustad, issued a very telling warning that applies to any tradition of worship, but that Presby-

---

45. David Martin, *Tongues of Fire: The Explosion of Protestantism in Latin America* (Cambridge, Mass.: Blackwell, 1990), 21.

terians especially should take to heart: "Charismatic believers have a right to develop their own worship to match their own theology and exegesis, and they have done this well. Noncharismatics should not thoughtlessly copy or imitate their worship formulae, unless they expect to enter the same 'Holy of Holies' in the same way. Instead, they should develop their worship rationale based on their scriptural understanding, and then sing up to their own theology."[46]

If Hustad is right, then Presbyterians and Reformed Protestants may have a valuable remedy for resisting the novelty, emotional excess, and disorder that characterizes so much worship in the contemporary church — a return to the Psalter. It is certainly not a magic cure-all that will suddenly cause teenagers to be attentive and put an end to worship committees' desire to experiment with new forms of worship. But exclusive psalmody may function like the broken-windows policy that reduced major crime in so many cities by enforcing laws against minor vices. If Presbyterians are jealous for singing the right songs in worship, debates over the regulative principle, questions about spontaneity, and worries about bored children and confused visitors may actually fall into their proper place.

---

46. Donald P. Hustad, foreword to Barry Leisch, *The New Worship: Straight Talk on Music and the Church* (Grand Rapids: Baker Book House, 1996), 10.

Part 2

Psalm Singing in Scripture

Chapter 5

Psalm Singing and Scripture

ROWLAND S. WARD

I n this chapter we look at psalm singing in Scripture with special reference to the New Testament.

The Old Covenant Background

While the use of song and lyric was common among the early Hebrews,
and certainly religious and non-religious song was regarded as proper,
only from David's time was there a service of song in the central place of
worship.

The Old Testament emphasizes the divine appointment of the song
service in the time of David, God's servant-king (1 Chron. 6:31–48;
25:1–31; cf. 2 Chron. 29:25). Although this worship often fell into decay,
when it was reformed, the warrant was found in the law given by God
through David. This can be seen in the reforms of 835 BC (2 Chron.
23:18); about 715 BC (2 Chron. 29:30); and 622 BC (2 Chron. 35:15),
and in the laying of the foundation of the second temple about 537 BC
(Ezra 3:10) and the dedication of the wall of Jerusalem about 434 BC
(Neh. 12:45–46). These references show that the songs of worship in the
temple were not considered a matter for mere human prescription. There
was freedom in regard to the words of prayers, but no freedom in regard
to the words of songs. The principle of the centralized worship of the
Old Testament is inspired songs authorized for the purpose. David's last
words were, "The Spirit of the LORD spake by me, and his word was in my
tongue" (2 Sam. 23:2).

Of course there was considerable diversity in Judaism in the time of the New Testament. The Essene-like group that produced the Dead Sea Scrolls used the Psalter extensively, but the order of the last half of their version (from Psalm 90 onwards) was not fixed, and they also had some distinctive psalms of their own (1QH and 11QPs). The *Psalms of Solomon*, a group of eighteen psalms written sometime after the death of Pompey in 48 BC, is a further example from another section of Jewry. But there are no grounds for supposing these compositions were employed in Israel's centralized worship.[1]

The present state of our knowledge is such that we cannot trace the successive stages through which the Psalter passed to its final form, traditionally in the time of Ezra around 430 BC. The Hebrew Bible was translated into Greek about 200 BC (the Septuagint) and was widely used, as extensive quotations from it in the New Testament demonstrate. In Hebrew the Psalter is called *Sepher Tehillim* (Book of Hymns or Praises); in Greek it is termed *Psalmois* (Psalms).

We do not know much about the use of the Psalter outside the temple, but it would be very natural for the compositions of "the sweet psalmist of Israel" (2 Sam. 23:1) to have enjoyed widespread use. The available Old Testament data emphasizes the connection of the Psalms with the centralized temple worship rather than with individual or synagogue worship. The synagogue is thought to have originated in its organized form in the period between the Old and New Testaments. It was certainly widely established throughout Palestine and the known world by the time of Jesus (cf. Acts 15:21). Essentially, it was an assembly for instruction in the Scriptures and for prayer, and there is no conclusive evidence that singing occurred there.

After all, the Psalter is not in the first place for individuals, but for a community whose hope is in God's Servant-King. This explains why a good number of psalms addressed to the choir director are songs that at first appear to be of purely individual concern.

---

1. Of course the *Odes of Solomon* were not so used either. These forty-two songs date at the earliest from late in the first century AD, were written first in Syriac, and seem to originate in Essene-like circles with some Christian influences.

It will not do to see the Psalter as merely predictive of Christ or as messianic in a few notable cases, such as Psalm 2 or Psalm 22. Far different is the true situation. In brief, Jesus Christ is the tuning fork by which we pitch the Psalms correctly. We will find Him in them in various ways, not just in a few psalms, but in all the psalms. The believer's union with Christ, the true David, is the key to unlocking the treasures of the Psalter. It is also the reason that these songs have a special place in the New Testament church and are so frequently quoted.

Theological Orientation

Any discussion of worship in Scripture must be Christ-centered. In the Gospel of John, Jesus sets the scene. Jesus' ministry commences with the cleansing of the temple at Passover time and the declaration of Himself as the true temple (John 2:12–22). He looks beyond the era of temple worship and feasts like Passover to communication between God and humanity through Himself as a result of His death and resurrection. The earthly must give way to the heavenly reality, and so He goes on to speak to Nicodemus (John 3) of the necessity of a birth from above by the Spirit if heavenly realities are to be understood and entry into the kingdom of God secured.

Similarly, in John 4, Jesus speaks to a Samaritan woman of how the promises of God come to fulfillment through Jewish history, not Samaritan history, and how the time has come for true worshipers to worship the Father "in spirit and in truth" (vv. 23–24). In this passage Jesus is not affirming that God from now on wants sincere worship, and still less that location no longer matters. God has always required worship from the heart and has always been near to those who call on Him in truth wherever they are. Rather, Jesus is affirming that true worship is according to the realm of the Spirit and thus according to the heavenly realities known through a birth from above. More simply, location and access to God are both found in the Lord Jesus who obtains the life-giving Spirit for us so that in faith-union with Christ, we might be living stones in the spiritual temple. It is not the physical location that matters but location in Christ, the way, the truth, and the life.

The temple and everything associated with it, including the Psalter, comes to its true realization in Jesus Christ. And if Christ our High Priest appears in heaven for us, the prayers He prayed through David remain the prayers of all who are in Him. There is no separate song for different individuals, but one song for the community in Christ, the one church for which He died; there is one song He prayed for us, and one song we pray in Him.

It is therefore no argument against using the Psalter in Christian worship to claim that it is pre-Christian, still less that it is sub-Christian and contains material unfit for Christian lips. Jesus used the Psalter in His life and teaching, sang from it at the Last Supper, quoted it from the cross, died with its words on His lips, and illumined its meaning in His teaching following His resurrection (Luke 24:44). The extensive use of psalms in the New Testament shows that the early believers recognized that the Psalter was full of Christ.

Singing in the New Testament

A further consideration of singing in the early church requires a discussion of the following: (1) specific references to singing in the New Testament, (2) actual songs present in the New Testament text, and (3) hymn fragments embedded in the New Testament text.

Specific References

Specific New Testament references to singing are very few. Matthew 26:30 and Mark 14:26 refer to singing a hymn at the institution of the Last Supper. This is the only singing reference in the Gospels. According to the Jewish Mishnah (*Pesahim* 10), compiled about AD 200, a part of the Great Hallel (Psalms 114/5–118) was sung in homes at Passover. While we cannot be absolutely certain that this was the case in Jesus' day, it is generally accepted, not least because worship practice normally tends to be conservative and changes only slowly. Andrew Brunson holds that many readers would have recognized from the context, particularly Jesus' words in Matthew 23:39, which include a quotation of Psalm 118, that Matthew was alluding to the Hallel.[2]

---

2. Andrew C. Brunson, *Psalm 118 in the Gospel of John* (Tubingen: Mohr Siebeck, 2003), 131.

It would be hard to imagine Paul and Silas not including compositions from the Psalter in the "hymning" they engaged in at midnight in the
prison at Philippi (Acts 16:25). Ralph Martin, who holds that there are
hymn fragments in the New Testament, comments: "There is no means of
knowing the genre of the hymns which Paul and Silas sang in the Philip-
pian jail, but if we are correct in reasoning that the human spirit, under
duress and trial, turns instinctively to what is familiar and well known,
there is then nothing to deny that the Psalms of the Old Testament
rang through the dark prison, greatly to the interest of the missionaries'
fellow-captives."[3]

James 5:13 exhorts those who are merry to sing psalms, and none
would suggest that the Psalter was excluded. It is noteworthy that he does
this immediately after exhorting those in trouble to pray. This shows that,
just as in the temple, singing is a religious duty distinct from prayer, even
if in some respects they overlap. To the same effect is Paul's distinction
between prayer and singing in 1 Corinthians 14:15. In both these elements
of communal worship, Paul requires the mind to be fruitful in edifying
others. Thus, praying and singing in (unknown) tongues is excluded as
contrary to the nature of these elements of worship; two or three spoken
messages in tongues are allowed, but are to be interpreted.

In 1 Corinthians 14:26, singing is a distinct element in worship, as
already noted. It is supposed a member wants to contribute a song (*psalmos*) in worship. This would not exclude an existing composition in the
Psalter, but it could refer to something other than a Psalter piece that met
the requirements of intelligibility, edification, and decent order. If we take
"a psalm,... a doctrine,... a revelation" as aspects of prophetic utterance, as
seems probable in the context, then we have a Spirit-inspired composition
but perhaps not necessarily a composition from the Psalter, although such
is inspired.

We now consider the phrase "psalms and hymns and spiritual songs"
in Ephesians 5:19 and Colossians 3:16, particularly the significance of the
adjective *spiritual*. Paul urges that "the word of Christ dwell...richly" in
his readers, meaning that the gospel of Christ is to permeate their think-
ing and direct their conduct. Paul thus exhorts the use of songs that arise

---

3. Ralph P. Martin, *Worship in the Early Church* (Grand Rapids: Eerdmans, 1975), 43.

from the gospel, are addressed to the Lord, but teach and admonish the believing community. Similarly, in Ephesians Paul desires that the believers go on being filled with the Spirit, speaking to one another in songs as they also make melody in their hearts to the Lord. We have either inspired songs, such as the Psalter, or Spirit-prompted songs which, while including the Psalter, express the truth of the gospel of Christ in appropriate ways.

The exegetical issues regarding the use of these three terms can be summarized in the following way:

1. *The meaning of the three terms cannot be distinguished in actual usage.*

If we look at the original derivation of the words we might argue that *psalmos* (from *psallo*, "to pluck") means a song sung to a stringed instrument such as a harp, *hymnos* means a song of praise to God, and *ode* is a more general word. Gregory of Nyssa (ca. AD 380) takes this line and has been followed by others, including Calvin. Distinctions may be made, as by J. B. Lightfoot, so that "psalms" refers to songs drawn directly from Scripture, "hymns" to distinctively Christian compositions, and "songs" to spontaneous Spirit-inspired odes, but usage is against this. Further, in the Septuagint the three terms are found in the titles in the Psalter, Psalm 76 having all three; the same feature is found to a lesser extent in the Hebrew text and the words *mizmorim*, *tehillim*, and *shirim*. English readers can note this in various psalms such as 67 and 108. In short, in practice the three terms are synonymous in the period before and during the first century AD. Further, the verb *psallo* is used in the New Testament (James 5:13; 1 Cor. 14:15) with the simple meaning "sing psalms," and the idea of instrumental accompaniment is not implied.

Some suggest the view that, according to H. A. W. Meyer's *Commentary*, originated with G. C. von Harless's *Commentary on Ephesians* in 1834. This is that the three terms are best explained as a reference to the Psalter since in the New Testament *psalmoi* is used in predominantly Greek settings, presumably from the title in the Greek translation of the Psalter, while in Jewish settings *humnoi* or related forms is used since this translates the Hebrew title *tehillim*. In a mixed Jewish/Gentile setting, the combination of the two terms together with the general term *ode*, the whole qualified by a word indicating the songs given by the Spirit, would provide a comprehensive phrase to identify and embrace the entire body of Spirit-given compositions urged upon believers. We can regard them as a piling up of synonyms like "iniquity, transgression, and sin" in the Old Testament or "signs, and wonders, and mighty deeds" in Paul (2 Cor. 12:12).

2. *The three terms cannot be limited with absolute certainty to the Psalter.*

Given the usage of *psalmos* in 1 Corinthians 14:26 for what is arguably a song given by prophetic utterance rather than an existing psalm and given that the terms appear as interchangeable in reference to religious songs in contemporary literature, such as the apocryphal *Psalms of Solomon*,[4] the terms may be general in nature.

3. *The adjective* spiritual *almost certainly qualifies all three terms.*

Where the tradition of distinguishing the terms is maintained, it is usual to regard *spiritual* as qualifying the general word *song* to indicate that it must be of religious character,[5] although this seems a bit redundant in a context that is already religious,[6] or alternatively that the song is Spirit-inspired.[7] The general view of scholars today is that while *spiritual*, in harmony with Greek usage, agrees grammatically with the last term, it actually refers to all three nouns. Indeed, it is also logical since it is difficult to suppose that Paul would link together compositions that were not of equal devotional value and spiritual profit. The sense will then be "Spirit-prompted psalms, hymns and songs" (Lohse) or "Spirit-inspired psalms, hymns and songs" (Martin, O'Brien, Schnackenburg, Lincoln).[8]

---

4. Composed in Hebrew ca. 30 BC; translated into Greek ca. AD 50.

5. So E. Schweizer, *Colossians* (Minneapolis 1982), 210; Murray J. Harris, *Colossians and Philemon* (Grand Rapids, 1991), 169.

6. Cf. Marcus Barth and Helmut Blanke, *Colossians* (New York, 1994) contra E. Schweizer.

7. F. F. Bruce, *The Epistles to the Colossians, to Philemon, and to the Ephesians* (Grand Rapids: Eerdmans, 1984), 159.

8. Eduard Lohse says, "The adjectival expression 'prompted by the Spirit' (*pneumatikais*) refers materially to all three terms." (*Colossians and Philemon*) [Philadelphia: Fortress Press, 1971], 151). Similarly, R. P. Martin, *Worship in the Early Church* (Grand Rapids: Eerdmans, 1975), 43; P. T. O'Brien, *Colossians, Philemon* (Waco, Tex.: Word, 1982), 310; A. T. Lincoln, *Ephesians* (Waco, Tex.: Word, 1990), 346. R. Schnackenburg, *Ephesians* (Edinburgh: T&T Clark, 1991), 238, states that the adjective "characterises all that the congregation sings as being inspired or produced by the Spirit." Even those who are not definite one way or another recognize the possibility (Barth and Blanke, James D. G.

4. The setting of the passage is communal, not individual, and thus the distinction made in 1 Corinthians 11:18–22 and 14:19, 35 between "in the church" and "at home" applies.

The Old Testament certainly regulated the centralized temple worship very closely, and we might argue that the New Testament does the same in regard to the spiritual temple of the believing community in Christ. While recognizing diversity in the churches, we must not underestimate the uniformity in some practices (cf. 1 Cor. 14:33b–34). What occurred "in the church" and what occurred "at home" might be somewhat different. Thus the common distinction between public worship and private worship has some justification, and the passages in Ephesians and Colossians appear to fit the gathered Christian meetings.

One concludes that if the sense is Spirit-inspired, then we are confined to songs given by the Spirit, which in practice means songs drawn from the text of Scripture. If the sense is Spirit-prompted, and Colossians 1:9 uses *spiritual* in this sense, then there is freedom to compose songs that arise from the gospel and reflect the fulfillment of the Old Testament in Christ. Naturally, the wisest course here is also to keep closely to the meaning of Scripture, if not its very words. Thus the new songs, though not formally canonical, can be regarded as accurately conveying the truth of God and thus of devotional value and spiritual profit along with material directly in the text of Scripture.

Of course it is true that a vibrant, living faith expresses itself in song, but the hymns that are suited for the gathered worship of the people of God and tend to endure are generally those closest to the biblical text. If we compare the language of Colossians 1:28 with 3:16, we could conclude that songs for church are essentially explanatory of Scripture. And we should not forget that God has always been very jealous of His worship.

Dunn, *The Epistles to the Colossians and to Philemon* [Grand Rapids: Eerdmans, 1996], 239; Margaret Y. MacDonald, *Colossians and Ephesians* [Collegeville, Minn.: Liturgical Press, 2000], 318; Jerry L. Sumney, *Colossians: A Commentary* [Louisville, Ky.: Westminster John Knox, 2008], 225). For older writers, where again the preponderance is for Spirit-prompted/originated/inspired, see Michael Bushell, *The Songs of Zion* (Pittsburgh: Crown and Covenant Publications, 1980), 73–76 and 188n110.

He has the right to fix its nature, and our response can only be one of obedience in the context of His gracious covenant.

Songs Present in the New Testament Text

The New Testament provides a number of examples of songs that take phrases of Scripture, supplement them, and express the result in forms appropriate to the new situation. Mary's song (the Magnificat) has at least nine references and allusions to the Psalms, and the Song of Zacharias at least eight (see Luke 1:46–55, 67–79). I have always found it surprising that one should argue for their regular use in public worship given that it is so obvious that they are unique songs for unique personal situations. However, they certainly demonstrate that the Psalter was woven into the spiritual life of ordinary pious people.

Three hymns are recorded in the book of Revelation. They cannot be thought of as hymn fragments since they are clearly embedded in the structure of the text in a way that shows they are integral to it. Still, they are hymns not in the Psalter. We should not make too much of this, however, since Revelation is picturing for us the ultimate fulfilment of God's purposes using a variety of literary devices.

The new song of Revelation 5:9–10 is sung by those with harps and bowls of incense, which are the prayers of the saints. The new song is then echoed by the angels, and comes to a finale with all creatures, even the fish in the sea, joining in. The expression "new song" is also found in Psalms 33:3, 40:3, 96:1, 98:1, 144:9, and Isaiah 42:10. It refers to the new situation brought about by God's saving action, and the new song is the song that celebrates this. Ultimately all believers, and they alone, participate in it (Rev. 14:3).

"The song of Moses the servant of God, and the song of the Lamb" in Revelation 15:3–4 is a single song, sung with harps given by God, which draws extensively on words in the old covenant to illustrate the climax in the new covenant ratified by the Lamb of God. Psalms alluded to include 86:9, 98:2, 111:2, 139:14, and 145:17. Similarly, in the wedding song of Revelation 19:6–9, several expressions are drawn from the Psalter (v. 6 — 93:1; 97:1; 99:1; v. 7 — 118:24; 96:8).

Song Fragments Embedded in the New Testament Text

It is also commonly argued that there are fragments of Christian hymns embedded in the text of the New Testament. The usual passages cited are Ephesians 5:14, Philippians 2:6–11, Colossians 1:15–20, and 1 Timothy 3:16; others are sometimes suggested. It is not clear what is established even if these are hymn fragments. If Paul could quote a heathen poet (Acts 17:28), how much more a Christian one, assuming there were some! But is it not possible to mistake memorable passages of great eloquence for hymns? Moreover, as Gerhard Delling remarks,[9] there is no attempt in the New Testament to use the Greek style of metrical hymns or follow clearly discernable laws in the passages cited, so that identification of hymn fragments is hypothetical and of limited validity.

What are much more obvious than these hymn fragments are the numerous citations from and allusions to the Psalter. Approximately one-third of all Old Testament quotations in the New Testament are from this single book. About forty psalms are directly quoted in the New Testament, and 100 to 110 in all are quoted or alluded to.[10] These facts are a telling testimony to the significance of the Psalter in the life of the New Testament church. It looks as though the early Christians took very seriously the presence of a hymnbook in the Scriptures they possessed. We do not have much evidence as to how they were sung. Some kind of antiphonal practice may be suggested by the phrase "speaking to one another" in Ephesians 5:19. We also see this in Pliny's letter to Trajan about AD 112, where the Latin words *carmen adicere* are used. But that the Psalter was known, loved, and extensively used is crystal clear.

Conclusion

The purpose of the foregoing analysis is not to argue for exclusive use of the Psalter in public worship, but to illustrate two things: (1) the paucity of information suggesting that the use of other hymns and religious songs was widespread or even existed in the public gatherings of the primitive

---

9. G. Kittel and G. Friedrich, *Theological Wordbook of the New Testament* (Grand Rapids: Eerdmans,, 1972), 8:500.

10. As an illustration of this one could refer to the indices in *The Greek New Testament*, 4th ed. (Stuttgart: United Bible Societies, 1994).

church, and (2) the extensive use of the psalms in the life of the primitive church, reflecting the recognition they had now come into their own as a vital element in new covenant theology and practice.

Hebrews 1 provides an example of the quite sophisticated use of the psalms. Here quotations are introduced with the expectation that the argument will be conclusive in the minds of the hearers. If we do not find it so, it may suggest that we have strayed somewhat from biblical standards.

There may be other principles of Scripture that justify embracing a wider body of songs than psalms, but if we lose sight of the norm of praise in the Psalter, we are likely to drift very seriously. By the same token, the hymns that tend to endure are those that stay most closely to Scripture themes and language. One only has to note the high frequency of Isaac Watts's compositions in modern hymnbooks compared with the relatively modest number by Charles Wesley, despite his far more prolific output, to see the point.

Practical experience may be the best argument. Dietrich Bonhoeffer wrote: "Wherever the Psalter is abandoned, an incomparable treasure vanishes from the Christian church. With its recovery will come unexpected power."[11] J. H. Eaton writes:

> If Scripture itself has a unique role in feeding the faith of the church and forming the life of converse with the Lord, then so does that part of it which has been to the fore from earliest times, the Psalter. Here in plain words and strong images Scripture teaches, prophesies, and lifts the veil of the good world to come; it puts into the worshippers' mouths robust words of praise and thanksgiving, along with passionate entreaty from the lowest pit of suffering. The hymns we write ourselves are pleasant and easy to the feelings. Much in the Psalms may be difficult for the modern imagination, seeming primitive or harsh. But if the challenge of them is met, they will be found to have a power and a fullness that modern compositions can hardly attain.[12]

---

11. Dietrich Bonhoeffer, *Psalms: The Prayer Book of the Bible* (Minneapolis, Minn.: Augsburg Fortress, 1974), 26.

12. J. H. Eaton, *The Psalms: A Historical and Spiritual Commentary with an Introduction and a New Translation* (New York: Continuum International Publishing Group, 2006), 58.

Chapter 6

The Hymns of Christ: The Old Testament Formation of the New Testament Hymnal

MICHAEL LEFEBVRE

In the Bible, the book of Psalms is traditionally located between Job and Proverbs, roughly in the center of the Old Testament. This placement in the middle of the Old Testament can give a wrong impression, however, if we thereby come to view the Psalter as a book formed in the midst of the Old Testament period. The book of Psalms is actually one of the later products of the Old Testament era. If we were to arrange the books of the Old Testament according to their dates of compilation, we would have to put the Psalter among the post-exilic volumes toward the very end of the collection. Many of the songs contained in it are, to be sure, much older, but the particular selection and arrangement of Hebrew hymns into the volume we call the book of Psalms is a post-exilic work. In fact, rather than looking at the Psalter as an Old Testament worship hymnal, it is probably more appropriate to regard it as a final product of the Old Testament temple, compiled in preparation for New Testament worship.

In this chapter, I would like to explore the history of hymnbook composition in Old Testament Israel, culminating with the book of Psalms. (Sometimes, you can get to know a child better by getting acquainted with his parents.) While we know little about the hymnals that preceded the Psalter, there are enough hints in Scripture to get some idea of the Psalmbook's heritage. Furthermore, the book of Psalms draws upon those previous collections in order to re-present a certain subset of temple hymns in a careful new arrangement. After placing the Psalter within its heritage, I would then like to explore the significance of its particular arrangement.

I hope that the study presented in this chapter will contribute to a renewed appreciation for the profound suitability of this Old Testament Psalter for Christ-centered, New Testament worship.

Hymnody of the Patriarchs?

Genesis is silent about any worship songs used during the days of the patriarchs. Certainly singing was an important part of human society from the earliest periods, and Genesis ranks the invention of musical instruments alongside the introduction of metal-working technologies and nomadic herding (Gen. 4:20 –22). We also read Laban's talk of throwing a farewell party for Jacob "with mirth, and with songs, with tabret, and with harp" (Gen. 31:27) and realize that singing was an important facet of the patriarchs' world. However, Genesis does not tell us anything about whether the patriarchs sang specifically in worship.

Other communities in the patriarchs' world—including Mesopotamia (where Abraham came from) and Canaan (where the patriarchs settled) —sang in worship and maintained written hymn collections. It may be that the patriarchs also composed and sang songs in worship. One seventh-century Jewish text claims that Adam began to sing praises immediately after God confronted his sin and provided for his forgiveness.[1] While there is no biblical warrant for such a claim, it certainly is not unreasonable to suspect that the saints in Genesis sang as part of their worship. However, the descriptions of worship in Genesis focus on sacrifice and prayer and are silent about any songs.

A Tabernacle Hymnal

The first explicit mention of a song composed for congregational praise is in Exodus 15. Moses had just led the people of Israel across the Red Sea, where God destroyed Pharaoh and his army beneath its waves. "Then sang Moses and the children of Israel this song unto the LORD" (Ex. 15:1).

---

1. Targum of Canticles 1:1 claims that Adam composed Psalm 92 ("A Psalm or Song for the sabbath day") in praise for God's forgiveness on that first Sabbath day.

This is the first explicit description of the congregation of Israel "singing unto the Lord" in worship.

The first biblical reference to a hymn being *written into a songbook* comes at the other end of Moses' ministry—in Deuteronomy 31. This is an important passage for our understanding of hymnody (and hymnals) in ancient Israel, and there are several lessons we can learn from this text. Deuteronomy 31 takes us to the close of Moses' ministry, as he was handing over leadership to Joshua. At that time, the Lord instructed Moses to compile *two* books for Israel: a law book and a songbook.

> And *Moses wrote this law*, and...commanded the Levites,... Take this book of the law, and put it [by] the side of the ark of the covenant of the LORD your God, that it may be there for a witness against thee (Deut. 31:9, 25–26, emphasis added).

> And the LORD said to Moses,... Now therefore *write ye this song* for you, and teach it [to] the children of Israel: put it in their mouths, that this song may be a witness for me against the children of Israel.... For it shall not be forgotten out of the mouths of their seed (Deut. 31:14, 19–21, emphasis added).

Here is something significant: Israel's first "Bible" and first "hymnal" were published at the same time. They were also published to serve the same purpose. The law book would serve as "a witness against thee"—a book that called each generation of Israel back to faithfulness when they strayed. The songbook, also, is called "a witness for me against the children of Israel." But unlike the law book, these songs would also be memorized in the course of their use in worship, thus providing a witness from within the hearts of the people.

There were actually two songs that Moses taught on that day: a song of warning in Deuteronomy 32 and a song of blessing in Deuteronomy 33. It is the first of these, the song of warning, that Moses was specifically told to write down, but it seems likely the song of blessing introduced with it was also included in that hymnal. Whether there were other songs that Moses included (e.g., the Exodus 15 song at the Red Sea; the song ascribed to Moses in the Psalter, Psalm 90), we cannot say. We can, however, see from this text that Israel's first hymnal, appointed by Moses, was designed as a companion volume for the law book.

There is another detail worth observing in this passage. Moses himself leads Israel in singing (as he has since the Red Sea), but now Joshua is called to accompany him: "And Moses came and spake [or sang] all the words of this song in the ears of the people, he, and Hoshea [Joshua] the son of Nun" (Deut. 32:44). It almost looks as though the transfer of leadership to Joshua includes a transfer of song leadership.[2] Actually, as we will see shortly, Joshua does indeed take over as the lead singer of Israel's praise. Meanwhile, the songbook begun by Moses was probably deposited (like the law book) with the Levites (cf. Deut. 31:9).

In addition to the Mosaic songbook just examined, there are three further references in the tabernacle-era narratives to books that contain songs. Numbers 21:14–15 introduces us to a song copied from a book called the Book of the Wars of Yahweh, and there are two references to songs contained in the Book of Yashar (Josh. 10:12–13; 2 Sam. 1:17–27).[3] The Book of Yashar (spelled *Jasher* in the KJV) appears to be another tabernacle-era hymnal, but we should look first at what we can learn about the Book of the Wars.

The Book of the Wars of Yahweh is mentioned as part of an Israelite travel itinerary in Numbers 21. After listing a series of stops on Israel's journey through the wilderness—"And the children of Israel…journeyed from Oboth…[to] Ijeabarim," and so on, "[to] the other side of Arnon" (vv. 10–13)—the narrator quotes a song: "Wherefore it is said in the *book of the wars of the LORD*, what he did in the Red sea, and in the brooks of Arnon, and at the stream of the brooks that goeth down to the dwelling of Ar, and lieth upon the border of Moab" (Num. 21:14–15, emphasis added). The main purpose for the quotation is to document that, indeed, "the border of Moab" was originally located at that spot where Israel had traveled. The border must have been elsewhere at the time of the book's composition, so this quotation served as a sort of footnote. But it is inter-

---

2. Cf. the double ascription of Psalm 72, a psalm about transferring the crown from the king to the king's son, which is called both the last psalm of David *and* a psalm of Solomon.

3. The LXX version of 1 Kings 8:53 mentions a "book of song" (τό βιβλίον τῆς ᾠδῆς) which some believe to be a third reference to the Book of Jasher through metathesis (*yšr* → *šyr*) in its Hebrew *Vorlage*. (F. C. Burkitt, "The Lucianic Text of I Kings VIII 53b," *Journal of Theological Studies* 10 [1909], 439–46.)

esting to us because it is a song fragment, and the book from which it was copied is named. Unfortunately, however, it is too short a fragment and too mundane in its details to know for certain what kind of book this Book of Wars might have been from which it was lifted. Based on the title of the book and the nature of this fragment, most scholars suspect the Book of Wars was an anthology of war songs from Israel's conquest of the land.[4] It does not look like a worship hymnal, though nothing can be said for certain.

The other tabernacle-era book of songs—the Book of Yashar—is, however, another matter. We find two references to this book in Scripture, both with explicit statements of congregational participation, one in praise and the other in lamentation. The first occurs in Joshua 10. Following the record of a great victory over the Amorites, we read, "Then spake Joshua to the LORD..., and he said in the sight of Israel, Sun, stand thou still upon Gibeon; and thou, Moon, in the valley of Ajalon. And the sun stood still, and the moon stayed, until the people had avenged themselves upon their enemies. Is this not written in *the book of Jasher?*" (Josh. 10:12–13, emphasis added).

The second reference is found in 2 Samuel 1. Once again, the setting involves a song that is taught to the nation by their divinely appointed leader; but this time, the song is a lament. After Saul and Jonathan died in battle with the Philistines, "David lamented with this lamentation over Saul and over Jonathan his son: (Also he bade them teach [it to]...the children of Judah...: behold, it is written in *the book of Jasher*)" (2 Sam. 1:17–18, emphasis added; the entire song is in vv. 19–27).

Based on the character of these song portions and their use in congregational singing, most scholars believe the Book of Yashar was an early collection of national hymns.[5] The fact that the first reference to this book is during the time of Joshua and the last is during the time of David suggests a hymnal with a long history of use and expansion throughout the tabernacle period. Unless a copy of a mysterious songbook is found

---

4. Duane L. Christensen, "Num 21:14–15 and the Book of the Wars of Yahweh," *Catholic Biblical Quarterly* 36, 3 (1974): 359.

5. Duane L. Christensen, "Jashar, Book of," in *Anchor Bible Dictionary* (New York: Doubleday, 1992), 3:646–47.

(and several fraudulent discoveries have occurred over the centuries),[6] we cannot say much more about it. However, it does appear to be another tabernacle-era hymn collection.

Thus far, we have identified at least two likely hymnals of the tabernacle era: the songbook begun by Moses and the Book of Yashar. But we may actually be talking about the same hymnal in these passages. That is, the Book of Yashar might be the name by which Moses' hymnal came to be called. The word *yāšār* is a Hebrew adjective that means "straight, upright, or law-keeping." The Book of Yashar is, literally, "the Book of the Upright." The songs from Deuteronomy 32–33 feature this term as a title for Israel (as those being called to uprightness). In the song of warning: "Ascribe ye greatness unto our God. He is the Rock.... But *Jeshurun* [literally, "the upright ones" from the noun form of *yāšār*] waxed fat...then he forsook God which made him, and lightly esteemed the Rock of his salvation" (Deut. 32:3–4, 15, emphasis added). Likewise, in the song of blessing: "The LORD...loved the people; all his saints are in thy hand:... And [God] was king in *Jeshurun*, when the heads of the people and the tribes of Israel were gathered together.... There is none like unto the God of *Jeshurun*, who rideth upon the heaven in thy help" (Deut. 33:2–3, 5, 26, emphasis added).

It may simply be a coincidence that these songs of Moses use the name for Israel that also became the title of the hymnal known to Joshua and David. Or, it may be that the songbook begun by Moses and the songbook added to by Joshua and David are, in fact, one and the same. Final answers are not possible, but whether there was one hymnal or there were more than one, it is evident that tabernacle-era worship featured a law book prepared by Moses and an accompanying hymn collection, which was written down and expanded at times by Israel's rulers.[7]

First Temple Hymn Collections

It was with David's rise to the throne that a major shift took place in Old Testament worship. These events are described in the opening chapters of

---

6. On *Yashar* forgeries: Arthur A. Chiel, "The Mysterious Book of Jasher," *Judaism* 26, 3 (1977): 365–74.

7. Cf. the song leadership of Deborah and Barak (Judg. 5:1) and possibly King Saul (1 Sam. 10:5b–6, 11), but especially the song leadership of the Davidic heirs (see 8n).

2 Samuel. There, David's initial coronation (chap. 2) follows his introduction as Israel's new song leader (chap. 1). But David's *first* national song, as we have already seen, was added into the existing hymnbook of tabernacle Israel: *The Book of Yashar*. However, David was soon to begin a whole new era of worship in Israel involving the centralization of worship in Jerusalem and the production of a new line of hymnody. All of this developed because of a new covenant that God established with David. Let's take a moment to think about the significance of this new covenant with David.

Since the death of Joshua (nearly five centuries before), Israel had floundered in its contest with the Canaanites. It was David who finally led the people to victory over the last of Israel's Canaanite foes, the Philistines. With Israel's transition from conquering tribes to a settled nation "at rest" in the land, an important milestone had been crossed. The time had come to centralize Israel's worship around a fixed capital. This is the instruction of Moses from so long before: "But when ye go over Jordan, and dwell in the land which the LORD your God giveth you to inherit, and when he giveth you rest from all your enemies round about, so that ye dwell in safety; then there shall be a place which the LORD your God shall choose to cause his name to dwell there; thither shall ye bring all… your burnt offerings" (Deut. 12:10–11).

With David's final conquest of the last Canaanite foes (2 Sam. 5), he brought the ark of the covenant to the nation's new capital (chap. 6), and he began to contemplate the need for a permanent sanctuary now that the land was at rest: "And it came to pass, when the king sat in his house, and the LORD had given him rest round about from all his enemies; that the king said unto Nathan the prophet, See now, I dwell in an house of cedar, but the ark of God dwelleth within curtains" (2 Sam. 7:1–2). David understood that the time had come to provide a permanent worship site. What he had not anticipated was the wonderful covenant that God would enter into with him on that occasion: "And it came to pass that night, that the word of the LORD came unto Nathan, saying, Go and tell my servant David,…when thy days be fulfilled, and thou shalt sleep with thy fathers, I will set up thy seed after thee, which shall proceed out of thy bowels, and I will establish his kingdom. He shall build an house for my name, and I will stablish the throne of his kingdom for ever" (2 Sam. 7:4–5, 12–13).

God was authorizing David's son (Solomon) to build a temple in Jerusalem, and, moreover, God was promising that the Davidic dynasty would continue *forever* as the royal line for Israel. This promise led David to begin immediate preparations for the new temple—including the composition of new hymns. This new line of hymnody that was produced as part of the Davidic covenant is of particular interest to us now.

With a single ruling house over God's people from this time forward, Israel would also have a single song-leading house in worship. This is the significance of the designation of David as "the sweet psalmist of Israel" (2 Sam. 23:1). This title is not a reference to David's ability as a good musician, though he evidently was quite skilled. It is a title highlighting the fact that "the Spirit of the LORD spake by" this song leader, and "[the LORD] hath made an everlasting covenant" with David's house (vv. 2, 5). Because of God's covenant that David's throne would eternally lead the congregation of His people, he began a new line of hymnody, known as the Psalms of David, for Zion-centered worship.

We often make the mistake, in the modern church, of supposing that Israel's king was primarily a *political* official—collecting taxes, leading the army, and so forth. It is true that the king of Israel led the nation's government, but he also functioned as the patron and head of Israel's worship (cf. Ps. 110:4). And it was the king who led the nation on their procession into the temple on holy days, including the leading of their praises (e.g., 1 Chron. 15:25–16:3).[8] This is not to ignore the role of Levitical hymn writers like Asaph. As part of his preparations for the temple, David appointed such Levitical hymn writers to assist him (1 Chron. 25:1–8).[9] David's heirs also continued to compose songs after him (e.g., Solomon, Ps. 127; Hezekiah, Isa. 38:20). Even though the psalms were not all personally written by David, they were all identified with his throne (hence the book's historic title, Psalms of David) because of the special covenant

8. E.g., Solomon (1 Kings 8:1–66); Asa (2 Chron. 15:8–11); Jehoshaphat (2 Chron. 20:18–19); Hezekiah (2 Chron. 29:20–36; 30:1–27); and Josiah (2 Chron. 35:1–19). Cf. John H. Eaton, *Kingship and the Psalms* (Sheffield: JSOT Press, 1986), 172–77; Aubrey R. Johnson, *Sacral Kingship in Ancient Israel* (Cardiff: University of Wales Press, 1967).

9. For a discussion of 1 Chron. 25:1–8, see Michael LeFebvre, *Singing the Songs of Jesus: Revisiting the Psalms* (forthcoming), chap. 2.

God had established with his throne as Israel's eternal head.[10] The royal office, in ancient Israel, was a sacral office as well as a political one.

There must have been a lot of these royally commissioned songs in the first temple. According to 1 Kings 4:32, King Solomon alone composed 1,005 songs. Not all of Solomon's songs were worship hymns, but it is reasonable to assume that a good number of them were. An extrabiblical memory credits David with composing 4,050 songs.[11] In Isaiah 38:20, Hezekiah speaks of "my songs," which were sung in the temple, one of which is quoted in the same chapter, but the rest of which are now lost. There are also several other temple-era hymns quoted in other parts of the Old Testament, besides those preserved in the Psalter (e.g., Hab. 3:1–19; Isa. 38:10–20). And bearing in mind the extensive hymn-writing workshops David began and the ongoing singing of Levitical choirs in the temple, day after day, we can be confident that the temple hymn library was quite extensive.

Such vast collections must have required an elaborate library. Rather than talking about a "hymnbook," we are probably talking about a "hymn library" in the First Temple period. Archaeological research at the site of Israel's temple has never been possible (since the location has been a Muslim holy place for centuries), but archaeology at other ancient temples indicates the elaborate libraries maintained at some ancient sanctuaries. In Ur, for example, hymns were inscribed on tablets that were stored on shelves, and "indexes" were kept (called hymn incipits) that listed hymns and their proper storage locations for ready retrieval.[12] According to the biblical record, the Jerusalem temple also had numerous storage rooms (1 Kings 6:5–6), and these likely housed the various Levitical utensils used in worship as well as the many books (probably scrolls) kept in the temple (e.g., 2 Chron. 34:14; 1 Sam. 10:25; Neh. 7:5; 12:23).

---

10. While I want to bring out the role of the king in Israel's praises, we must not ignore the composition of songs amongst the laity of Israel as well. From Hannah's praise recorded in 1 Sam. 2:1–10 to the LORD's allusion to the songs of grape gatherers in Isaiah 65:8, Israel clearly enjoyed a rich culture of music. Nevertheless, we miss an important theme of Old Testament worship if we fail to note the centrality of the king, and the king's songs, in Old Testament references to *assembled* (i.e., congregational) worship.

11. 11QPs^a col. XXVII, lines 2–11.

12. Gerald H. Wilson, *The Editing of the Hebrew Psalter*, Society of Biblical Literature Dissertation Series 76 (Chico, Calif.: Scholars Press, 1985), 25–26.

There are many questions that we simply cannot answer about the First Temple hymn collections. However, certain facts can be identified. First, from David at least as far as Hezekiah (and probably longer), the kings in Jerusalem continued to serve as Israel's "sweet psalmists," leading in congregational singing and composing hymns along with their Levitical assistants. Second, although it is impossible to determine a precise number of psalms used in First Temple worship, there certainly were many more than just the 150 songs now preserved in the Psalter. The collection maintained on Mount Zion likely continued to expand for nearly five centuries, building to a significant library of song—until the fall of Jerusalem in 587 BC.

Second Temple Hymnody and the Psalter

In 587 BC, the Babylonians sacked Jerusalem, destroyed the temple, and drove the people into exile. After a series of twenty-one Davidic rulers—from David to Zedekiah—the throne was empty. There was no longer a Davidic king on Mount Zion. We can only imagine what might have happened to the law books, songbooks, and other texts kept in the temple library. Many texts may have been lost forever in the temple conflagration. Others must have been hastily stashed into caves ahead of the approaching Babylonian armies, and some were evidently carried away to Babylon.

In any case, within a generation, the Babylonians were themselves overthrown by yet another kingdom—the Persians. Under the new Persian rulers, the Jews were permitted to return to Jerusalem and rebuild. Recovering the books was the special charge of a Levitical scribe named Ezra: "This Ezra went up from Babylon; and he was a ready scribe in the law of Moses, which the LORD God had given.... For Ezra had prepared his heart to seek the law of the LORD, and to do it, and to teach in Israel statutes and judgments" (Ezra 7:6, 10). Although nothing is explicitly said about the books of the prophets, the historical narratives, the wisdom literature, and the Psalms, it is evident that these materials, as well as the Law of Moses, were successfully compiled again.[13] Ezra is generally regarded, both in Jewish and Christian traditions, as the one who compiled the Hebrew Scriptures into the basic canonical form that we now

---

13. Cf. 2 Maccabees 2:13.

possess—including the book of Psalms.[14] He is as likely a candidate as any for identifying with the task, and we will hereafter refer to Ezra as the compiler of the Psalter, although it is not crucial to know whether it was him or another individual or group who did the work.

Our only direct evidence about Ezra's work with Israel's worship songs is that which is provided by the Psalter itself. And there are several features of the new post-exilic hymnal that are worth noting.

First, bearing in mind the historic relationship between law book and songbook in Israel, it should not surprise us to note the same close tie between the Ezran Psalter and the Pentateuch (i.e., the law book that Ezra recompiled). Psalm 1—the introduction to the Psalter[15]— opens this new hymnal with an exhortation to meditate on God's law: "Blessed is the man...[whose] delight is in the law of the LORD; and in his law doth he meditate day and night" (vv. 1–2). In fact, as Martin Luther used to say, the whole book of Psalms thus introduced is, itself, a collection of meditations on the law.[16] Furthermore, the arrangement of the 150 psalms into five volumes—Book 1 (1–41), Book 2 (42–72), Book 3 (73–89), Book 4 (90–106), and Book 5 (107–150)—has long been recognized as a parallel to the five-book arrangement of the Mosaic law.[17] The 150 psalms, chosen from the numerous hymns likely recovered in the Second Temple and arranged into the canonical Psalter, are introduced and formatted as a com-

---

14. Some scholars date the completion of the Psalter as late as the first century AD because certain Qumran scrolls include a different arrangement for portions of the Psalter into the New Testament period. (E.g., Gerald H. Wilson, "The Qumran Psalms Manuscripts and the Consecutive Arrangement of Psalms in the Hebrew Psalter," *Catholic Biblical Quarterly* 45 [1983]: 377–88.) However, the LXX Psalter (translated between 200–150 BC) presents the same overall form of the Psalter as the MT Psalter. Even if the Qumran community was varying *their* form of the Psalter into the first century, the received version had to have been completed and extant prior to the second century BC at the latest.

15. Wilson, *Editing,* 204–205; "The Structure of the Psalter," 232–33, in Philip S. Johnston and David G. Firth, *Interpreting the Psalms: Issues and Approaches* (Leicester: IVP, 2005).

16. "What is the whole Psalter but meditation and exercises based on the First Commandment?" (Martin Luther, preface to his Large Catechism). Cf. Michael LeFebvre, "Torah-Meditation and the Psalms: The Invitation of Psalm 1," in Johnston and Firth, *Interpreting the Psalms,* 213–25.

17. *Midrash Tehillim* 1:1; Wilson, *Editing,* 207–208; "Structure," 230–31.

panion to the similarly re-published law book (the Pentateuch).[18] The close relationship between Bible and hymnal continues in the Ezran Psalter.

The new Psalter also continues the royal character of previous hymn collections in Israel. Of the 117 psalms with superscriptions, 73 of them are identified as "Of David."[19] Additionally, two are ascribed to David's heir, Solomon. One is ascribed to the original song leader of national Israel, Moses (Psalm 90). Twenty-eight others are ascribed to Levitical assistants working under royal appointment. More importantly, there are frequent first-person "I" statements throughout the Psalms where the king is speaking. Scholars debate how many of the first-person references in the Psalms should be understood as spoken by the king, but even a conservative assessment identifies close to a third of the Psalter as royal psalms.[20] The post-exilic Psalter also continues the historic pattern of lifting songs in the voice of the divinely appointed ruler, but it is remarkable that the voice of the king takes such a central place in a hymnal compiled in an era when there was no longer a king on Mount Zion.

Further insight into the royal character of the post-exilic Psalter can be found in its arrangement. One of the most lively frontiers of Psalms scholarship today is study of the Psalm book's organization—the order in which the individual psalms were arranged. Although the "shape" of the Psalter is a historic concern of the church,[21] it has only been since the 1980s that attention to the ordering of the Psalms has become a priority of modern scholarship. It was the publication of the late Gerald H. Wilson's *The Editing of the Hebrew Psalter* in 1985 that persuasively estab-

---

18. Note the five-book Pentateuch closes with song (Deut. 31–33), and the five-book Psalter opens with law (Ps. 1). Cf. Patrick D. Miller, "Deuteronomy and Psalms: Evoking a Biblical Conversation," *Journal of Biblical Literature* 118, 1 (1999), 15.

19. These numbers are based on the MT Psalter; the LXX has additional superscriptions, increasing the "Of David" psalm count by fourteen.

20. Steven J. L. Croft, *The Identity of the Individual in the Psalms*, Journal for the Study of the Old Testament Supplement Series 44 (Sheffield: Sheffield Academic Press, 1987). See especially Croft's summary chart on 179–81.

21. Cf. David C. Mitchell, *The Message of the Psalter: An Eschatological Programme in the Book of Psalms*, Journal for the Study of the Old Testament Supplement Series, 252 (Sheffield: Sheffield Academic Press, 1997), 33–48. One of the earliest studies of the Psalter's arrangement was written in the fourth century by Gregory of Nyssa, *Commentary on the Inscriptions of the Psalms*, trans. Casimir McCambley (Brookline, Mass.: Hellenic College Press, n.d.).

lished that the Psalter is not a random hodgepodge of hymns, but that it is a carefully arranged collection. Since that time, a flood of books, seminars, and journal articles have contributed further insights into the shape of the Psalter. Many of the proposals offered are debatable, and a full survey of them is not possible here. However, a clear consensus emerging from this scholarship is recognition of the Psalter's focus on the Davidic covenant.

The Shape of the Psalter

It was Gerald Wilson who pointed out the importance of "seam" psalms in the arrangement of ancient hymn collections like the Psalter. That is, songs placed at the beginnings or ends of the Psalter's five volumes are important clues to its primary, shaping themes. Based on this insight, it becomes evident that the first three books of the Psalter are structured around Israel's faith in the (now fallen) Davidic dynasty, and the last two books uphold hope in the restoration and future fulfillment of the Davidic covenant. It is fitting to conclude, therefore, that the post-exilic Psalter was a hymnal prepared for a coming heir to David's throne.

With Psalm 1 serving as an introduction to the whole collection,[22] Psalm 2 stands at the opening "seam" of Book 1. It is a coronation psalm, singing the bold announcement of God's covenant with the Davidic king now being installed on Mount Zion: "Yet have I set my king upon my holy hill of Zion.... Ask of me, and I shall give thee the heathen for thine inheritance, and the uttermost parts of the earth for thy possession" (vv. 6, 8). Complementing Psalm 2, then, Psalm 72 stands at the closing "seam" of Book 2 with another coronation psalm—this time a confident expectation of God's continued faithfulness to the king's heir: "Give the king thy judgments, O God, and thy righteousness unto the king's son.... He shall have dominion also from sea to sea, and from the river unto the ends of

---

22. Some scholars view Psalms 1–2, together, as introductory to the Psalter: e.g., Gerald T. Sheppard, *Wisdom as a Hermeneutical Construct: A Study of the Sapientializing of the Old Testament* (Berlin: de Gruyter, 1980), 136–44; J. Clinton McCann, Jr., "Psalms," *The New Interpreter's Bible: Volume 4–1 and 2 Maccabees, Introduction to Hebrew Poetry, Job, Psalms* (Nashville, Tenn.: Abingdon Press, 1996), 664–65. However, it is more likely that Psalm 1 introduces the whole Psalter and Psalm 2 introduces Book 1, as demonstrated by John T. Willis, "Psalm 1—An Entity," *Zeitschrift für die Alttestamentliche Wissenschaft* 91, 3 (1979), 381–401; Wilson, *Editing*, 205–206; "Structure," 232–33.

the earth" (vv. 1, 8). Book 3, then, closes with the plaintive cry of Psalm 89, which recounts God's covenant with David and his sons and then bemoans the fact that the throne has been cast in the dust and overthrown. Books 1 through 3 of the Psalter end with a desperate appeal to God yet to fulfill His covenant with David: "How long, LORD? wilt thou hide thyself forever?... Lord, where are thy former lovingkindnesses, which thou swarest unto David in thy truth?" (vv. 46, 49). Books 4 and 5 of the Psalter are arranged as a response to this "covenant crisis." In addition to important "seam" psalms opening these two books, liturgical groupings of psalms play an important role here.

Book 4 (Psalms 90–106) begins at its opening "seam" with Psalm 90, "a Prayer of Moses the man of God." As a psalm of Moses, this is the only psalm in the Psalter identified with an author *before* the Davidic covenant. In Psalm 90:1 ("LORD, thou hast been our dwelling place in all generations"), a theme of confidence in God's *ancient* faithfulness (i.e., long before David) is introduced. In the body of Book 4, Psalms 91–92 might be intended to continue the theme of Psalm 90; thereafter, clear groups of psalms follow. A group of "Yahweh is King" psalms (93–100) repeatedly rejoice in the unassailable reign of Israel's heavenly king.[23] An "Of David" group of psalms (101–103) introduces the Davidic king's promises to faithfulness and his expected restoration. Finally, a closing group of historical psalms (104–106) reviews the whole spread of Pentateuchal history, first extolling God's faithfulness in creation (104) and from Abraham through the Exodus (105), then lastly confessing our own unfaithfulness through that same history, with repentance and expected restoration (106). Like one of those photomontages where numerous little pictures are arranged in a way that forms a bigger picture, the individual psalms and psalm groupings of Book 4 provide a picture of the inviolable reign of the heavenly King and remember His faithfulness to the Abrahamic covenant, even long before the anointing of King David. On this basis, they lead us in repentance—with great expectation.

Book 5 (Psalms 107–145) begins at its opening "seam" with a psalm of ingathering: "O give thanks unto the Lord.... Let the redeemed of the

---

23. David M. Howard, Jr., *The Structure of Psalms 93–100* (Winona Lake, Ind.: Eisenbrauns, 1997).

Lord say so.... [He] gathered them out of the lands, from the east, and from the west, from the north, and from the south" (vv. 1–3). It is this theme of gathering together God's scattered people from throughout the nations that Book 5 sustains in a series of psalm groupings. The first and last groupings in Book 5 are "Of David" collections (108–110; 138–145). At the center of the book, we find the Egyptian Hallel (113–118) and the monumental declaration of love for God's law (119), followed by the Songs of Ascent (120–134). Together, this series of groupings in the center of Book 5 carries on the theme of pilgrimage introduced in Psalm 107, leading the singers from Egypt to Mount Sinai and, in a faithful embrace of God's law, from Sinai on the ascent to Mount Zion.[24] The grouping that introduces this pilgrimage sequence is a set of "Praise the LORD" psalms (111–112), and the grouping that follows this pilgrimage sequence is a set of psalms (liturgically located on Mount Zion, Psalm 135:1–2) that praises God for His victory over Israel's great foes: Egypt, the Canaanites (135–136), and finally Babylon (137). The overall theme of Book 5 is Diaspora saints joyously anticipating the victorious ingathering of God's people from all corners of the earth in a new fulfillment of the Exodus–Sinai–Zion story.

The whole Psalter, then, fittingly closes with a doxological grouping of "Praise the LORD" psalms (Psalms 146–150). These psalms enjoin all nations and all creation to join in praise of Him who fulfills all the blessings and judgments promised in His law, as specially revealed to Israel. "Let everything that hath breath praise the LORD. Praise ye the LORD" (150:6).

While scholars continue to debate many facets of the Psalter's structure (especially that of Books 4–5), it is generally recognized that Books 4–5 answer the crisis raised by Books 1–3, anticipating the fulfillment of the Davidic covenant.[25] Ezra (or whoever worked on this post-exilic

---

24. Elizabeth Hayes identifies these three psalm groupings with the three temple festivals: Passover, Pentecost, and Tabernacles, respectively ("The Unity of the Egyptian Hallel: Psalms 113–18," *Bulletin for Biblical Research* 9 [1999]: 145–56, 145n1). Cf. Robert Davidson, *The Vitality of Worship: A Commentary on the Book of Psalms* (Grand Rapids: Eerdmans, 1998), 7.

25. For other variations on the same approach to the Psalter's structure, cf. Wilson, *Editing*, 199–228; William L. Holladay, *The Psalms through Three Thousand Years: Prayerbook of a Cloud of Witnesses* (Minneapolis, Minn.: Fortress Press, 1993), 76–80; James Luther Mays, *Psalms* (Louisville, Ky.: John Knox, 1994), 14–19; McCann, "Psalms,"

hymnal) was not simply slapping together songs at random; serious and involved planning—and theological reflection—went into the compilation of the final Zion praise book. And it is a praise book conscientiously formed in expectation of the coming son of David.

As Gerald Wilson explains, "The shape of the canonical Psalter [now presents the Davidic psalms]…as hopeful anticipation of the Davidic descendant who would—as God's anointed servant—establish God's direct rule over all humanity in the Kingdom of God."[26] James Luther Mays agrees: "Because the sequence [of the Psalms] moves from promise through disaster to renewed promise and expectation, and because these psalms about the anointed king are included in the Psalter formed long after the kings of Judah had vanished, they must have been read and preserved and included as a form of prophecy…. In [the Psalter] we hear the messiah speak about the kingdom of God…[and] we are invited to enter into and join in this messianic prayer and praise."[27] These views are typical of the field,[28] and they are certainly consistent with the New Testament attitude toward the Psalms.

659–65. For some other approaches, see Walter Brueggemann, "Bounded by Obedience and Praise: The Psalms as Canon," *Journal for the Study of the Old Testament* 50 (1991), 63–92; Nancy L. deClaissé-Walford, *Introduction to the Psalms: A Song from Ancient Israel* (St. Louis, Mo.: Chalice, 2004).

26. "King, Messiah, and the Reign of God: Revisiting the Royal Psalms and the Shape of the Psalter," in Peter W. Flint, et al., eds., *The Book of Psalms: Composition and Reception*, Supplements to Vetus Testamentum (Leiden: Brill, 2005), 404–405. In his earlier work, Wilson overstressed the "direct" relationship between God and men that he perceived in Psalms 93–100 to a point of almost totally eliminating any expectation of a Davidic messiah in the final Psalter. His comment quoted here represents his revised position, affirming the messianic expectation of the Psalter, based on the corrections and criticisms of scholars like Mitchell, *Message of the Psalter*; Bernhard W. Anderson, *Out of the Depths: The Psalms Speak for Us Today* (Louisville, Ky.: Westminster John Knox, 2000), 208–211.

27. Mays, *Psalms*, 18.

28. There are, naturally, other arguments; however, the quotes from Wilson and Mays are representative of the field. The most prominent alternative in vogue is that the shape of the Psalter teaches *every* Israelite to "become a David" in prayer and piety and to expect the Davidic covenant to be fulfilled *without* a new heir to the throne. As Bernhard Anderson points out in criticizing this individualistic and democratizing interpretation, "The truth is that Israelite interpreters, even in the face of harsh realities of history, never surrendered the hope for a coming monarch of the Davidic line who would rule as God's vicegerent." In other words, if the goal of the Psalter's shapers was to downplay expectation for a new king, their efforts miserably failed; the psalm-singing people of God continued,

For the New Testament disciples, who grew up singing psalms in expectation of a royal song leader who would one day personify and fulfill them, it must have been thrilling to meet Jesus. John 2 captures this delight, as the disciples observed Jesus undertaking the *royal* responsibility for the temple's purity (cf. 2 Kings 23:4–20) and casting out the money changers. They immediately "remembered that it was written, The zeal of thine house hath eaten me up" (John 2:17, quoting Ps. 69:9). The disciples saw in Jesus the Son of David expected by the Psalter.[29]

Let me underscore something here that should not be missed. The church today often recognizes that the Psalms are *about* Jesus. But the New Testament enthusiasm for the Psalter goes beyond that. Notice in the following passages, for example, how the New Testament authors want us to recognize Jesus, not simply as one who fulfills things *about* Himself in the Psalms, but *as the song leader who leads us in singing them:*

> Now I say that *Jesus Christ* was a minister [to] the circumcision…[and to] the Gentiles…; as it is written, For this cause *I will confess* to thee among the Gentiles, *and sing* unto thy name (Rom. 15:8–9, quoting Ps. 18:49, emphasis added).

> *He [Christ]* is not ashamed to call them brethren, saying, *I will declare* thy name unto my brethren, in the midst of the church *will I sing praise* unto thee (Heb. 2:11–12, quoting Ps. 22:22, emphasis added).

> Wherefore when *he [Christ]* cometh into the world, *he saith,* Sacrifice and offering thou wouldest not, but a body hast thou prepared me…. Then *said I,* Lo, I come (in the volume of the book it is writ-

---

with fervor fueled by the Psalms, to anticipate a coming Messiah. As David Howard notes in a recent survey of the field, despite the continuing presence of this "every man" position (you will encounter it in various commentaries), the consensus around the intentionally messianic character of the Psalter is growing (as illustrated by Wilson's movement back in this direction; see n26) (Anderson, *Out of the Depths,* 209; cf. Mitchell, *Message of the Psalter,* 81; David M. Howard, Jr., "The Psalms and Current Study," in Johnston and Firth, *Interpreting the Psalms,* 27).

29. On the New Testament's recognition of Christ in the Psalms, see Richard P. Belcher, Jr., *The Messiah and the Psalms: Preaching Christ from All the Psalms* (Ross-shire, Scotland: Christian Focus, 2006); James Luther Mays, "'In a Vision': The Portrayal of the Messiah in the Psalms," in James Luther Mays, *The Lord Reigns: A Theological Handbook to the Psalms* (Louisville: Westminster John Knox, 1994), 99–107.

ten of me,) to do thy will, O God (Heb. 10:57, quoting Ps. 40:6–8, emphasis added).

In each of these passages, Jesus is recognized by His followers as the "singing king" for whom the Psalter was prepared. They were not "re-interpreting" old temple songs in light of Christ; this was a hymnal already prepared in expectation of the Christ, and it was only natural for the church to accept it as their hymnal. Furthermore, as Luke shows us in a poignant glimpse of an apostolic praise service in Acts 4, the New Testament believers sang the psalms of the Christ as those sharing in *His* sufferings and trusting in *His* victories and consequently singing *His* songs with Him (vv. 23–31). In the modern church, we can hardly do any better.

Conclusions

Too little has been done, to date, to assess the character of the hymnals that preceded the canonical Psalter. This chapter has endeavored to forge into that subject and to draw upon recent scholarship on the shape of the Psalter as well in order to better appreciate the glorious gift that the church has received in this great hymnbook. There are several practical implications of this study that deserve to be summarized.

First, and I trust the most obvious implication of this study, is that the Psalter should be sung in the church. It is not simply a book to be read in devotions or preached (though it is all that), but it is also a hymnal to be sung *by the church* in worship. The nineteenth-century attitude that led to a sharp decline in psalm singing in the church (i.e., that the Psalms are "Jewish" songs that lack faith in Christ) needs to be rejected and replaced with a recovery of the recognition shared by the New Testament apostles, the early church, and the Reformation churches: the Psalter is designed for the Israel of Christ, and the church should sing it.

But there is an orientation toward worship called for in the Psalter that is very different from what is common in the modern church. Often, congregations in the church today see themselves as a choir (the "performers") singing praises to God (the "audience"). The Psalter calls us to refine this outlook: it teaches us to view ourselves as "a backup ensemble" singing *with a great Soloist* who is the primary "Performer." It is the Son of David who stands as "the sweet psalmist" beloved by the Father. We, who enter into the Father's delight in Christ, are privileged to join with Jesus in *His* songs as we sing the Psalms. We still need to make them our own songs as well, but we do so only by placing our own sufferings and victories into the sufferings and victories of Christ with Him and by acknowledging His entering into our guilt on our behalf with us.[30] We need to learn, again, to sing the Psalms *with* Christ.[31]

Third, while the anticipated King of the Psalter has come, the full promises of the Davidic covenant expected in the Psalms are not yet fulfilled. The Son of David now reigns from heaven, and He must continue to reign until all creation has been brought to its intended purpose. Consequently, we still look forward to the full ingathering of God's people from all nations, the submission of kings and nations in reverence before Christ, the purging of sin from our communities, and the final consummation of all things held out in the Psalms, climaxing in the final joyous moment when "every thing that hath breath [will] praise the LORD" (Ps. 150:6). That day is coming, but it is not here yet. Therefore, there is still a tone of expectation in the Psalter. The Christ has come, but the completion of all that was covenanted to Him is still unfolding. As we sing the Psalms today, we continue to share in the vexation of the way things are and the anticipation of the way things will be, which the saints of old inscribed into the Psalms, all sharing the same Christ-centered faith.

It is that imminent expectancy of Christ and His redemptive work at the dusk of the Old Testament era that makes the Psalms almost more a part of the New Testament than the Old. While the contemporary practice of printing pocket Bibles with just the New Testament, Psalms, and Proverbs seems to give short shrift to the rest of the Old Testament, perhaps there is, in this practice, an implicit recognition of the Psalter as so New Testament-like to justify this placement. In any case, the Psalter's conventional location in the middle of the Old Testament canon ought not distract us from its suitability—even its design—for New Testament worship.

---

30. On Christ's singing with us in the psalms of repentance, see Belcher, *Messiah and the Psalms*, 87–88; LeFebvre, *Singing the Songs of Jesus*, chap. 4.

31. For a more detailed discussion of the "praising conversations" with Christ, into which the Psalms bring us, see LeFebvre, *Singing the Songs of Jesus*, chap. 3.

Chapter 7

Christian Cursing?

David P. Murray

How can we sing the Psalms when so many of them ask God to curse our enemies? Calling down curses on our enemies does appear to be contrary both to the spirit and letter of the New Testament (Matt. 5:43–44). If cursing psalms (often called imprecatory psalms) are sub-Christian or pre-Christian, as some allege, should Christians sing them at all? Should we restrict ourselves only to the "Christian" psalms? In this chapter I hope to show that the imprecatory psalms, when rightly understood, are both Christian and suitable for Christian praise, not least because they point us to Christ our Savior.

Because many view the imprecatory psalms as problematic, they have offered misguided explanations for their inclusion in the Psalter. First, I will examine some of these wrong solutions to the imprecatory psalms "problem." Second, I will propose ten helps for Christian singing of the imprecatory psalms.

How extensive is the use of imprecation in the Psalms? Three psalms are primarily imprecatory throughout (Pss. 35, 69, 109). Others have imprecatory verses (Pss. 5, 7, 10, 28, 31, 40, 55, 58, 59, 70, 71, 79, 83, 137, 139, 140). It has been argued that ninety of the 150 psalms have imprecatory language. Nevertheless, it is important to remember that imprecations are found in relatively few verses and represent only a minor theme in the Psalms.

Wrong Solutions

The following are some of the wrong solutions to this perceived problem.

Changed Days

Some say that imprecatory language was fine in the Old Testament but not in the New Testament and that these psalms are included in the Scriptures only to show the contrast between the two eras.

This solution is unacceptable because it portrays God as contradicting His ethical standards over time. Also, the contrast between the Old and New Testaments is not as stark as is often claimed. The Old Testament has commandments to love our enemies and turn from vengeance (Lev. 19:17–18; Prov. 24:17–18; 25:21–22), while the New Testament also contains imprecations (2 Tim. 4:14), as we will see in more detail.

Sinful David

Some argue that as the imprecations of the psalms were sinful expressions on the lips of sinful men, we should not take them upon our lips. C. S. Lewis went so far as to deny the inspiration of psalms like Psalm 137. He called the imprecatory psalms "devilish," "diabolical," "terrible," and "contemptible." He said, "The hatred is there—festering, gloating, undisguised—and also we should be wicked if we in any way condoned or approved it, or (worse still) used it to justify similar passions in ourselves."[1]

We reject this explanation because it raises questions about the inspiration of Scripture. David claimed, without qualification, that his psalms were inspired by God's Spirit (2 Sam. 23:1–2). David is not merely claiming that the recording of these psalms was inspired, but that God inspired the actual words. Note also that the titles of some imprecatory psalms indicate that they were to be used in public worship. For example, Psalm 69 is "To the chief Musician."

And where is the evidence for David's vengeful character? Look at his loving response to Saul's hatred, especially the Song of the Bow (2 Sam. 1:17–27), which he composed when Saul died: "And David lamented with this lamentation over Saul and over Jonathan his son.... The beauty

---

1. C. S. Lewis, *Reflections on the Psalms* (New York: Harcourt, Brace and Company, 1958), 20–22.

of Israel is slain upon thy high places: how are the mighty fallen!... Saul and Jonathan were lovely and pleasant in their lives, and in their death they were not divided: they were swifter than eagles, they were stronger than lions" (vv. 17, 19, 23). Look at his treatment of rebellious Absalom and his response to his death (2 Sam. 18:32–33). If anything, David was too hesitant at times to execute justice.

Demons—Not People

Some interpreters say that the imprecations are called upon the heads of demons—not people. We may certainly have evil spirits in view as we sing the imprecatory psalms. That would be a legitimate application. However, the New Testament tells us that the imprecations in Psalm 69:25 and 109:6–9 were also fulfilled in Judas (Acts 1:20), a real human being.

Prophecies—Not Prayers

Another common explanation is that these psalms were to be sung in the future indicative, an expression of what will be, rather than the imperative, which conveys a command or strong request. The authors were saying what would happen rather than what they desired to happen. They were predicting calamity rather than praying for it.

It is certainly a truth of Scripture that God will punish the wicked; however, that is not the whole truth of the imprecatory Scriptures. These imprecations may be prophetic, but they are also prayers. In fact, some grammarians claim that the Hebrew will not allow for the future indicative, a predictive translation.

Our reluctance to pray these prayers is especially strange if heaven itself rejoices in God's vengeance upon His enemies (Rev. 16:5–6; 18:20). Indeed, heaven itself prays for it (Rev. 6:10). So may not we also both pray and rejoice in God's judgments? Robert Dabney answers:

> Righteous retribution is one of the glories of the divine character. If it is right that God should desire to exercise it, then it cannot be wrong for his people to desire him to exercise it. It may be objected that, while he claims retribution for himself, he forbids it to them, and that he has thereby forbidden all satisfaction in it to them. The fact is true; the inference does not follow. Inasmuch as retribution inflicted by a creature is forbidden, the desire for its infliction by a

creature, or pleasure therein, is also forbidden; but inasmuch as it is righteously inflicted by God, it must be right in him, and must therefore be, when in his hand, a proper subject of satisfaction to the godly.[2]

Hyperbole

Some say the imprecations are examples of hyperbolic language, or purposeful exaggeration, a figure of speech that is often used in Hebrew poetry. However, while a figurative interpretation may help us understand some imprecatory expressions such as "break their teeth," it is stretching too far to use this to explain away the unmistakeable substance of the imprecatory psalms.

Ten Helps

Having dispensed with some of these wrong solutions to what some see as the problem of the imprecatory psalms, let me now propose some helps that will improve our understanding and motivate our singing of them.

Rooted in the First Gospel Promise

The curses of the Psalms are rooted in the gospel curse on the serpent and his seed in Genesis 3:14–15. Moses develops this further by showing that the gospel promises salvation and cursing (Gen. 12:3). In the context of the psalmist being persecuted by enemies of the gospel, he is basically saying in the imprecations, "God, be faithful to your promise to curse those who curse me." For example, in Psalm 83, the psalmist describes how Israel's innumerable and inveterate enemies plot to annihilate her (vv. 1–8) before going on to plead with God to cut off these nations as He had done before (vv. 9–18).

David's Forgiving Character

David was the author of most of the imprecatory psalms. However, the biblical narratives and the Psalms in general portray him not as a vindic-

---

2. Robert Dabney, *Discussions Evangelical and Theological* (London: Banner of Truth, 1967), 1:715.

tive man, but rather, as we noted above, one who prayed for his enemies and sought to do them good (e.g., Pss. 35:13; 109:4–5).

The King Represented God

As the king was God's representative, God's reputation was tied up with the king's. Offending God's anointed king was equivalent to offending God. James Adams explains that David was God's anointed in a particularly special, christological way.[3] He reminds us that none of David's pre-anointing songs appear in the Old Testament canon. It was only when he became God's anointed that his songs became God's songs.

As God's anointed king, the psalmist was chiefly concerned with God's glory and reputation and did not cringe from praying prayers that had God's glory, not human welfare, as their ultimate end. For example, notice how the psalmist speaks of his perfect hatred of God's enemies and how he counts them his enemies as well: "Surely thou wilt slay the wicked, O God: depart from me therefore, ye bloody men. For they speak against thee wickedly, and thine enemies take thy name in vain. Do not I hate them, O LORD, that hate thee? and am not I grieved with those that rise up against thee? I hate them with perfect hatred: I count them mine enemies" (Ps. 139:19–22). Adams relates how Martyn Lloyd-Jones explained this in a sermon: "Look at the psalmist. Look at some of those imprecatory psalms. What are they? There is nothing wrong with them. It's just the zeal of the psalmist. He's grieved and troubled because these people are not honoring God as they should be. That's his supreme concern."[4]

Multiple New Testament Quotations

Apart from the more frequently quoted psalms of a strongly messianic nature (Pss. 2, 22, 110, 118), the largely imprecatory Psalms 35, 69, and 109 are the next most frequently quoted psalms in the New Testament, and they are quoted without any reserve or qualification. Harry Mennega notes, "The New Testament appears not in the least embarrassed with the Old Testament imprecations; on the contrary, it quotes freely from

---

3. James Adams, *War Psalms of the Prince of Peace* (Phillipsburg, N.J.: P&R, 1991), 26–27.
4. As quoted in ibid., xi.

them as authoritative statements with which to support an argument. The New Testament not only quotes passages which though themselves not imprecations, are found in a Psalm with an imprecatory section; but also, and this is more remarkable, it quotes with approval the imprecations themselves."[5]

New Testament Imprecations
As previously noted, the New Testament also contains its own imprecations. See the seven woes Christ pronounced on the Jewish religious leaders in Matthew 23:13–29. These were not angry outbursts of impatient frustration, but rather loving warnings to them to repent before they were overtaken by these divine curses.

The following provide further examples of New Testament imprecations:

> But though we, or an angel from heaven, preach any other gospel unto you than that which we have preached unto you, let him be accursed. As we said before, so say I now again, if any man preach any other gospel unto you than that ye have received, let him be accursed (Gal. 1:8–9).

> And I, brethren, if I yet preach circumcision, why do I yet suffer persecution? then is the offence of the cross ceased. I would they were even cut off which trouble you (Gal. 5:11–12).

> Alexander the coppersmith did me much evil: the Lord reward him according to his works (2 Tim. 4:14).

> If any man love not the Lord Jesus Christ, let him be Anathema [accursed] Maranatha (1 Cor. 16:22).

In a day when there is an over-emphasis on the love of God at the expense of the justice of God, we have to fight against extreme separations and contrasts of Old and New Testament ethics. God's justice and God's love are found in both testaments, despite repeated attempts by many to ignore this important truth. As Dabney clearly stated, "The admission must be squarely and honestly made, that the inspired men of both Testa-

---

5. Harry Mennega, "The Ethical Problem of the Imprecatory Psalms" (master's thesis, Westminster Theological Seminary, 1959), 38.

ments felt and expressed moral indignation against wrong-doers, and a desire for their proper retribution at the hand of God."[6]

Based on Justice

The substance of the imprecatory psalms is that justice be done and the innocent righteous vindicated, which is a New Testament theme also (Luke 18:1–8). While rehabilitation and restitution are at the forefront of judicial policy today and though they were important components of biblical justice, the foundation of biblical justice was retribution: an eye for an eye, a tooth for a tooth. If the idea of retributive justice is lost or devalued, then the imprecatory psalms will never be properly understood.

Thy Kingdom Come

The imprecations of Scripture reflect the zeal of God's people for the kingdom of God and their passionate hatred of sin and evil. Imprecation is implied even in the prayer, "Thy kingdom come," because God's kingdom comes by defeating and destroying competing kingdoms. Anyone who loves the kingdom of God will hate the kingdom of Satan.

Martin Luther said that when one prays, "Hallowed be thy name, thy kingdom come, thy will be done," then "he must put all the opposition to this in one pile and say: 'Curses, maledictions and disgrace upon every other name and every other kingdom. May they be ruined and torn apart and may all their schemes and wisdom and plans run aground.'"[7] As Mennega asserts, "Advance and victory for the Church means retreat and defeat for the kingdom of darkness."[8]

This is really saying that blessing and cursing are two sides of the same coin. Real compassion for the wronged can exist only beside indignation against wrong-doing (Matt. 23). Both are beautiful qualities in God's sight, which He rewards with fuller measures of His Holy Spirit (Heb. 1:9).

Christians are to love their personal enemies and bless those who curse them and spitefully use them. Nevertheless, they will desire at the same time the downfall of all evil and will pray for such. John Piper wrote,

---

6. Dabney, *Discussions*, 709–10.
7. Martin Luther, *Luther's Works*, ed. Jaroslav Pelikan (St. Louis: Concordia, 1956), 21:101.
8. Mennega, "Ethical Problem," 93.

"There is a kind of hate for the sinner (viewed as morally corrupt and hostile to God) that may coexist with pity and even a desire for their salvation…. [But] there comes a point of such extended, hardened, high-handed lovelessness toward God that it may be appropriate to call down anathema on it."[9]

Piper is saying that prayers of imprecation should not be our first reaction to evil, but our last. However, he is also saying that it is possible to both love and hate the same person at the same time. We may hate what someone stands for and is doing against God and His people while at the same time desiring his salvation. We may love his soul while at the same time praying that God would defeat him in his persecution of God's people. That is a very difficult balance to strike. Perhaps that is why after praying, "Do not I hate them, O LORD, that hate thee? and am not I grieved with those that rise up against thee? I hate them with perfect hatred: I count them mine enemies," David goes on to pray, "Search me, O God, and know my heart: try me, and know my thoughts: and see if *there be any* wicked way in me, and lead me in the way everlasting" (Ps. 139:21–24, emphasis added).

Vengeance Is God's

An imprecation is a prayer for God to take vengeance. The psalmist does not take vengeance himself but turns the situation over to God. He is effectively saying, "Vengeance is not mine but Thine, O Lord." He rejects carnal and worldly measures as he fights spiritual battles with spiritual weapons (Eph. 6:12), including the "weapon" of the imprecatory psalms. Adams emphasizes that it is the Lamb's wrath that should come through these psalms, not our own: "The enemies of the Lord need to hear these prayers of Christ proclaimed today. They are not the prayers of a careless and compassionless tyrant, but the effectual prayers of the Lamb of God who bore the curse of God for the sins of all who bow their knee to Him. *The wrath of the psalms must be preached as the wrath of the Lamb of God.* God's kingdom is at war!"[10]

---

9. John Piper, "Do I Not Hate Those Who Hate You, O Lord?" *Taste & See*, October 3, 2000, http://www.desiringgod.org/ResourceLibrary/TasteAndSee/ByDate/2000/1161_Do_I_Not_Hate_Those_Who_Hate_You_O_Lord/; (accessed November 30, 2009.)

10. Adams, *War Psalms*, 34, emphasis added.

Many Western Christians seem to have lost this sense of "being at war." Persecuted Christians have it, and they also have no difficulty singing the imprecatory psalms. In the late 1980s, I had the privilege of ministering to Romanian Christians who were fleeing to Hungary to escape Ceausescu's persecution. At the time I was struggling with the imprecatory psalms and asked a few of the Romanians what they thought. They looked at me with puzzled expressions and told me that the Romanian Christians sang the imprecatory psalms more than any others, and they did so without any qualms or questions!

Judgments Aiming at Salvation

An imprecatory prayer will often have the good of the sinner at its heart, because God will often use judgments to bring sinners to Himself. This is summed up in the psalmist's petition, "Fill their faces with shame; that they may seek thy name, O LORD" (Ps. 83:16). It is exemplified in Nebuchadnezzar's salvation (Dan. 4) and in how God's judgment upon Elymas the sorcerer led to the salvation of Sergius Paulus (Acts 13:9–12). Luther puts it like this:

> We should pray that our enemies be converted and become our friends, and if not, that their doing and designing be bound to fail and have no success and that their persons perish rather than the Gospel and the kingdom of Christ. Thus the saintly martyr Anastasia, a wealthy, noble Roman matron, prayed against her husband, an idolatrous and terrible ravager of Christians, who had flung her into a horrible prison, in which she had to stay and die. There she lay and wrote to the saintly Chrysogonus diligently to pray for her husband that, if possible, he be converted and believe; but if not, that he be unable to carry out his plans and that he soon make an end of his ravaging. Thus she prayed him to death, for he went to war and did not return home. So we, too, pray for our angry enemies, not that God protect and strengthen them in their ways, as we pray for Christians, or that He help them, but that they be converted, if they can be; or, if they refuse, that God oppose them, stop them and end the game to their harm and misfortune.[11]

---

11. Martin Luther, *What Luther Says* (St. Louis: Concordia, 1959), 1100.

Point Us to Christ

Finally, and most importantly, the imprecatory psalms point us to Christ. The *Spirit of the Reformation Study Bible* says,

> Even the psalms that include imprecations, or cursing, find fulfillment in Christ. These psalms cry out for the vindication of the righteous and for God's judgment on the wicked (e.g., Ps. 69:22–29). Such prayers reflected the calling of the Israelites to holy war as God's instruments of judgment. With the coming of Christ to bear God's judgment, the nature of the warfare of God's people has changed. It is now more intense, but directed first and foremost against the "spiritual forces of evil in the heavenly realms" (Eph. 6:12). When Christ returns in glory, the time of mercy will be ended and the imprecations (curses) of the psalms will be fulfilled against all the enemies of God.[12]

James Adams goes further. He says that we must hear Christ singing and praying these psalms:

> The Lord Jesus Christ is praying these prayers of vengeance. The prayers that cry out for the utter destruction of the psalmist's enemies can only be grasped when heard from the loving lips of our Lord Jesus. These prayers signal an alarm to all who are still enemies of King Jesus. His prayers will be answered! God's wrath is revealed upon all who oppose Christ. Anyone who rejects God's way of forgiveness in the cross of Christ will bear the dreadful curses of God.... When we understand that it is this merciful and holy Savior of sinners who is praying, we will no longer be ashamed of these prayers, but rather glory in them. Christ's prayers lead us to give God the honor and trust now because we know that God answers His prayers. Therefore, we are assured that the powers of evil will fall and God alone will reign forever![13]

This means that we can patiently wait for God to fulfill His promises, despite the temporary triumphing of the wicked and the affliction of the godly.

---

12. *Spirit of the Reformation Study Bible* (Grand Rapids: Zondervan, 2003), 805.
13. Adams, *War Psalms*, 33, 35.

Conclusion

We must admit that the imprecatory psalms are among the most difficult parts of Scripture to understand. It is difficult to explain everything and answer every objection. Faith is required. Spurgeon summed it up well: "Truly this is one of the hard places of Scripture, a passage which the soul trembles to read, yet it is not ours to sit in judgement upon it, but to bow our ear to what the Lord would speak to us therein."[14] It is also difficult to pray these prayers with pure motives, with righteous indignation. However, we must believe that Christ was able to sing these psalms with perfect holiness. Even on the cross, He was praying these prayers against His enemies silently, while also praying for His people, "Forgive them."

The Puritan William Romaine noticed with alarm the decline of psalm singing in the church and said it was caused by the failure to see the relation of the Psalms to Jesus Christ. What a blessing it would be to the church if many began to preach Christ from the Psalms again, even the imprecatory ones, and so inspire a new generation of psalm singers.

---

14. C. H. Spurgeon, *Treasury of David* (Grand Rapids: Zondervan, 1966), 2a:436.

Chapter 8

The Case for Psalmody, with Some Reference to the Psalter's Sufficiency for Christian Worship

Malcolm H. Watts

What is the worship of God? Worship is the acknowledgment of God's supreme worth and our suitable response to that worth, in honor and respect. John Owen, the Puritan, defined it as "paying that homage which is due unto the divine nature";[1] Stephen Charnock, another Puritan, wrote of it as "a reverent remembrance of God."[2]

Acts of Worship

The Scriptures teach that there are certain acts of worship. These are strictly regulated by God Himself, so that positive and express warrant of God's written Word is required for each one of them. In the Old Testament the Lord forbids His people to adopt man-made devices in their worship. "Take heed to thyself," He says, "that thou be not snared by following them.... What thing soever I command you, observe to do it: thou shalt not add thereto, nor diminish from it" (Deut. 12:30, 32; cf. 4:2; 2 Chron. 8:13; 29:25; Ezra 3:2, 4; Jer. 7:31). The New Testament insists on the same biblical authority, our Lord clearly stating as much with reference to the scribes and Pharisees: "Why do ye also transgress the commandment of God by your tradition?... In vain do they worship me, teaching for

---

1. John Owen, *The Works of John Owen* (London: The Banner of Truth Trust, 1966), 6:65.
2. Stephen Charnock, *The Complete Works of Stephen Charnock* (Edinburgh: James Nichol, 1864), 1:318.

doctrines the commandments of men" (Matt. 15:3, 9; cf. 28:20; 1 Cor. 11:2, 23; Col. 2:20–23). The sole rule for worship has ever been the revealed will of God; hence, any invention of men is precluded, and only the observance of divine appointments will prove acceptable and efficacious.

Since it is God's exclusive right to appoint public (as well as private and family) worship, we do well to inquire carefully as to the lawful ordinances of His house. We will find that the normal stated and solemn assemblies of the Sabbath day (Ex. 20:8–11; Lev. 23:3; Isa. 58:13–14; John 20:19, 26; Acts 20:7; 1 Cor. 16:2) include the reading of God's written Word (Deut. 31:11–12; Neh. 8:1–3; Acts 13:14–15; 17:11; Col. 4:16; Rev. 1:3); the offering of prayer, which includes supplications, intercessions, and the giving of thanks (Matt. 6:9–13; Acts 2:42; Eph. 6:18; 1 Tim. 2:1–8); the singing of praise (Ps. 22:22, 25; Matt. 26:30; Acts 2:46–47; Col. 3:16); the preaching and teaching of God's Word (Neh. 8:7–8; Acts 15:21; 1 Tim. 4:11; 6:2; 2 Tim. 3:16–17; 4:2; 1 Peter 4:11); and the pronouncing of solemn benediction or blessing (Num. 6:22–27; 2 Cor. 13:14; 2 Tim. 4:22; Rev. 22:21). Also included, of course, will be the administration and reception of the two sacraments: baptism and the Lord's Supper (Matt. 28:19–20; Mark 14:22–25; Acts 2:41–42; 1 Cor. 11:23–28).

However, as Arthur Hildersam rightly observes, "If these outward things be performed never so constantly, without the inward and spiritual worship of the heart, they cannot please God, nor do us any good."[3] He further observes, "Every part of God's worship is spiritual, and there is in it an outward and bodily action done by man, and an inward spiritual work that is done by the Lord himself."[4] Both truths are of paramount importance (Ps. 51:6, 17; John 4:23–24; Ex. 20:24; 1 Cor. 3:16–17). Hildersam stresses both the inward and the outward aspects of worship when he writes, "In observing of them, we do our *homage* to God, and shew our *obedience* unto him."[5]

Certainly the Lord's people worship through these means, following the divine directives and observing what has been enjoined, but, more specifically, in Scripture reading and hearing, His people recognize *His*

---

3. Arthur Hildersam, *CLII Lectures upon Psalm, LI* (London: J. Rayworth, 1642), 532.
4. Ibid., 539–40.
5. Ibid., 534, emphasis added.

sovereign and rightful authority over their hearts and lives (Dan. 10:21); in prayer, they declare *His all-sufficiency, His readiness, ability, and willingness to bestow good things for Christ's sake* (Job 10:12; Acts 17:25; James 4:6); in praise, they make known *His great goodness, mercy, and grace* in the communication of various and innumerable blessings (Pss. 30:4–5; 31:19; 63:3–4); in the preaching and hearing of sermons, they reverence Him as *the God of truth and the only wise God* (Deut. 32:4; 1 Tim. 1:17); and in the benediction, they believe and declare that their God is *present in the midst of them*, to manifest Himself and bestow joy and peace (Pss. 3:8; 133:3; Rom. 15:13; Heb. 13:20). Finally, baptism and the Lord's Supper are observed to show that God in Christ is *faithful to covenant promises*, affording to His people *the benefits of union and communion* (symbolized in baptism and the Lord's Supper) (Rom. 6:3–4; 1 Cor. 10:16–17).

What *Praise* Means

Praise, then, constitutes a part of God's worship, but what exactly is meant by the word *praise?* Thomas Boston describes it as "the acknowledging and declaring of *the glorious excellencies of God*, as he has manifested them in his word and works."[6] Praise is indeed a response to the divine excellencies. It actually makes them manifest, even in their totality as God's super-excellence or surpassing glory. This is what is meant by glorifying God. While men can in no way add to God's *essential* glory (what He is in Himself [Ex. 3:14; Job 35:7; Rom. 11:25, 36]), they can in song set forth His *declarative* glory (what He is made known to be [Pss. 89:1; 96:3, 7, 8; Isa. 44:23]). Thomas Adams emphasizes this point when he writes, "Not that praise can add to God's glory, nor blasphemies detract from it…as the sun is neither bettered by the birds singing, nor battered by dogs barking. He is so infinitely great, and constantly good, that his glory admits neither addition nor diminution. Yet we that cannot make his name greater can make it seem greater; and though we cannot enlarge his glory, we can enlarge the manifestation of his glory."[7]

---

6. Thomas Boston, *The Whole Works of the Late Reverend Thomas Boston* (Aberdeen: George and Robert King, 1849), 5:591, emphasis added.

7. Thomas Adams, *The Works of Thomas Adams* (Edinburgh: James Nichol, 1862), 3:11.

Through grace, and in the consequent exercise of faith, the Lord's people are able to discern and even to sense Him in all His attributes or perfections (Heb. 11:27; 1 Peter 2:3); it is in their contemplative experience of Him that they are moved to express themselves in honorable and worthy praise (1 Chron. 29:10–13; Ps. 63:3). It is the Lord, in His transcendent splendor, then, who always provides the matter for true praise; hence, He is called in Scripture "thy praise" or the praise of his saints (Deut. 10:21; Jer. 17:14).

A valid distinction is sometimes made between praise, blessing, and thanksgiving. Although conceding that these terms are sometimes used "promiscuously" (or indiscriminately), Thomas Manton, for example, observes that at times there appears to be "a distinctness of notion," and when that is the case, he asserts that "praise relateth to his *excellences*, as we may praise a stranger for his excellent endowments" (Pss. 145:3; 148:13); "blessing...respects the *works* of God as beneficial to us" (Pss. 26:11–12; 66:8–12—"God's blessing is operative, ours declarative"[8]); and "thanksgiving...has respect to *benefits* as well as *blessings*" (Pss. 116:12, 17; 147:7–9).[9] Strictly speaking, then, praise is the celebration of all the wonderful perfections that are in the living and true God.

God, in everything that He has done, has always aimed at the revelation of His attributes or qualities (Isa. 48:11; Rom. 11:36). Creation—and the creatures generally—are able to display something of His glory ("even his eternal power and Godhead" [Rom. 1:20]), and, by their very existence and continuance, they may be said to bear constant testimony to His praise (Pss. 19:1; 145:10). However, it is man especially who has been made spiritually to discern God's glory, and when confronted by His self-disclosure as the wonderful and wonder-working One (that is, by God's "name" [Pss. 8:1; 48:10]) and graciously enabled to apprehend this revelation (Eph. 1:16–19; Heb. 11:27), he is then in a position to proclaim it in an active way through his lips and in spoken praise (Isa. 43:7, 21; 60:21; 1 Peter 2:9). "Our tongues are called our glory" (Psalm 16:9; cf. Acts 2:26),

---

8. Thomas Manton, *The Works of Thomas Manton, D.D.* (London: James Nisbet and Co., 1872), 1:244; 9:190, 191.

9. Ibid., 9:191, emphasis added.

Manton observes, "not only as speech is our excellency above the beasts, but because God is thereby *glorified* and *praised*."[10]

It follows that the more our souls are blessed in the knowledge of God—with His sacred persons, His sublime attributes, and His marvelous works—the more we will feel constrained not only to admire but also to extol Him. Scripture suggests that renewed and increased experience of the divine goodness and love will create within us a further wonder and gratitude and, therefore, a greater disposition and aptness to praise the Lord. In the hope of new mercies coming his way, David is able to say, "[I] will yet praise thee more and more" (Ps. 71:14; literally, "I will add upon all thy praise").

Beautifully does Richard Sibbes express this truth when he writes, "We see the poor birds in the spring-time, when those little spirits they have are cherished with the sunbeams, how they express it in singing. So when God warms us with his favours, let him have the praise of all."[11]

Given that God's mercies are new every day and given that our experience of these mercies is progressive, we can only believe that praise is being perfected throughout our lives. In the life to come, then, when blessing and blessedness are complete, we wonder what will be the nature of the church's eternal and united praise. Certain it is that praise, unlike other ordinances, will continue through endless ages (Isa. 26:19; 35:10), and it is in the book of Revelation that we catch the sound of that singing that one day will be heard by God, the angels, and all the redeemed. "Blessing, and glory, and wisdom, and thanksgiving, and honour, and power, and might, be unto our God for ever and ever. Amen" (Rev. 7:12; cf. 4:11; 5:13; 15:3–4).

In concluding this consideration of the general subject of praise, it should perhaps be noted that praise does have certain distinctives that show it to be the most eminent part of worship:

- Praise is a leading ordinance in public worship (Ps. 95:2; Acts 2:46–47).
- Born of a vision of the superlatively excellent God, it particularly glorifies Him (Pss. 50:23; 145:3).

---

10. Ibid., emphasis added.

11. Richard Sibbes, *The Complete Works of Richard Sibbes* (Edinburgh: James Nichol, 1862), 2:274.

- Our love to God—not self-love—is what moves us to perform this duty (Ps. 116:1, 19).

- In this act we are actually giving rather than receiving: we are giving to God the glory due to His name (Ps. 29:1–2; Heb. 13:15).

- It is a source of great happiness, and there is no exercise more enjoyable to our souls (Ps. 33:1; 135:3).

- An infinitely excellent God must furnish matter for the most exalted response in His people's adoration (Pss. 18:3; 96:4).

- The glorified redeemed and the holy angels sing just such everlasting praises to the God enthroned above (Ps. 104:33; Isa. 26:19).

The Matter of Our Praise

It is necessary now to consider the matter of our praise. The Scriptures authorize the use of inspired songs in public worship, even such as are found in the book of Psalms, and these are remarkably suited to all the various needs of the church in every age. The biblical warrant for singing the psalms of David, Asaph, and the other psalm writers in public assemblies needs to be established and clearly stated.

God, in His essence and nature, is altogether incomprehensible. Accordingly, He is represented as dwelling in light of such intense brilliancy as to be incapable of being even approached, let alone assessed. Yet at the same time, He is said to be surrounded with "clouds and darkness," which at first might seem to be contradictory but in actuality only emphasizes that God is hidden to men, enveloped in His own impenetrable mystery (Pss. 18:11; 97:2; 1 Tim. 6:16). Now it is perfectly true that God has disclosed something of Himself in general and special revelation, and therefore the unknown God has become knowable, but even so, it is still impossible to acquire a perfect and entire knowledge of Him. Hence, we are told that no amount of study will "find out God" or find Him out "unto perfection." "Touching the Almighty, we cannot find him out," and why is that? It is because He is "excellent"—or because He excels—and therefore His being is vast, even infinite, and beyond human understanding (Job 11:7; 37:23; Ps. 145:3).

Once this is understood, the question naturally arises: how can men, even with the aid of revelation, set forth in praise the wonders of a Being so illustriously great? He is surely "exalted *above* all blessing and praise" (Neh. 9:5, emphasis added), and it must surely follow that our most sublime songs fall unspeakably below His transcendent majesty. The problem, of course, is further aggravated by the fact that men are fallen and therefore subject to sin and error. If the divine glory rises far above the highest flights of human praise, certain is it that men corrupted in all their faculties of soul, with a defective understanding of spiritual things, are altogether incapable of producing worthy material for praise. The general principle lies in the question, "Who can bring a clean thing out of an unclean?" (Job 14:4; cf. 11:12; Eph. 4:18).

In view of these things, God, from the beginning, granted certain men the supernatural and unerring influence of the Holy Spirit, with the result that the songs they wrote could only be said to be by inspiration of God.

Moses, apparently the first of such men, was a "prophet" who, "moved by the Holy Ghost," composed, with the help of Miriam "the prophetess," the praise sung by the Israelites at the farther side of the Red Sea and also subsequent praises during the wilderness period (Ex. 15:1, 20–21; Num. 21:17–18; Deut. 31:30; Ps. 90 [title]; cf. Deut. 34:10; 2 Peter 1:21). After Moses, other prophets or prophetesses were raised up to compose sacred songs for public worship, such as Deborah (Judg. 4:4; 5:1, 5, 12). In the early days of the monarchy, young men, with the prophetic gift and in training for the prophetic ministry, were often under the influence of inspiration and enabled with "a psalter, a tabret, and a pipe, and a harp" to "prophesy" in various spiritual hymns and songs (1 Sam. 10:5).

Eventually David was raised up, "the sweet psalmist of Israel," the one who testified, "The Spirit of the LORD spake by me, and his word was in my tongue" (2 Sam. 23:1–2). He composed many psalms. In the book of Psalms, seventy-three bear his name, but references elsewhere make clear that he was responsible for others, perhaps even a considerable number of those not formally ascribed to him (Acts 4:25 [Ps. 2]; Heb. 4:7 [Ps. 95]).

On the occasion when David brought the ark up to Jerusalem, Heman, Asaph, and Ethan (or Jeduthan), representative Levites, were the men appointed to lead the singing. The significance of their appointment lies in the fact that all three men were seers or prophets, able in their own right to provide suitable material for praise (1 Chron. 15:16; cf. 1 Chron. 25:5; 2 Chron. 29:30; 35:15). Later in his reign, when making preparations for the temple and its worship, David set apart these men's sons, also supernaturally endued, "who should *prophesy* with harps, with psalteries, and with cymbals" (1 Chron. 25:1, emphasis added).

Such inspired psalms were delivered to those responsible for the arranging of worship in order that they might be sung in the public services of the Jewish people (1 Chron. 16:7). Psalms such as 4–6, entitled "To the chief musician"—words prefixed to fifty-five psalms—demonstrate this practice. Accordingly, Israel's leaders directed the Levites to use in public praise "the words of David, and of Asaph the seer," by which words the inspired Psalms are clearly intended (2 Chron. 29:30).

It is significant that in one of his psalms David says, "My praise shall be *of thee* in the great congregation" (Ps. 22:25, emphasis added). This is the genitive of source and the words may be more literally translated "from thee," meaning not merely that God is the source of David's deliverance, but also—and more particularly—that He is the source of what he intends to sing in the way of thanksgiving. In other words, David is resolved to sing what the Lord Himself has provided in the God-breathed psalms, and his subsequent reference to "the great congregation" makes clear that this psalm singing will take place when the people assemble for worship, evidently pointing back to verse 3 with its mention of "the praises of Israel."

There is evidence to show that, far from being one man's personal intention, this was a divine institution. Toward the end of David's life, when he, by God's instruction (1 Chron. 28:11–19), made preparation and provision for the temple, he particularly organized the Levites responsible for leading worship. These included Asaph, Jeduthun, and Heman, along with their families. Heman is given a position of some prominence as "the king's seer [or prophet] *in the words of God*, to lift up the horn" (1 Chron. 25:5, emphasis added). The expression appears to mean either that he will excel in "the composition of his psalms"[12] or that he will "sing such Divine songs as were inspired by God."[13] (The words that follow, "to lift up the horn," may refer to musical accompaniment, or they may be figurative, alluding to the seer's key role as leader of the praise of God, as perhaps in 1 Sam. 2:1). What is clear is that in the old economy the songs

---

12. Christopher Wordsworth, *The Holy Bible, with Notes and Introductions* (London: Rivingtons, 1873), 3: 217.

13. Matthew Poole, *A Commentary on the Holy Bible* (Edinburgh: The Banner of Truth Trust, 1974), 1: 810–11.

sung in the celebration of God's praise were given by divine inspiration and consisted of the actual words of God.

These songs were therefore subsequently and correctly called "the songs of the LORD" or, in general, "the song of the LORD" (1 Chron. 25:7; 2 Chron. 29:27). At first, of course, a song composed under the divine influence stood alone as a sacred song for the worship of God, but then, as more of these songs of praise appeared, many of them formed a collection, which grew in size until there appeared at last a whole book of them, entitled in the Hebrew *Sepher Tehillim*, "Book of Praises," and later called "the book of Psalms" (Luke 20:42; Acts 1:20). Some songs composed under the Spirit's influence at various times were not included in this book, because they were designed just for one particular occasion, for example, the songs of Moses, Hannah, Hezekiah, and Habakkuk (Deut. 32:1–43; 1 Sam. 2:1–10; Isa. 38:9–20; Hab. 3:1–19); those that were included were recognized as divine and sacred songs designed and suited to be used as the vehicle of public praise in successive generations. It remains only to be said at this point that it was God—by the teaching of His Holy Spirit and by His directing providence—who caused this book to occupy an important and prominent place in the inspired canon of Holy Scripture.

The fact that this book of Psalms, or Book of Praises, exists is surely proof that God intended these songs for standing and exclusive use in His church. Hence David, who wrote so many of them that the whole is sometimes called "the Psalms of David," is designated in Scripture "the sweet psalmist *of Israel*" (2 Sam. 23:1, emphasis added). Furthermore, the pieces themselves are designated "the songs *of Zion*," "the songs *of the temple*," and the "songs *of praise and thanksgiving unto God*" (Ps. 137:3; Amos 8:3; Neh. 12:46, emphasis added). What are these but declarations from God that His will is that these songs be set to music and sung in His worship?

Their divine appointment for this purpose is confirmed by express commands, such as "Sing unto him, *sing psalms* unto him"; "*Take a psalm*, and bring hither the timbrel, the pleasant harp with the psaltery"; "Let us come before his presence with thanksgiving, and make *a joyful noise unto him with psalms*"; "Sing unto the LORD with the harp; with the harp, and *the voice of a psalm*"; "Sing unto him, *sing psalms* unto him" (1 Chron. 16:9; Pss. 81:2; 95:2; 98:5; 105:2, emphasis added).

At this point it may be as well to remember that by *psalms*, Scripture means "songs given by inspiration." In support of this statement, the following points may be made:

1. First, the "Book of Praises," which contains the psalms, has a place within the canon of inspired Scripture (Luke 24:44).

2. The oldest in the collection is probably Psalm 90, composed by Moses, "the man of God," a title that designates him as a "prophet" (1 Sam. 2:27; 1 Kings 17:18, 24; 20:28; cf. Deut. 34:10).

3. David, "the sweet psalmist" who wrote so many of the psalms, claims inspiration when he says, "The Spirit of the LORD spake by me, and his word was in my tongue" (2 Sam. 23:1–2), a fact borne out by other scriptures, such as, "The Holy Ghost by the mouth of David spake" (Acts 1:16; cf. Mark 12:36; Acts 4:25; Heb. 4:7).

4. Other authors, including Solomon, Asaph, Heman, and Ethan (or Jeduthan), were all endowed with the spirit of prophecy (1 Kings 11:9; cf. Num. 12:6; 1 Chron. 25:1–5; 2 Chron. 29:30).

5. The compositions of the psalmists were "the LORD's song" or "the songs of the LORD," a title denoting their full inspiration (1 Chron. 25:7; Ps. 137:4).

6. Since the psalmist describes the "songs" he sang as divine "statutes," the Psalms must be nothing other than the inspired Word of God (Ps. 119:54).

7. In one of his psalms, Asaph intimates that it is the church's duty to preserve and transmit to future times, teachings hitherto communicated and now found in the Scripture Psalms, thereby "shewing to the generation to come the praises of the LORD" (Ps. 78:4). The conclusion to be drawn is that when the Bible directs men to "sing psalms," it is the inspired psalms, bearing the seal and signature of God, which they are under obligation to sing.

The church has divine and scriptural warrant, then, to sing the inspired psalms in her worship. What she does not have is a warrant to sing uninspired hymns or even psalm paraphrases. Indeed, the appointment of the Psalms (which has never been annulled) necessarily excludes the use of any other material, just as the appointment of Jerusalem for the site of Israel's worship excluded all places besides, or the appointment of

Aaron's sons to the priesthood excluded non-Aaronic family members, or the appointment of a lamb for the Passover excluded other kinds of creatures. What, then, about the frequent exhortation to "sing unto the Lord a new song"? It has sometimes been said, rather naively, "We find it difficult to believe that what David really meant was, 'Only sing unto the Lord an old psalm.'" It is to be noted, however, that where these words appear (Pss. 33:3; 40:3; 96:1; 98:1; 144:9), the reference is *always* to the particular psalm in which they appear. God's people are not told to compose their own original songs, but rather to sing that inspired one presently set before them, albeit with a fresh sense of adoration, gratitude, and delight. As John Cotton once rightly observed, "These [Scripture-] *Psalms* being chosen out suitably to the new occasions and new conditions of God's people, and sung by them with new hearts and renewed affections, will ever be found new songs."[14]

It is clear that the Jewish church sang these inspired psalms. As already noted, on the occasion of carrying the ark to Jerusalem, David "delivered first *this psalm* [a psalm later presented as Pss. 105:1–15; 96:1b–13; and 106:1, 47–48]…into the hand of Asaph and his brethren." The fact that David is said to have done this for the "first" time suggests that, after this, he passed on other inspired psalms to be used in public worship (1 Chron. 16:7).

Later, under special divine direction, David made specific arrangements for the singing of praise in stated worship (1 Chron. 23:1–6, 30; 28:11–13, 19). History records that thereafter every effort was made to keep to those arrangements so that Jehoiada, the priest, for example, appointed "singing, as it was ordained by David," and after the exile, when the people began to rebuild the temple, like deference was shown to "the ordinance of David king of Israel" (2 Chron. 23:18; Ezra 3:10–11; cf. Neh. 12:24). The verse in Ezra shows that this necessitated the singing of an inspired psalm which, on that occasion, was Psalm 136, the opening words of which are quoted: "Giving thanks unto the LORD; because he is good, for his mercy endureth for ever." This would appear to have been a favorite psalm since it is recorded as having being sung on another important occasion (2 Chron. 20:20–21).

---

14. John Cotton, *Singing of Psalmes a Gospel-Ordinance* (London: M.S. for Hannah Allen, 1647), 25, emphasis added.

It is therefore not at all surprising to read that when King Hezekiah reformed Israel's worship according to the Word of God, he not only ordered the praise "according to the commandment of David, and of Gad the king's seer, and Nathan the prophet: for so was the commandment of the LORD by his prophets," but he specifically commanded the Levites to "sing praise unto the LORD with *the words of David, and of Asaph the seer*" (2 Chron. 29:25, 30, emphasis added), which shows that there was, even then, a collection of inspired sacred poems for use in public worship and that, by divine and express appointment, these were the compositions actually sung in Israel's public worship. In that significant verse, as William Hanna observes, "there is a concise and comprehensive account of the service of praise, as performed in the temple."[15] Although there is no clear biblical evidence for psalm singing in the ancient synagogue, we know that temple worship gave rise to synagogal worship, that psalmody was practiced outside the temple (as, for example, in the Songs of Degrees or Ascents, sung by the pilgrims on their journey to Jerusalem [Pss. 120–134; cf. 42:4: Isa. 30:29]), and that, in Ezra's day, in something like a synagogue service, the people were called upon to "Stand up and bless the LORD" (Neh. 9:5; cf. 8:1–8). Such lines of evidence have led some scholars to conclude that "psalmody was not unknown in the worship of the ancient synagogue."[16]

The Old Testament church recognized the superlative excellence of these inspired praises. Worshipers in that ancient church knew very well that there were no songs equal to those in the book of Psalms. The author of the Psalms was God; in consequence, they were therefore full of awesome majesty (Ps. 29:4); absolutely pure and faultless (Pss. 12:6; 119:42); intended for the public praise of the sanctuary (Ps. 137:3—"the songs of Zion"); replete with the best teaching available to men (Ps. 119:54, 99); effective for the soul's sanctification and comfort (Ps. 119:9, 11, 104); possessed of life and unfading beauty (Isa. 40:8); and acceptable to the One seated upon the eternal throne (2 Chron. 5:13–14; Pss. 22:3; 69:30–31).

---

15. William Hanna, *A Plea for the Songs of Zion* (Belfast: Printed by J. Johnston, 1860), 10.

16. Cuthbert C. Keet, *A Liturgical Study of the Psalter* (London: George Allen and Unwin, Ltd., 1828), 137.

For these and like reasons, Scripture psalmody alone was used in the former dispensation in worship, and Scripture gives evidence, not only of precept to that effect, but also of definite, approved example.

At this point certain questions arise: Were the inspired Psalms meant to be perpetually sung? Were they suitable only for the worship of the Jewish church? Were they set aside under the new Christian economy? These questions are important, and, by way of a preliminary response, the following points may be made:

- Singing God's praise is a moral duty, and psalmody is a positive institution. Neither the duty nor the institution is of a ceremonial or judicial nature, and consequently there is no reason to suppose that they have been abrogated.

- David, the author of so many of the psalms, is styled "the sweet psalmist of Israel," but the term *Israel* is applied to the body of Christian believers, both Jews and Gentiles, suggesting that he composed his psalms also for them (2 Sam. 23:1; Gal. 6:16; cf. 3:29). In the same way the Psalms are called "the songs of Zion," and, since *Zion* is a name for the New Testament church, it would appear that these psalms are intended also to be sung by the church under the new covenant (Ps. 137:3; Heb. 12:22).

- In anticipation of their future use in these Christian times, the Psalms themselves refer to their being sung "to all generations" (Ps. 79:13; 89:1; cf. 102:18). God's servants are enjoined to praise the Lord in psalmody "from this time forth and for evermore" (Ps. 113:1–2).

- Salvation, in fact, is reckoned in the Psalms to be already accomplished (Ps. 98:1–2). Furthermore, to facilitate their usefulness in *this* era, the great prophetic utterances and predictions of Christ are all referred to in the past tense; for example, "He asked life of thee, and thou gavest it him, even length of days for ever and ever"; "Reproach hath broken my heart.... They gave me also gall for my meat; and in my thirst they gave me vinegar to drink"; "The LORD said unto my Lord, Sit thou at my right hand, until I make thine enemies thy footstool" (Pss. 21:4; 69:20–21; 110:1).

- The call is frequently given to "all the earth" to unite in singing the inspired "song" (Ps. 96:1; cf. 66:4; 100:1–2), something brought about only through the Great Commission and the universal preaching of the gospel (Matt. 28:18–20; Rom. 16:25–27). Indeed, verses from the Psalms are quoted in the New Testament to confirm the extension of God's kingdom to the Gentiles (Rom. 15:9, 11).

• There is so much in the Psalms concerning Christ and the gospel (Luke 24:44 – 45; 1 Peter 1:11–12), a truth borne out by the fact that the New Testament quotes from the Psalter more often than from any other Old Testament book.[17] In this connection, it is noteworthy that when the author of the epistle to the Hebrews, in the first chapter, seeks biblical proof for our Lord's divinity, a fundamental Christian truth, at least seven of his citations are from the book of Psalms. In the divine wisdom, the Psalms appear perfectly adapted for Christian worship.

• Since the church is essentially one in both ages, and since the Psalms have been appointed — *and never set aside* — for its public praise, we may assuredly believe that, by divine authority, the continued use of them has been enjoined.

Psalms in the New Testament

In the New Testament, Christ (and His disciples) would doubtless have sung psalms in the temple and probably in the synagogue (Matt. 21:13; Mark 1:39; Luke 4:16; John 10:23; Acts 13:14). Our Lord named this inspired collection "the book of Psalms" or, more simply, "the psalms" (Luke 20:42; 24:44), which is significant because His quoting from them shows His belief in their inspiration and authority (see especially Mark 12:36); the fact that under the new covenant they are retained as a unique testimony to His person and work (Luke 24:27, 44); and, in particular, that they are still to be used for their original purpose: namely, the celebration of divine praise. It should also be observed that when our Lord spoke of them as "*the* book of Psalms" or "*the* psalms" (the Greek word *psalmoi*, from *psallo*, "to sing"), He appears to recognize these inspired songs as the proper and sole vehicle of the church's public praise.

---

17. A. F. Kirkpatrick, ed. *The Book of Psalms* (Cambridge: Cambridge University Press, 1903), 838– 40. Dr. A. F. Kirkpatrick listed ninety-three such quotations but made no attempt to include in his list the numerous indirect allusions to the Psalms.

Throughout His ministry our Lord never once intimated that the institution of psalmody was to be set aside, nor did He ever suggest that He or His disciples should compose new songs for praise, nor did He give as much as a hint of a promise that the Holy Spirit would lead and gift men to do such a thing. As a result, there is nothing like the book of Psalms in the New Testament. An equally salient fact is that our Lord neither annulled nor replaced the divine principle, honored from the beginning, that only inspired material, breathed out by the Holy Spirit, should be used in the worship of God. It is therefore true to say, "No instance can be adduced in which the King of Zion has abrogated the use of the church's inspired songs, *or given permission to supplant them by the effusions of men*."[18]

The gospels record the memorable occasion when our Lord, in the company of His disciples, first observed the Passover and then instituted the Lord's Supper, and at the close of the latter service, "when they had sung an hymn" (literally, "when they had hymned" or "sung praise"), they went out to the Mount of Olives" (Matt. 26:30; Mark 14:26). The word in the original is *humnesantes*, a verb form of *humnos*, "a song of praise," and in and of itself, the term does not give any clear indication as to what exactly they sang. However, in the Septuagint, the Greek translation of the Old Testament (LXX), the word, in one or other of its forms, is used repeatedly of the inspired Psalms; for example, "Moreover Hezekiah the king and the princes commanded the Levites to *sing praise* unto the Lord with the words of David, and of Asaph the seer" (2 Chron. 29:30, emphasis added). Indeed, it appears in the titles of six of the actual psalms where the Authorized Version reads "on Neginoth" and "Neginah," both terms apparently referring to music with stringed instruments, but the Septuagint uses the Greek word for *hymn* in these places because it is inclusive of song with an instrument (see Pss. 6, 54, 55, 61, 67, and 76). That version also uses *hymn* in the text of the actual psalms: "And he hath put a new song in my mouth, even *praise* unto our God" (Ps. 40:3, emphasis added).

Josephus, the Jewish historian, uses the term similarly when referring to the Psalms: "And now David, being freed from wars and dangers, and enjoying for the future a profound peace, composed songs and *hymns* to

---

18. *The Covenanter, A Religious Periodical for 1835*, ed. Thomas Houston and James Dick (Belfast: Printed by Stuart and Gregg, 1835), 6, emphasis added.

God, of several sorts of metre."[19] The least that we can say about the singing in the Upper Room is that the expression used does not exclude the idea that Jesus and the disciples sang an inspired psalm.

Elsewhere in the New Testament, this word, in the form of a verb, appears in the book of Acts in the account of Paul and Silas, who, thrown into the inner prison at Philippi, at midnight "sang praises unto God" (Acts 16:25). Since they would have been in pitch darkness and therefore wholly reliant upon their memories, it is almost certain that what they sang was what they had learned from childhood: the Psalms of David. The only other place where this expression is used is in the epistle to the Hebrews, where the writer quotes from Psalm 22: "I will declare thy name unto my brethren, in the midst of the church will I *sing praise* unto thee" (Heb. 2:12; Ps. 22:22, emphasis added). Here, the word (and it is but one word in the Greek) undoubtedly refers to that psalm in which it is found and from which it is taken. In the New Testament, therefore, the word seems always to relate to the singing of the Old Testament psalms.

Taking the study further, we note that Maimonides, the twelfth-century rabbi who codified Jewish law, authoritatively states that it was customary from ancient times to sing the Great Hallel at the Passover (Pss. 113–118). The best Christian authorities accept this, believing one part of it was sung at the beginning of the feast (113–114) and another part at the end (115–118). Dr. John Lightfoot, the highly esteemed biblical and rabbinic scholar (1602–1675), alluding to the words "when they had sung an hymn," writes: "What? The very same that every company did,—viz. the 'great Hallel', as it was called.... No expositor but grants this, and no reason to the contrary; for Christ complied with all the rites of the Passover." He continues, "Here the Lord of David sings the Psalms of David.... He that gave the Spirit to David to compose, sings what he composed.... [He] could have indited himself, could have inspired every disciple to have been a David, but [he] submits to order, which God had appointed, [and] sings the Psalms of David."[20]

19. *The Antiquities of the Jews*, book 7, chapter 12, section 3, in *The Works of Flavius Josephus* (London: George Routledge and Sons [n.d.]), 184, emphasis added.
20. John Lightfoot, *The Whole Works of the Rev. John Lightfoot* (London: J. F. Dove, 1822), 7:39–40. The reference to Maimonides and his treatise is in 9:142–43.

A later scholar, Alfred Edersheim, confirms this to have been the case. Writing of the Paschal Feast, he observes, "The service concluded with the fourth cup, over which the second portion of the 'Hallel' was sung, consisting of Psalms cxv, cxvi, cxvii and cxviii," and he later adds, "In this manner was the Paschal Supper celebrated by the Jews at the time when our Lord for the last time sat down to it with his disciples."[21]

Herman Ridderbos arrives at the same conclusion. Commenting on Matthew 26:30, he writes, "The hymn spoken of here formed the final act of the Passover ritual: the singing of the second part of the Hallel.... Shortly before his death Jesus and his disciples thus sang together Israel's ancient songs of deliverance and praise (see Pss. 116 and especially 118). Then they left the city for the Mount of Olives."[22] Similarly, William Lane writes on Mark 14:26:

> The table-fellowship was concluded by the recitation (or chanting) of the second half of the Hallel Psalms.... Jesus took the words of these psalms as his own prayer of thanksgiving and praise…and he concluded with a song of jubilation reflecting his stedfast confidence in his ultimate triumph: "I shall not die, but live, and declare the works of the Lord" (Ps. 118:17).... When Jesus arose to go to Gethsemane, Ps. 118 was upon his lips. It provided an appropriate description of how God would guide the Messiah through distress and suffering to glory.[23]

These psalms were relevant to that occasion. Psalms 113 and 114, sung before the meal, describe the Lord looking down in condescending love upon poor sinners upon the earth and then accomplishing His mighty deliverance, prefigured by the temporal deliverance from Egypt's dreadful bondage. The psalms sung after the meal, Psalms 115–118, speak generally of the Lord's exaltation, but, in particular, they concentrate on His call to faith (Psalm 115), His applied salvation (Psalm 116), the extension of His gospel and mercy to the Gentiles (Psalm 117), and, finally, His open-

21. Alfred Edersheim, *The Temple, Its Ministry and Services as They Were at the Time of Jesus Christ* (London: The Religious Tract Society, 1874), 210.

22. Herman Ridderbos, *Matthew*, in *Bible Student's Commentary*, trans. Ray Togtman (Grand Rapids: Regency Reference Library, 1987), 484.

23. William Lane, *The Gospel according to Mark* (London: Marshall, Morgan and Scott, 1974), 509.

ing of the gates of the everlasting kingdom to all who believe in His name (Psalm 118). At the end of these psalms, knowing the dark night that lay before Him, how deeply moving it must have been to hear the Lord sing, "Bind the sacrifice with cords, even unto the horns of the altar" (v. 27).

It is therefore most reasonable to believe that at the conclusion of this memorable service our Lord, with the disciples, sang the biblical psalms. Was there special significance in this for Christian worship? Indeed there was. As William Binnie perceptively observes, "The singing of the Hallel by Christ and the Eleven in the guest-chamber, on the night of his betrayal, may be said to mark the point at which the Psalter passed over from the old dispensation into the new; for it accompanied the celebration of the new ordinance of the Lord's Supper as well as the celebration of the expiring ordinance of the Passover."[24]

The early Christians, of course, continued for a while in the temple and the synagogue, where psalms were sung (Luke 24:53; Acts 2:46; 13:5, 14), but, in course of time, separate Christian churches were established, and the evidence shows that psalm singing remained a leading feature of the new worship. The apostle is himself an example in this respect, writing to the Corinthians: "I will sing (psalo) with the spirit, and I will sing (psalo) with the understanding also" (1 Cor. 14:15, emphasis added). Although the Corinthians had many faults, it appears nevertheless that psalm singing was an important and approved element in their public worship: "How is it then, brethren? When ye come together, every one of you hath a psalm" (1 Cor. 14:26, emphasis added).

It is possible that this was a song composed under the extraordinary influence of the Holy Spirit (and therefore immediately inspired), but it is more likely that believers were choosing their preferences from the canonical psalms. There is no evidence for charismatic songs in the New Testament (Luke 1 and 2 contain only prophecies that were spoken, not sung, and Acts 4:31 tells us that the previous verses [vv. 24–30] record prayer, not praise). Furthermore, the word psalm, in the New Testament, seems always to indicate a song from the book of Psalms (Luke 20:42;

---

24. William Binnie, *The Psalms: Their History, Teachings, and Use* (London: Hodder and Stoughton, 1886), 376.

24:44; Acts 1:20; 13:33; Eph. 5:19; Col. 3:16). The church of the first century, then, certainly appears to have used the Psalter for its book of praise.

In such passages as Matthew 26:30, Mark 14:26, and 1 Corinthians 14:26, Scripture does provide God's people with approved examples for psalmody, but does Scripture also provide us with a direct command? The answer must be yes. In two places the apostle positively enjoins the singing of "psalms, hymns and spiritual songs" (Eph. 5:19; Col. 3:16). It is generally agreed that the word *psalms* denotes the Psalms of Scripture and, as has been already observed, that word in the New Testament seems always to mean the biblical psalms. Furthermore, the word *hymns* can be a synonym for psalms, as in the references to Christ and His disciples "hymning" at the Last Supper.

What then of the term *spiritual songs?* The psalms were known in the Old Testament as the songs of Zion, and many of the psalms are designated as songs in their titles: "a Psalm and Song" or "a Psalm or Song," and sometimes, simply, "a Song" (Pss. 30, 66, 120–34). In the Greek Septuagint version (which we know the apostles both read and used [Rom. 3:10–14, 18; 9:12–13; 1 Cor. 9:9; 10:7; 2 Cor. 4:13; 6:2; Gal. 4:27]), thirty-five of the Psalms are designated "a Song" (*ode*), and the verb form of this word also appears in the texts of the psalms themselves, as in "*Sing* unto him a new song" (Ps. 33:3, emphasis added; cf. 96:1; 98:1; 149:1).

From the Septuagint, therefore, it appears that a psalm can be called both a hymn and a song. Indeed, the title of Psalm 76 in that version includes all three terms. It reads as follows: "For the end, among the *Hymns*, a *Psalm* for Asaph; a *Song* for the Assyrian."

The apostle Paul, by including the word "spiritual" ("spiritual songs"), clearly intends by that term Spirit-inspired psalms or psalms proceeding from the Holy Spirit; in other words, he has in mind the psalms of the book of Psalms, found in the Holy Scripture (2 Sam. 23:1–2; Matt. 22:42–43; Acts 1:16; Heb. 3:7–11). Appearing where it does, "spiritual" certainly qualifies the term "songs," but since in the original it comes after the three terms and at the end of the clause, Leon Morris is surely right to point out that "'spiritual' *could* grammatically be taken with 'songs,' but *more probably* we should understand it as qualifying all three of the musical modes of which Paul is speaking."[25] If this is so, Paul is urging believers to sing the inspired praises that are to be found in the Psalter.

This conclusion finds support from these further facts: first, the apostolic command here to "sing psalms" supposes that a collection of praises was then in existence (cf. "search the Scriptures," John 5:39); second, the content of these praises is said to be "the word of Christ" (Col. 3:16) because Christ, by His Spirit, is the author of them and the speaker in many of them (1 Peter 1:10–11; cf. 3:18–20; Pss. 2:7; 22:1; 40:7); third, the added and explanatory words "making melody in your hearts" (*psallontes*), literally translated, would be rendered "psalming in your hearts," which is said here to be the result of singing the aforementioned praises; fourth, one of the reasons for singing these praises is that there may be a "teaching and admonishing [of] one another" (Col. 3:16), which is really the function of actual Scripture (Rom. 15:3–4; 2 Tim. 3:16–17); and fifth, if the Scripture's identification of these praises is rejected, there is absolutely nothing to indicate what these terms actually refer to, and so we are left to conjecture and speculation.

Viewing now the whole phrase "psalms, hymns and spiritual songs," the point should be made that it is not at all unusual in Scripture for there to be a piling up of such synonyms. Take, for example, the reference to God's revealed law in the following three-fold description of it: "Walk in my statutes, and execute my judgments, and keep all my commandments"; or the reference to supernatural works by use of the three terms "miracles and wonders and signs"; or the reference to reverent request using three like terms: "supplications, prayers, intercessions" (1 Kings 6:12: Acts 2:22; 1 Tim. 2:1). Evidently these terms are different designations for the same thing, and they are used for the purpose of emphasis. Even so, "psalms, hymns and spiritual songs" is a triad of terms indicating the number, variety, and totality of the psalms contained in the book of Psalms.

A further command is found in the epistle written by James. "Is any merry?" James asks, "Let him *sing psalms*" (5:13, emphasis added). Again, there is but one word in the Greek, *psalleto*, "let him psalm." We would not expect the presiding minister of the Jerusalem church, who felt responsibil-

---

25. Leon Morris, *Expository Reflections on the Letter to the Ephesians* (Grand Rapids: Baker Books, 1994), 117.

ity for gathered and scattered Jews, to think or say otherwise than he does in this particular verse. According to James, inner cheerfulness and rejoicing should be expressed in psalm singing—and he certainly has biblical support for this. "Let us come before his presence with *thanksgiving*, and make a *joyful noise* unto him with psalms" (Ps. 95:2, emphasis added).

There is, then, for psalm singing, both example and command in the Holy Scriptures, but there is not one single example or command justifying the use of uninspired songs in the public worship of God. Some detect hymn fragments in such passages as Ephesians 5:14, Philippians 2:5–11, and Colossians 1:15–20, but this is pure surmise and conjecture, rejected by many competent scholars. The idea takes no account of the fact that when an inspired writer is moved with strong emotion, he often does express himself in a poetical and even in a rhythmical way. This gives no support to the theory that the writer is quoting some first-century uninspired hymns. Besides, church history gives no indication whatsoever that these—or other similar portions—were ever sung in early Christian worship.

Others appeal to passages in the book of Revelation that contain words of heavenly praise, and these are cited as clear examples of original Christian hymns (Revelation 5:9–10; 12–13; cf. 4:8, 11; 7:10–12; 11:17–18; 15:3–4). However, there is no authority or warrant for singing these words in formal church worship. They were sung by celestial angels and glorified saints. How can they be said to provide material for believers on earth? Should we take these "songs" to be intended for our worship, strict consistency would require that we introduce other features of the worship described in this book, namely, the golden crowns, the white robes, the harps, the altars, and so on. The truth is that any argument based on the highly figurative book of Revelation to justify praise other than inspired psalms will not only present us with insurmountable problems of interpretation, but it will also expose us—and the whole visible church here below—to serious errors and dangers, such indeed as would corrupt the purity of prescribed worship.

A final word on this: if the argument from these passages could still somehow be sustained, it would not even then prove the acceptability of uninspired praise. The passages in question appear in Scripture, and, that being the case, they are evidently inspired by the Spirit of God.

The Sufficiency of the Psalms

There is one question remaining: is the book of Psalms adequate and sufficient for the worship of the Christian church? In answer to that question, several points may be made and offered for consideration.

1. As inspired, this book of Psalms is "perfect," like the moral law contained in the Ten Commandments (Pss. 19:7–8; 119:96), and therefore, having no defect, it needs neither correction nor supplementation.

2. Its admission into Scripture with the unique title *Sepher Tehillim* (Book of Praises) declares that its contents are designed by God to be suitable and adequate material for the church's worship until the end of time. God meant His people to sing these songs—not to paraphrase or imitate them (1 Chron. 16:9; 2 Chron. 29:30).

3. Like other parts of God's written Word, the things contained in this book were not only given for believers in a former age, but they were given "for us also," "for our learning," and even "altogether for our sakes" (Rom. 4:24; 15:4; 1 Cor. 9:10; cf. 1 Peter 1:12). These inspired praises are intended for Christian believers, hence the exclusive use the Lord and His apostles made of them.

4. Our Lord as "the messenger of the covenant" (Mal. 3:1) supplied all the needs of the Christian church, but the fact that He made no provision for another book of psalms, or even for a supplement to the existing book, shows that He considered this book both suitable and complete.

5. The Lord Jesus Christ is the composer of these psalms (Col. 3:16), and He is also the precentor of them when they are sung in His church (Heb. 2:12—"in the midst of the church will I sing praise unto thee"). We would not expect the Son of God to sing anything but inspired and perfect praise. It is clear He would not expect us to sing anything else either. If Christian experience can be summed up in terms of union and communion, then in the Psalms we have exactly what is required as a means to that end. We have fellowship with the Lord in singing the inspired Psalms. Why would believers want to look elsewhere for their praises?

6. Such is the treasury in this book, including so much about Christ and His great salvation (Luke 24:44; Rom. 4:6–8), that there is no need for the composing of other praises. The early

church, believing this, sang only the psalms at the beginning of
its history and then for many years afterwards.

7. If psalm singing is an ordinance of worship, then the presence
and blessing of God will attend our observance of it: "Thou art
holy, O thou that inhabitest the praises of Israel" (Ps. 22:3). In
the singing of the Psalms, we may therefore expect our God to
be with us, for the good of our souls. It is enough!

Conclusion: The Paradise of Praise

We conclude with the words of Donald McLaren, who writes concerning
the Psalms:

Those that worship him in truth, tremble at his word. He not only
requires them to present, but directs them where they will find, the
appointed offerings of praise, pure and acceptable. They follow his
directions. They go to the broad, bright field of *revelation*. Directly
before them, when they enter it, they behold, as it were in the centre
of the field, a garden enclosed, and over its gates, PRAISE.... Its
fruit is for the throne of God, and they that gather it may eat it and
praise the Lord. Various, pleasant and good, is its fruit—so good
that angels would be pleased to gather it, and so abundant that all
the angels of heaven, and all the redeemed from amongst men, would
not be able, by their gathering, to make it less. Its trees of life, beautiful as fruitful, were pruned when planted of old, by the hand of God,
and it needs not the hand of man to prune again, or to plant more.
This is the appointed, perfect Paradise of praise, for the church on
earth, from which we may get a good view of all the wondrous works
of God, and especially a good view of the sufferings and glories of
Christ, and by the light of that glory, a good view of the Paradise of
praise and bliss, prepared in heaven for the redeemed. Here let us
stay and keep all these things in view, and *praise the Lord*.[26]

---

26. Donald McLaren, *The Psalms of Holy Scripture, the Only Songs of Zion* (Geneva,
N.Y.: Ira Merrell, Printer, 1840), 59–60.

Part 3

Psalm Singing and the
Twenty-First-Century Church

Chapter 9

Psalm Singing and Redemptive-Historical Hermeneutics: Geerhardus Vos's "Eschatology of the Psalter" Revisited

ANTHONY T. SELVAGGIO

I am both an advocate for psalm singing and an advocate for biblical theology and the redemptive-historical approach to Scripture. Many consider these simultaneous commitments to be irrefutable evidence of my theological schizophrenia. After all, how can someone who is committed to biblical theology, which emphasizes the progressive nature of revelation, believe that the church should sing only songs from the old covenant? Because the Psalms reside in the text of the Old Testament, many advocates of the redemptive-historical approach contend that they are redemptive-historically deficient for use in Christian worship. For example, in his essay "Redemptive History and the Regulative Principle of Worship," Dominic Aquila writes, "Since the consummation of God's redemptive revelation is in Christ, we need to speak and sing of Christ in all his fullness. Singing the Palms is good but incomplete; we need to see and sing about the anticipation of Christ's coming, but in the fullness of Christ's completed redemptive work (Luke 24:44)."[1] At first glance, it seems that biblical theology and psalm singing are mutually exclusive positions and that the idea of a redemptive-historical psalm singer is an oxymoron.

My purpose in this essay is to convince you otherwise. My goal is to demonstrate that there are cogent biblical, theological, eschatological, and redemptive-historical reasons to sing the Psalms in the era of the new

---

1. In *The Hope Fulfilled: Essays in Honor of O. Palmer Robertson*, ed. Robert L. Penny (Phillipsburg, N.J.: P&R, 2008), 265.

covenant. I will make this case by revisiting a lesser-known writing of the most well known of biblical theologians—Geerhardus Vos.

Geerhardus Vos: The Father of Reformed Biblical Theology

It is widely accepted that Geerhardus Vos (1862–1949) is the father of Reformed biblical theology. Vos assumed this patriarchal position because Princeton Seminary recruited him to join the faculty to defend the Reformed faith against the rising tide of liberal biblical theologians.[2] In 1893, Vos acquiesced to Princeton's call and filled the newly created chair of biblical theology. Vos proceeded to have an illustrious career at Princeton, during which he penned numerous journal articles and sermons. After his retirement, Vos's teaching notes were edited and compiled, primarily by his son Johannes, into his two most influential books, *Biblical Theology: Old and New Testaments* and *The Pauline Eschatology*. While Vos made many significant contributions to the discipline of biblical theology, perhaps his greatest contribution was his understanding of the role of eschatology in redemptive history. One simply cannot begin to understand Vos's writings or theological contributions without first grasping the prominent place eschatology occupies in his understanding of revelation.

While many theologians and laymen consider eschatology a matter of last things, Vos understood it as a matter of first things. For example, Vos considered eschatology to be the key to understanding *pre-redemptive* revelation (revelation occurring before the Fall). He wrote, "In so far as the covenant of works posited for mankind an absolute goal and unchangeable future, *the eschatological may be even said to* have *preceded the soteric religion*" (emphasis mine).[3] Likewise, Vos also viewed eschatology as the key regulative dynamic controlling the trajectory of *redemptive* revelation (revelation occurring after the Fall): "In sum, the original goal remains regulative for the redemptive development of eschatology aiming to rectify the results of sin (remedial) and uphold, in connection with this, the realization of the original goal as that which transcends the state of rectitude

---

2. David B. Calhoun, *Princeton Seminary: The Majestic Testimony* (Carlisle, Penn.: Banner of Truth, 1996), 2:138.

3. Geerhardus Vos, *The Pauline Eschatology* (Phillipsburg, N.J.: P&R, 1994), 325, fn1.

(i.e., rising beyond the possibility of death in life eternal)."[4] Vos understood eschatology as being central to understanding the history of revelation and salvation.

The centrality of eschatology is also apparent in Vos's understanding of Pauline theology. For example, in *The Pauline Eschatology*, Vos argued that eschatology serves as the key to understanding the entirety of the Pauline corpus: "The eschatological strand is the most systematic in the entire fabric of the Pauline thought-world. For it now appears that the closely interwoven soteric tissue derives its pattern from the eschatological scheme, which bears all the marks of having had precedence in his mind."[5]

According to Vos, eschatology is central to understanding the meaning and direction of all of God's self-revelation recorded in the Scriptures; the entire trajectory of the Bible is propelled by an eschatological thrust.

Given Vos's emphasis on eschatology, it should come as no surprise that he applied a similar hermeneutic to the Psalter. He explored this topic in a lesser-known article entitled "Eschatology of the Psalter," which was originally published in the *Princeton Theological Review* in 1920.[6] In the paragraphs that follow, I will provide a brief summary of the significant points that Vos developed in this article and then apply some of his conclusions to the practice of psalm singing.[7] My purpose is to demonstrate how Vos's insights from this article support the idea that the Psalms are eschatologically and redemptive-historically sufficient for new covenant worship.

A Survey of Vos's "Eschatology of the Psalter"

Vos commenced his article on the eschatology of the Psalter by noting the modern tendency of printing New Testaments that include the Psalter as an appendix after the book of Revelation. He noted how most Christians would find this location of the Psalter a bizarre choice because it places the

4. Ibid., 74.

5. Ibid., 60.

6. This article was reprinted as an appendix in Vos's *The Pauline Eschatology*, 323–65. All references in this essay to Vos's "Eschatology of the Psalter" are made to the page numbers in *The Pauline Eschatology*.

7. For further reading on Vos's view of the eschatology of the Psalter, see Geerhardus Vos, *The Eschatology of the Old Testament*, ed. James T. Dennison, Jr. (Phillipsburg, N.J.: P&R, 2001), 131–44.

book of Revelation's "storm-ridden landscape" next to the "green pastures" and "still waters" of the Psalms.[8] Vos, however, thought this juxtaposition quite appropriate because he contended that the book of Revelation and the Psalms have much more in common than we might at first think. He was troubled by the fact that many had reduced the Psalter to mere devotional literature, and he desired to set the Psalter free from this restrictive interpretative schematic. He wrote that he wanted to "shake us out of this habit and force us to take a look at the Psalter's second face."[9] Vos assured his readers that if they allowed the Psalter to express itself fully, they would recognize its content's affinity with the book of Revelation because both are rife with eschatological import.

In the remainder of his article, Vos outlined his case that the theology of the Psalter is predominantly eschatological in nature. He built his case using six main points, which will be discussed sequentially in the paragraphs that follow.

The Psalter's Subjective/Objective Dynamic

The first area where Vos saw the eschatological nature of the Psalter emerging is in its unique subjective/objective dynamic. Vos explains this subjective/objective dynamic as follows: "The deeper fundamental character of the Psalter consists in this that it voices the subjective response to the objective doings of God for and among his people."[10] Vos observed that the Psalms reveal Israel's response (the subjective component) to the mighty acts of God in history (the objective component). According to Vos, the interaction between these two elements does not occur on a static plateau, but instead unfolds progressively in revelation, propelling the reader ever forward to the consummation. In essence, Vos argued that the subjective and objective dialogue of the Psalms proceeds on an upward eschatological trajectory wherein each interaction builds on the last, in staircase fashion, proceeding toward the expectation of the final age to come. Vos described this dynamic as follows: "Consequently, where religion entwines itself around a progressive work of God, such as redemption, its general

---

8. Vos, *Pauline Eschatology*, 323.
9. Ibid.
10. Ibid., 324.

responsiveness becomes prospective, cumulative, climacteric; it gravitates with all its inherent weight toward the end. A redemptive religion without eschatological interest would be a contradiction in terms."[11] While aspects of this subjective/objective interplay occur throughout Scripture, it takes on a unique shape and emphasis in the Psalter because the Psalter provides the richest repository of the subjective expressions and expectations of God's people.

The Psalter's Dynamic/Static Pattern

A second area where Vos saw the eschatological emphasis of the Psalter emerging is in its frequent and varied employment of eschatological concepts. He grouped these eschatological concepts into two basic categories: dynamic and static. According to Vos, the dynamic concepts include "Jehovah's accession to the kingship, the judgment, the conquest of the nations, the cup of wrath, the recovery of territory, the vindication of Israel, and the repulsion of the last great assault by the nations," and the static concepts include "peace, universalism, paradise restored, the dwelling of Jehovah's presence in the land, the vision of God, the enjoyment of glory, light, satisfaction of all wants, the outlook beyond death towards an uninterrupted contact with God and a resurrection."[12]

Vos contended that revelation provides us with a vacillating eschatological paradigm of dynamism (or cataclysm) and stasis. According to Vos, redemption and consummation are intrusive, violent, and disruptive acts (or dynamic concepts) that ultimately culminate in peace and stability for God's people (or static concepts). Vos argued that both the vocabulary and concepts of this dynamic/static pattern are abundantly present in the Psalter.

The Psalter's Pedagogical Function

A third area where Vos noted the Psalter's eschatological nature is in its eschatological pedagogy. Vos argued that the Psalter teaches the church how to live appropriately in light of its future. According to Vos, the Psal-

---

11. Ibid., 325.

12. Ibid., 332. In Vos's *Eschatology of the Old Testament* he lists additional eschatological expressions extant in the Psalms including "new song," "new things," "new creation," "new name," "set time," and "morning" (140–41).

ter, more than any other part of revelation, illustrates for the believer how to respond properly to eschatological expectations.

Vos pointed out that the church has historically made two great errors in responding to eschatology. The first error is to become "dead" to eschatology. The church often lives as if it has no eschatological expectation, and this can severely hobble its well-being and growth. Eschatology is meant to propel our hope, expectations, and even our godly living for Christ in this age. On the other end of the spectrum is a second error. The church can also become "overmuch pathologically alive" with regard to eschatology.[13] This error can lead the church to pursue the misguided path of over-realizing its eschatology and engaging in the type of end-times silliness often displayed in certain premillennial and dispensational traditions. Vos contended that the Psalter acts as a preventative against such errors by providing the believer with a template displaying the "normal working" of the church with regard to eschatology.[14] Thus, by immersing itself in the Psalter, the church can learn how to avoid these all too common eschatological errors and instead adopt a biblical ethos regarding its relationship to eschatology.

The Psalter's Unifying Power

A fourth element of Psalter eschatology noted by Vos is the unique way the Psalter makes us "aware of our vital unity with the church of the old dispensation."[15] Vos compared the power of the Psalms with the power of Old Testament prophetic revelation in maintaining the unity of the people of God in both dispensations. He argued that while the prophets do connect the New Testament believer to the Old Testament church through the fulfillment of prophecy—"by means of prophecy...we are sons of the prophets and of the *diatheke* God made with Abraham"—this connection is experienced only *objectively* by the believer: "But this is a purely objective bond; it is the bond between a program and its execution; it does not directly enable us to feel our oneness with the Old Covenant people of God."[16]

---

13. Vos, *Pauline Eschatology*, 332.
14. Ibid.
15. Ibid.
16. Ibid., 333.

In contrast to the prophets, Vos contended that the Psalms bequeath to the Christian the *subjective* reality of what it means to be the people of God:

> No sooner, however, do we pass out from the region of prophecy into that of psalmody, than we come into touch with something that is internally akin to us, a preformation of our own living religious embrace of the realities of redemption. This must be so all the more, because our whole New Testament life and heritage was, from the Old Testament point of view, an eschatological thing. Here, therefore, we find ourselves and them occupied with identical fact; what they eschatologically contemplated we retrospectively enjoy, and the religious apprehension of it, while formally different, is in essence the same. In the eschatology of the Psalms we may trace the embryonic organism of our own full-grown state.[17]

Vos adroitly illuminated the fact that the Psalter serves an eschatological nexus point for the church in both dispensations. Because of the Psalter's eschatological limberness, it transcends the limitations of the old covenant.

The Psalter's Messianic Element

A fifth aspect of the Psalter's eschatology noted by Vos is what he referred to as the "Messianic element" of the Psalms.[18] Vos described this messianic element in the following manner: "To speak of the preexistence of the Messiah in the Psalms may sound preposterous in many critical ears, but there is no escape from the force that draws in that direction, once the actual occurrence of the individual Messianic figure in the Psalter is recognized. The Messiah leads, as it were, a mysterious life, that is somehow woven into the life of his people."[19] Vos contended that the Messiah, the eschatological Lamb of God, looms over and shines through the Psalms, not just in the psalms that are explicitly messianic, but in all the songs of the Psalter. Vos expanded on this argument in his other writings, where he argued that the Psalms had a unique messianic role, noting that it is in "the Psalter that the term Messiah enters into the eschatological vocabulary."[20] Vos also argued that this messianic element of Psalter eschatology served

---

17. Ibid.
18. Ibid., 351.
19. Ibid., 356.
20. Vos, *Eschatology of the Old Testament*, 131.

as an additional point of union between the saints of both dispensations. According to Vos, the Psalter forces the saints of both dispensations to recognize their mutual dependence on the redemptive work of the Messiah. For example, Vos quoted the following messianic reference from Psalm 84:9: "Behold, O God our shield, and look upon the face of thine anointed," and then noted "how profoundly at one the Christian's Messianic orientation of faith" is with the Israelites who sang this song under the old covenant.[21]

Three Other Outstanding Characteristics
Finally, as his sixth point, Vos specifically enumerated three other "outstanding characteristics of Psalter-eschatology."[22] First, he noted the Psalter's use of history as a basis for eschatology. According to Vos, the Psalter displays for the Christian the living and true God who has acted in history, is acting in history, and who will act in history.[23] The believer's hope rests in trusting in the God who acts on behalf of His people. Vos recognized that the consistent temperament of the psalmist, regardless of his current distress, is "on the whole, one of serene confidence and quiet expectation" because the psalmist is aware that the future "proceeds with stately, unhastened, unretarded step from the council chamber of God."[24]

A second of these additional outstanding characteristics of Psalter-eschatology that Vos highlights is the Psalter's "God-centeredness."[25] The repetitive beat of the Psalter is that God controls the progress of redemption, and that redemption is performed by the Son, the eschatological covenant servant. The Psalter also reminds Christians that the redemptive work of the covenant servant is experienced corporately. Vos was careful to bring to the church's attention the reality that the psalmist's prayer for salvation is not primarily selfish or individualistic, but rather encompasses the collective struggle and deliverance of Israel as a whole.[26]

---

21. Vos, *Pauline Eschatology*, 357.
22. Ibid., 334.
23. Ibid., 335.
24. Ibid., 337.
25. Ibid., 338.
26. Ibid., 339.

The third of the three additional outstanding characteristics of Psal-ter-eschatology, according to Vos, is the Psalter's emphasis on the kingdom. Vos describes the Psalter as having "prevailingly kingdom-eschatology."[27] Here Vos stressed that the Psalms speak specifically to last things through frequent references to a kingdom motif in which God reigns as the exalted king over Israel, all nations, and the entire creation.

From this brief survey it is clear that Vos viewed the Psalms as pos-sessing unique and rich eschatological content. According to Vos, the Psalms are not static songs intended to be sequestered in the old covenant, but rather they are eschatological songs that are flexible enough to be rel-evant to God's people in any age. It is this inherent eschatological elasticity of the Psalms that renders them redemptive-historically sufficient for the worship of the new covenant church. In the next section, I will apply some of Vos's insights regarding Psalter eschatology directly to the practice of psalm singing.

The Redemptive-Historical Benefits of Psalm Singing

Although Vos was certainly not overtly arguing for psalm singing in his article on the eschatology of the Psalter, his insights are nonetheless very supportive of the practice. Perhaps anecdotal evidence of this contention can be found in the fact that one of Vos's sons and editors, Johannes G. Vos, chose to spend his entire adult life in theological service to an exclusively psalm singing denomination. Clearly J. G. Vos found no conflict between his father's biblical theology and the practice of exclusive psalmody.

In the paragraphs that follow I will specifically enumerate four redemptive-historical benefits of singing the Psalms that flow directly from Vos's insights on Psalter eschatology. These benefits not only serve as evidence that being a redemptive-historical psalm singer is not oxy-moronic, they also demonstrate an actual redemptive-historical advantage possessed by those who sing the Psalms.

1. *Singing the Psalms keeps our focus on the mighty acts of God.*
   One of the main emphases of Vosian biblical theology is its focus on the objective and mighty acts of God in history. According to biblical the-

---

27. Ibid., 342.

ology, the subjective aspects of our faith must always be derivative to the objective work of God. In other words, the Bible is not about us and what we are doing; it's about God and what He has done in the past, is doing in the present, and will do in the future. Biblical theology always demands that we relate to God theocentrically rather than anthropocentrically.

When new covenant saints sing the Psalms, they can be assured that they are always keeping the subjective and objective aspects of the faith in perfect biblical balance. The Psalms remind us that our faith is about God, not about us. This balance is in stark contrast to the modern trend of allowing the subjective experience of the believer to be sovereign in the music of the church. Much of contemporary worship music, and even much of traditional hymnody, is overwhelmingly focused on the subjective experience of the believer. Often the subject of modern church music is the believer and not God. In these modern songs the subject is predominantly oneself, with frequent use of pronouns such as I, me, or my. The focus is not primarily on the objective mighty acts of God, but rather it is on us. The Psalter is not void of personal pronouns—much to the contrary, it is rife with them—but the difference in the Psalms is that the subjective experience and response of the believer is always inextricably connected to, and subordinated to, the objective actions of God. Psalm singers are equipped to be better able to maintain their theological equilibrium in this regard. The psalm singer is compelled to keep the proper balance between God's mighty acts and our worshipful response.

2. Singing the Psalms saturates us with biblical eschatology.

As we've seen in this article, Vosian biblical theology stresses the centrality and all-pervasiveness of eschatology in the Scriptures. Eschatology is not something relegated to the last few pages of the Bible, but rather it permeates the entirety of biblical revelation and even precedes the introduction of soteriology in the unfolding of biblical history. This perspective on the importance of eschatology in our faith is not widely shared among Christians. For most Christians, eschatology is last things, not first things, and this very limited view of eschatology is what emerges in most humanly composed songs dealing with the subject (e.g., "When the Roll Is Called up Yonder"). The Psalms serve as a helpful corrective to this skewed mentality regarding the role of eschatology in our lives.

Psalm singing forces Christians to recognize the significance and all-pervasiveness of eschatology in the Christian life. The Psalms hold before our eyes the reality that God has intruded, and *will* intrude, into history in cataclysmic ways, ultimately yielding everlasting peace and rest for His people. The Psalms remind us that these historical intrusions have not ceased. The greatest intrusion is yet to come. Jesus will return. Psalm singing equips the believer to be on watch for God's kingdom intrusion to come. The Psalms encourage eschatological expectation and longing.

One of the ways the Psalter inculcates this eschatological expectancy is through its admonition to sing a "new song." Vos noted the connection between the phrase *new song* and the eschatological expectancy of Israel: "The worshiping congregation of Israel sing a 'new song' because their hearts are full of the 'new things' that are on the wing with which the air is already vibrant."[28] What Vos is saying here is that the Psalms became new songs to Israel every time they sang them because they were singing them in light of the new things that God was doing in Israel and in their own individual hearts. This dynamic implies that the Psalms were not meant to be relegated to one age, but were crafted with the ability to be ever new and self-refreshing.

The eschatological expectancy emphasized by the "sing a new song" admonition of the Psalms carries over to the new covenant saint who now sings these songs as new songs in light of the redemptive work of Christ. Michael Bushell helpfully reflects on this transitional dynamic: "The Old Testament Psalms may therefore in a particular sense be seen as 'new songs' because they have all taken on new significance in the light of their fulfillment in Christ and in the interpretive light that the New Testament sheds upon them."[29] The new covenant church can sing these old songs as new songs. Just like Israel, we Christians in the new covenant era understand the Psalms to be new songs because *our* hearts are full of new things.

But singing the Psalms not only helps Christians maintain a proper perspective on biblical eschatology, it also aids the Christian in cultivating a proper response to biblical eschatology. The psalm singer is continually confronted with the words and actions of the people of God in response

---

28. Vos, *Eschatology of the Old Testament*, 131.
29. Michael Bushell, *Songs of Zion* (Pittsburgh, Penn.: Crown and Covenant, 1999), 97.

to God's advancement of redemption. The church is to be encouraged with the progress of redemptive history, but it is simultaneously admonished to trust in God, and not in itself, to realize its eschatological destiny. Psalm singing helps us to avoid imbibing in a theology of glory and serves as a guard against the temptation to over-realize our eschatology. Vos described this beneficial attribute of the Psalms: "The Psalter teaches us before all else what the proper, ideal attitude of the religious mind ought to be with reference to its vision of the absolute future."[30]

3. *Singing the Psalms reminds us of the unity of God's people and plan.*

Those who sing the Psalms join their voices in praise with the saints of the old covenant. By singing the same songs as our fathers, we inevitably experience a unique sense of communion with them, and it forces us to remember that the covenant of grace did not begin to be unfolded in Matthew 1:1, but rather in Genesis 3:15. The Old Testament is not about a different God who made different promises. The Old Testament is also not about an entirely different church with entirely different salvific hopes and expectations. Simply put, the old covenant saints are not so different from us. Their hopes are our hopes. Their longings are our longings. Consider, for example, the words of William Perkins in his commentary on Hebrews 11 in which he discusses why new covenant saints should continue to sing the Psalms:

> The church, in all ages, consisted of a company of believers, and their faith is always one and the same; and this makes all that apprehend God's promises, to be like to one another in graces, meditations, dispositions, affections, desires, spiritual wants in the feeling and use of afflictions, in a course of life and conversation, and in performance of duties to God and man: and therefore, the same Psalms, prayers, and meditations, are now as fit for the church in these days, and are said and sung with the same use and profit to the church in these days, as when they were made.[31]

---

30. Vos, *Pauline Eschatology*, 332.

31. As quoted in Thomas Ford's *Singing of Psalms* (Australia: Presbyterian Armoury Publications, 2004), 64.

Singing the Psalms forces us to recognize what Vos referred to as the "vital unity" between the church in both dispensations. It forces us to inculcate a redemptive-historical and covenantal hermeneutic that embraces the organic unity of revelation and the people of God.

4. *Singing the Psalms enables us to see the glory of Christ in new ways.*

As Vos noted, the Psalms provide us with a unique and unparalleled window into the work and life of the Messiah. The redemptive-historical and biblical theological messianic robustness of the Psalms is evidenced by their prolific use in the New Testament. The human authors of the New Testament were divinely inspired redemptive-historical preachers of the finest sort. When they desired to show forth the truth of Christ from the Scriptures, they repeatedly and consistently turned to the verses of the Psalms. For example, in Bruce Waltke's fine article, "Christ in the Psalms," he notes that of the 283 direct quotes of the Old Testament in the New Testament, 116 (41 percent) are from the Psalter. Waltke also notes that in the Gospels the Psalms are used over fifty times to allude to the person and work of Jesus Christ. Waltke concludes, "The specific predictions of some Psalms that find their fulfillment in Jesus Christ combined with the use of the Psalter in the New Testament suggest that the entire Psalter pertains to Jesus Christ and his church."[32]

But the christocentric power of the Psalms is not limited to quotations and allusions to them in the New Testament text; it also extends to the reality that it is only in the Psalms that we can grasp the innermost thoughts of the Messiah, which cannot be found anywhere else in revelation. Vos described this unique feature of the Psalms: "Our Lord himself found his inner life portrayed in the Psalter and in some of the highest moments of his ministry borrowed from it the language in which his soul spoke to God, thus recognizing that a more perfect language for communion with God cannot be framed."[33] The most vivid example of this is how

---

32. In *The Hope Fulfilled: Essays in Honor of O. Palmer Robertson*, ed. Robert L. Penny (Phillipsburg, N.J.: P&R, 2008), 41. Terry Johnson, a contributor to this volume, does a superb job of demonstrating how the entire life and ministry of Christ is spoken of in the Psalter; see Terry L. Johnson, "Restoring Psalm Singing to Our Worship," *Give Praise to God* (Phillipsburg, N.J.: P&R, 2003), 262–63.

33. Vos, *Grace and Glory* (Edinburgh: Banner of Truth, 1994), 169–70.

the Psalms unfold for us the inner mind of Christ during His crucifixion. While the Gospels provide us with third-person external eyewitness testimony of the crucifixion of Jesus, the Psalms allow us to enter into the very existential experience of the Messiah on the cross. The Psalms give us Jesus from the first-person perspective. Just read Psalm 22, and you will understand the suffering of our Lord in new and profound ways. When a Christian sings the Psalms, he is exposed to Christ in a unique way.

A Redemptive-Historical Psalm Singer

Vos's "Eschatology of the Psalter" demonstrates that one can truly be a redemptive-historical psalm singer. Singing the Psalms does not reveal theological schizophrenia; rather, it is consistent with a redemptive-historical view of Scripture. The Psalms are redemptive- historically designed for use in the era of the new covenant. Jesus Himself demonstrated this point by employing them in the very first new covenant worship service—the Lord's Supper. Consider the following insights from Scottish Presbyterian William Binnie (1823–1886) as he reflected on the inaugural dawning event of the new covenant age: "The singing of the Hallel by Christ and the eleven in the guest-chamber on the night of His betrayal, may be said to mark the point at which the Psalter passed over form the old dispensation into the New: for it accompanied the celebration of the new ordinance of the Lord's Supper as well as the celebration of the expiring Passover. Thenceforward, it is assumed that at every gathering of Christians for mutual edification, some one will 'have a Psalm' to give out to be sung."[34]

Think about the power of the point Binnie is making here. At the very inflection point, at the hinge between old and new dispensations, as Jesus turned the page into the new covenant era, our Lord chose the Psalms as the celebratory hymns of the inaugural new covenant worship service. Whereas entirely new sacraments were required for this new age, the Psalter required no revision or replacement.

Christ's use of the Psalms at the first celebration of the Lord's Supper demonstrates that the Psalter was constructed to be enduring and relevant. When the disciples joined their Lord in singing, the Hallel Psalms

---

34. William Binnie, *A Pathway into the Psalter* (Birmingham, Ala.: Solid Ground, 2005), 376.

became "new songs" reflective of the new dispensation that Christ had just inaugurated. In other words, this nucleus of the new covenant church sang the Psalms redemptive-historically. This means the church can continue to sing them in a redemptive-historical manner in our own age.[35]

The inherent redemptive-historical elasticity of the Psalms explains why they have occupied a unique place in the life of the church throughout its history. This was true in the Old Testament church, the New Testament church, and throughout ancient, medieval, and modern church history as well. The Psalms are where the people of God are drawn when they desire to find words with which to commune with God. In one of his sermons, Vos reflected upon the indefatigable power of the Psalms in drawing God's people near to Him and in conveying the emotions of their hearts:

> Hence the Psalter has been at all times that part of Scripture to which believers have most readily turned and upon which they have chiefly depended for the nourishment of the inner religious life of the heart. I say that part of Scripture, not merely that part of the Old Testament, for even taking the Old and the New Testament together the common experience of the people of God affirms that there is nothing in Holy Writ which in our most spiritual moments—when we feel ourselves nearest to God—so faithfully and naturally expresses what we think and feel in our hearts as these songs of the pious Israelites.[36]

Those who sing the Psalms with the eschatological and biblical theological awareness that Vos demanded will find themselves drawn ever closer to their Lord. What could be more redemptive-historically satisfying and fulfilling than that?

---

35. Singing the Psalms in this manner does require some work, as is noted by D. G. Hart and John Muether: "Churches that only sing from the Psalter, then, need to have a good understanding of the Old Testament and how it reveals Christ. To be sure, this is not easily done. But the early church did sing Psalms, and therefore it is possible to sing them from the perspective of redemptive-historical fulfillment" (D. G. Hart and John Muether, *With Reverence and Awe* [Phillipsburg, N.J.: P&R, 2002], 163).

36. Vos, *Grace and Glory*, 169.

Chapter 10

Psalm Singing and Pastoral Theology

Derek W. H. Thomas

*J*ohn Calvin's statement concerning the book of Psalms is well known: "I have been accustomed to call this book, I think not inappropriately, 'An Anatomy of all the Parts of the Soul.'"[1] It summarizes the issue before us in this chapter well: the Psalms provide material for a *comprehensive* understanding and application of pastoral theology. Many of the psalms are written from the first-person perspective. They are, therefore, highly personal, and we read them as descriptive of *our own* spiritual journey. They speak of highs and lows, covering the entire range of human experiences—even some that we might find uncomfortable.

Given that the Psalms are a rich source of pastoral advice and counsel, we may well ask this question: what accounts for the general lack of psalm use in public worship these days? Carl Trueman provides an answer:

> I am not certain about why this should be, but I have an instinctive feel that it has more than a little to do with the fact that a high proportion of the psalter is taken up with lamentation, with feeling sad, unhappy, tormented, and broken. In modern Western culture, these are simply not emotions which have much credibility: sure, people still feel these things, but to admit they are a normal part of one's everyday life is tantamount to admitting that one has failed in today's health, wealth, and happiness society. And, of course, if one does admit to them, one must neither accept them nor take

---

1. John Calvin, "The Author's Preface" to *The Psalms of David and Others*, trans. Arthur Golding, in *Calvin's Commentaries*, 22 vols. (Grand Rapids: Baker Books, 1981), 4:xxxvii.

personal responsibility for them: one must blame one's parents, sue one's employer, pop a pill, or check into a clinic in order to have such dysfunctional emotions soothed and one's self-image restored.[2]

This essay is not a polemic for either an exclusive or inclusive psalms position regarding public worship; rather, it is on the use of the Psalms in pastoral theology. It is not possible to engage the topic without drawing attention to the fact that without a regular familiarity with the Psalms in the liturgy of public worship, many Christians find themselves at odds with their experience of what the Christian life means to them. What they *feel* as well as what they *understand* about what Christianity is meant to be is negated by a worship culture that is frequently too exclusively positive and upbeat. What they sing and hear during public worship does not match what they experience during the rest of the week. This often leads to cynicism, a loss of assurance, a schizophrenic experience of Christianity, and experiences of guilt that find little or no resolution. It would be an exaggeration to point the finger entirely in the direction of the church's failure to use psalms in worship for these ills, but this omission does account for a significant part of its current failure in adequate pastoral care.

Consider, for example, the Twenty-third Psalm—perhaps, in our own time, the most well-known and well-loved of all the psalms. It employs the image of shepherd: "The LORD *is* my shepherd" (v. 1, emphasis added). Pastoral care, after all, "came to be understood as poimenics or shepherding (*poimen*, shepherd)," writes Andrew Purves, adding, "even the names given to the practice of care, *pastoral* care, and to the caregiver, *pastor*, take their identity from this rural and agricultural metaphor."[3] The pastoral imagery of the Twenty-third Psalm describes "in a series of memorable tableaux the ever-changing terrains through which God may lead his people."[4] The shepherd not only leads his flock into lush green pastures beside still waters, where life is good and supplies are plentiful, but the shepherd

---

2. Carl Trueman, *The Wages of Spin: Critical Writings on Historic and Contemporary Evangelicalism* (Fearn, Ross-shire: Mentor, 2007), 158–59.

3. Andrew Purves, *Reconstructing Pastoral Theology: A Christological Foundation* (Louisville, Ky.: Westminster John Knox Press, 2004), xxvii.

4. Donald McLeod, "The Doctrine of God and Pastoral Care," in *Engaging the Doctrine of God: Contemporary Christian Perspectives*, ed. Bruce L. McCormack (Grand Rapids: Baker Academic, 2008), 246.

also leads his sheep into such scenarios as the valley of the shadow of death, where predators lurk and sorrow abounds and death awaits. Even the final scene, where the metaphor may well change from a shepherd to a host, with the psalm envisaging Christians enjoying warm hospitality and a fully laden table, is constrained by the fact that this feast is spread *in the presence of enemies* intent on doing harm. And it is here—in the face of hostility—that blessings come. As Donald McLeod comments, "There may be difficulty and danger all around, but we do not need to wait for changed circumstances to experience the divine blessing. The cup may overflow even in the midst of persecution, loss, stress, and pain. Indeed, at such times it may be especially full."[5] Such a rich expression of the nature of the pilgrim's life in communion with the Lord can be found almost nowhere else than here in the Psalms, but despite the familiarity of the Twenty-third Psalm, far too many Christians seem not to have understood its theological and pastoral instruction.

Window on the Soul

The Psalms are remarkably realistic. They address us at points of need and, more importantly, points of failure. The psalmists express anger and resentment at seeming injustice in the world and in their own experience. They cry for vengeance, expressing anger in ways that we modern believers find offensive. They move into the impenetrable darkness of the soul and make us cower in horror that believers should ever speak in such a fashion. They boil with disbelief that their circumstances are what they are, and all the while they do so, taking their pent-up feelings to the Lord in worshipful prayer.

Consider for a moment the so-called imprecatory psalms. Whatever else they may mean, they are surely, considered at their most basic level, pleas for justice to be done and the right to be vindicated. They are a cry against the seeming unfairness of life in this world where good is penalized and wrong given a status of honor. Everyone—Christians too—knows what we moderns call "the need for closure" when a terrible injustice has been done. We do not want to live in a world where the wicked prosper at so many levels. Thus the plaintive cry of Asaph in Psalm 73: "I was envi-

5. Ibid.

ous at the foolish, when I saw the prosperity of the wicked. For there are no bands in their death: but their strength is firm. They are not in trouble as other men; neither are they plagued like other men" (vv. 3–5).

All of us can relate to this sentiment in one way or another, even if we would be reluctant to say, "Let there be none to extend mercy unto him: neither let there be any to favour his fatherless children. Let his posterity be cut off; and in the generation following let their name be blotted out" (Ps. 109:12–13).

Or, "O daughter of Babylon, who art to be destroyed; happy shall he be, that rewardeth thee as thou hast served us. Happy shall he be, that taketh and dasheth thy little ones against the stones" (Ps. 137:8–9).

While some argue that these sentiments violate basic New Testament ethics, others have argued strongly in a different direction. Derek Kidner argues,

> The history of David…gives proof enough that his passion for justice was genuine, not a cover for vindictiveness. There have been few men more capable of generosity under personal attack…and no ruler was more deeply stirred to anger by cruel and unscrupulous actions, even when they appeared to favour his cause. What he asked of God was no more—and could certainly be no less—than the verdict and intervention which a victim of injustice could expect from him, David himself, as king of Israel."[6]

Similarly, Johannes Vos argued that these psalms may still be employed in Christian worship:

> Because the act of God which was prayed for conflicted with no actual rights of men, and because the prayers themselves were uttered by the inspiration of the Holy Spirit and therefore must have been right prayers and could not have been immoral. The total destruction of evil, including the judicial destruction of evil men, is the prerogative of the sovereign God, and it is right not only to

---

6. Derek Kidner, *Psalms 1–72*, Tyndale Old Testament Commentaries, ed. D. J. Wiseman (Leicester: IVP, 1977), 26–27. For a brief summary and response to the ethical issues raised by the imprecatory psalms, see Alec Motyer, *The Story of the Old Testament*, ed. John Stott (Grand Rapids: Baker Books, 2001), 71–72. See also chapter 7 of this book (David P. Murray, "Christian Cursing?").

pray for the accomplishment of this destruction, but even to assist in
effecting it when commanded to do so by God himself.[7]

This is not the place to discuss the profound ethical issues that emerge
from the imprecatory psalms, but a more general point needs to be made
in relation to our topic in this chapter. Every Christian has experienced
to some degree or other an example of terrible injustice; in such circumstances, the desire for the wrong to be made right must form the basic
language of Christian piety and worship. If it does not, serious pastoral
problems ensue that are as difficult as the imprecatory desires.

But there are other negative passions expressed in the Psalms. Writing
of his experience of imprisonment following a conviction of libel, leading
British politician Jonathan Aitken—former defense minister and a cabi-
net minister as chief secretary to the treasury—wrote movingly of his first
night in Belmarsh Prison. Following the unimaginably lurid taunting of
fellow prisoners as they "chanted" obscene suggestions of what lay ahead
of him, Aitken writes:

> So I knelt down on the concrete floor and tried to say a prayer.
> Because I was so petrified by the shouts of menace around me at first
> I found it impossible to say even the simplest words of supplication.
> Then I remembered that just before going off to the Old Bailey to
> be sentenced a friend had put in my pocket a calendar style booklet
> entitled 'Praying the Psalms'. When I was searched on arrival at Bel-
> marsh it was confiscated for drug examination by sniffer dogs. But
> it was later returned to me.... So I turned up the page for 8 June. It
> recommended reading Psalm 130. [I] studied its eight short verses
> which began:

> > 'Out of the depths I cry to you O Lord
> > O Lord hear my voice.
> > Let your ears be attentive
> > To my cry for mercy'

> A warm and comforting wave of reassurance flooded over me. Sud-
> denly I realized that I was not as lonely, scared, helpless or vulnerable
> as I had thought. The author of the psalm had been there before me.

---

7. Johannes Vos, "The Ethical Problem of the Imprecatory Psalms," *Westminster
Theological Journal* 4 (1942): 134–35.

Some 3,000 years earlier he had experienced very similar emotions of despair to mine. He had found a route to climb out of his depths with God's help and he had signposted that route in beautiful poetry recorded for posterity in the 19th book of the Bible known as 'The Psalms.'[8]

This highly personalized testimony as to the pastoral nature of the Psalms highlights how in times of crisis the book of Psalms has proved immediately helpful. Unlike some parts of Scripture, the Psalms seem to reflect experiences that we all share. "Where we would pray *blandly*," writes Alec Motyer, "the Psalms pray *realistically*, facing up to the implications of what they are asking."[9]

Lamentations and Woe

The psalmist found God at the center of even the most severe testing. Psalm 74 is typical in two ways. First, it paints a thoroughly realistic portrait of life. There is no attempt at hiding the severity of the pain or the consequent doubt that it produces. Second, in the midst of the horror stands God in all His majesty and power: "Lift up thy feet unto the perpetual desolations; even all that the enemy hath done wickedly in the sanctuary.... For God is my King of old, working salvation in the midst of the earth" (vv. 3, 12). With a deft touch, the psalmist urges us to compare the size of our problem to that of the infinite majesty of God! No matter how potentially disastrous the threat, God is simply beyond comparison.

Because so many psalms fall into the category of lamentation,[10] their use as pastoral guides and templates is particularly fitting.[11] Various attempts have been made to identify psalms of lament, sometimes subcategorizing them into psalms of individual lament and laments of the

---

8. Jonathan Aitken, *Psalms for People under Pressure* (London, New York: Continuum, 2004), xii.

9. Alec Motyer, *A Scenic Route through the Old Testament* (Leicester: IVP, 1994), 64.

10. Some identify as much as a third of the Psalter as comprising lament psalms. See Bruce Waltke with Charles Yu, *An Old Testament Theology* (Grand Rapids: Zondervan, 2007), 876.

11. See D. Capps, "Pastoral Use of Psalms," *Dictionary of Pastoral Care and Counseling*, ed. Rodney J. Hunter and Nancy J. Ramsey (Nashville, Tenn.: Abingdon Press, 2005), 969–70.

corporate people of God.[12] Such psalms evoke an emotional response that opens the door to some tough questions: Does life make sense? Is there any real purpose to my pain? Why must every relationship end? Is God good? We may not want to admit that such questions arise in our hearts, but unless these questions find expression in the language of our worship (individual and corporate), it is likely that some significant distortions will arise in our relationship with God and each other. In addressing this issue, Tremper Longman and Dan Allender ask, "What are we to listen for in our emotions? The answer is, in part: *We are to listen for the direction of our heart. The question, What do I feel? is in fact another way of asking, Who am I? What direction am I moving in?*"[13]

Though such emotion-based use of the Psalms may result in an abuse in interpretation, it is important to realize that the Psalms have always functioned in this way—as release valves for pent-up feelings. They enable the worshiper to engage in, for example, the grief process in a way that honors the integrity of the psalm and a biblical anthropology. Psalm 13, for example, is a brief but compelling example. It is at once a prayer, a lament, an "impatient complaint flung upward by one who can bear his agony no longer—and protests, yes protests, that without the help of God he cannot live."[14]

> How long wilt thou forget me, O LORD? for ever? how long wilt thou hide thy face from me? How long shall I take counsel in my soul, having sorrow in my heart daily? how long shall mine enemy be exalted over me? Consider and hear me, O LORD my God: lighten mine eyes, lest I sleep the sleep of death; Lest mine enemy say, I have prevailed against him; and those that trouble me rejoice when I am moved. But I have trusted in thy mercy; my heart shall rejoice in thy salvation. I will sing unto the LORD, because he hath dealt bountifully with me (vv.1–6).

---

12. For an introductory-level entry point into psalm identification, see C. Hassell Bullock, *Encountering the Book of Psalms: A Literary and Theological Introduction* (Grand Rapids: Baker Books, 2001). For his analysis of lament psalms see pp. 135–50.

13. Tremper Longman and Dan Allender, *The Cry of the Soul: How Our Emotions Reveal Our Deepest Questions about God* (Colorado Springs, Colo.: Navpress, 1994), 25.

14. James L. Mays, *Preaching and Teaching the Psalms*, eds. Patrick D. Miller and Gene M. Tucker (Louisville, Ky.: Westminster John Knox Press, 2006), 167.

This is a prayer worthy of Job. Pain and sorrow are the psalmist's constant companions. The world about him is one of unrelenting hostility. As he looks at his life, he can see only one possible outcome—death. As you read the psalm, you can hear him beg for life, and as he does so, he feels the energy of faith and assurance swelling up within him. How is it possible that someone can be in such darkness, angry with God and forsaken by Him, and at the same time "rejoice" in Him? Is it possible to be angry with God and love Him at the same time? *Of course it is!* And only a saccharin-infused view of Christianity would dare think otherwise. If there can be no place for the haunting line that closes Psalm 88, paraphrased accurately as "darkness is my only friend" (v. 18), then those believers who find themselves in such darkness will have no basis for spiritual comfort.

The truth is, though we may *feel* that darkness surrounds us—and it is important that such feelings find expression other than engagement in denial—no Christian has ever felt the darkness as Christ did on the cross. In citing the opening verse of Psalm 22, we may ask (reverentially), what Scripture was suitable to utter at such a moment? Where would Jesus find the language of worship to fit *this* occasion? Bereft of all that was fitted to comfort Him—for example, the assurance of His Father's love or His own native sonship—He cries "My God!" rather than the usual "Father." "The inability to say 'Abba!'," writes Donald MacLeod, "suggests that at last the veil of (imputed) sin, ignominy and suffering was so impenetrable that his sonship was obscured even from himself: not necessarily in the sense that he doubted it but in the sense that it was not present as any consolation to his consciousness."[15] It is salutary to consider that the only material Jesus found suitable at such an hour was the language He had Himself employed in the synagogues of northern Judea.

The Pilgrim's Progress

John Bunyan employed the psalms at definitive moments in *Pilgrim's Progress* to great pastoral effect. When Christian stepped out of the path that led toward the Wicket Gate, he met Mr. Legality, who urged him to take a very different route to gain his salvation. Evangelist warned Christian

15. Donald MacLeod, *From Glory to Golgotha: Controversial Issues in the Life of Christ* (Fearn, Ross-shire: Christian Focus Publications, 2002), 91.

using the words of Psalm 2: "Take heed that thou turn not aside again, lest thou 'perish from the way, when his wrath is kindled but a little.'"[16] Later in the story, Christian and Hopeful are reassured of the King's presence, despite the possibility of robbers and thieves along the highway: "O, my brother, if he will but go along with us, what need we be afraid of ten thousands that shall set themselves against us" (Pss. 3:5–8; 27:1–3).[17] Alluding to the river imagery and the waters of cool refreshment from such passages as Psalm 65:9, Ezekiel 47, and Revelation 22, Christian and Hopeful take refreshment, at which point Bunyan writes:

> Behold ye how these Crystal Streams do glide,
> (To comfort Pilgrims) by the High-way side.
> The Meadows green; besides their fragrant smell,
> Yield dainties for them: and he that can tell
> What pleasant Fruit, yea, Leaves, these Trees do yield,
> Will soon sell all, that he may buy this field.[18]

Bunyan uses the familiar lines of the Twenty-third Psalm to similar effect. In the Valley of the Shadow of Death, he describes how one of the wicked ones comes up behind Christian and whispers blasphemies into his mind. Christian thinks he is the source of the blasphemies and is disconsolate. After Christian had traveled in this condition some considerable time, he thought he heard the voice of a man, as going before him, saying, "Though I walk through the Valley of the Shadow of Death, I will fear no evil, for thou art with me" (Ps. 23:4).[19]

Perhaps of greater interest is the way Bunyan employs Psalm 88, arguably the darkest of all the psalms. In part 2—the story of Christiana and her children—Bunyan describes how Mr. Great-Heart tells Mr. Honest about Mr. Fearing's troublesome path. Mr. Great-Heart apparently has no doubts about Mr. Fearing's salvation; nevertheless, the man's soul "was always kept very low…and that made his life so burdensome to himself, and so troublesome to others. [At this point Bunyan cites Psalm 88 in the

---

16. John Bunyan, *The Pilgrim's Progress*, ed. Roger Pooley (London: Penguin Books, 2008), 27.
17. Ibid., 135.
18. Ibid., 114.
19. Ibid., 69.

margin.] He was, above many, tender of sin: he was so afraid of doing injuries to others, that he often would deny himself of that which was lawful, because he would not offend."

Mr. Honest then asks, "But what should be the reason that such a good man should be all his days so much in the dark?" to which Mr. Great-Heart replies:

> There are two sorts of reasons for it. One is, the wise God will have it so: some must pipe, and some must weep. Now Mr. Fearing was one that played upon the bass. He and his fellows sound the sackbut, whose notes are more doleful than the notes of other music are: though indeed, some say, the bass is the ground of music. And for my part, I care not at all for that profession which begins not in heaviness of mind. The first string that the musician usually touches is the bass, when he intends to put all in tune. God also plays upon this string first, when he sets the soul in tune for himself. Only there was the imperfection of Mr. Fearing; he could play upon no other music but this till towards his latter end.[20]

Bunyan's use of the Psalms in these pastoral ways, dealing with issues of assurance, fear, bravery, courage, and faith, demonstrates how the Psalms, though written in specific contexts, can help us too in our own specific circumstances. Sinclair Ferguson summarizes it this way: "The psalms...show us how the people of God have grappled with their questions, doubts, desertions, and how God lifted them up and brought them into new light and joy."[21]

The Psalms, then, are a portion of Scripture with which Christians should be familiar. Digging from these mines will yield treasures of inestimable value. Whatever the issue may be—loneliness, bitterness, helplessness, melancholy, anger, frustration, joy, contentment, faithfulness, or a hundred other issues—the Psalms address them all. Calvin was correct: they are an anatomy of all the parts of the soul. Having made this statement in the preface to his commentary on the book of Psalms, the Reformer went on to write:

---

20. Ibid., 255.
21. Sinclair Ferguson, *Deserted by God?* (Grand Rapids: Baker Books, 1993), 12.

[T]he Holy Spirit has here drawn to the life all the griefs, sorrows, fears, doubts, hopes, cares, perplexities, in short, all the distracting emotions with which the minds of men are wont to be agitated. The other parts of Scripture contain the commandments which God enjoined his servants to announce to us. But here the prophets themselves, seeing they are exhibited to us as speaking to God, and laying open all their inmost thoughts and affections, call, or rather draw, each of us to the examination of himself in particulars in order that none of the many infirmities to which we are subject, and of the many vices with which we abound, may remain concealed. It is certainly a rare and singular advantage, when all lurking places are discovered, and the heart is brought into the light, purged from that most baneful infection, hypocrisy. In short, as calling upon God is one of the principal means of securing our safety, and as a better and more unerring rule for guiding us in this exercise cannot be found elsewhere than in The Psalms, it follows, that in proportion to the proficiency which a man shall have attained in understanding them, will be his knowledge of the most important part of celestial doctrine.[22]

Calvin's point is salutary: the more familiar we are with the Psalms, the better equipped we will be to face the journey that leads to the Celestial City.

---

22. Calvin, "The Author's Preface" to *The Psalms of David and Others*, 27–28.

Chapter 11

Psalmody and Prayer

J. V. Fesko

We live in a culture that desires near-constant entertainment, so it should not be much of a surprise to find an entertainment-driven understanding of music in the church. Sociologist Alan Wolfe, in his insightful *The Transformation of American Religion*, explains how pastors of megachurches use marketing research to identify the different contemporary music preferences of the people in their communities in an effort to make worship appealing, contemporary, and relevant. Wolfe explains, "The whole idea behind this approach is that secular culture, for all its faults, knows something about getting and retaining an audience."[1] What lies behind such assumptions is that the music in a worship service must be entertaining, and, if it is, churches will be able to retain visitors. Yet there is an underappreciated dimension of music in worship that has been passed by, ignored, or unknown, namely, songs as a form of congregational prayer.

If song in worship is a form of congregational prayer, then music in worship turns on an entirely different axis. No longer is music in worship a question of entertainment but rather an expression of personal and corporate worship and devotion. In such a light, singing psalms in worship takes on an important and significant role not only in corporate worship, but also in the corporate and individual prayer lives of Christians. This chapter will show the importance of psalmody for the growth and

---

1. Alan Wolfe, *The Transformation of American Religion: How We Actually Live Our Faith* (Chicago: University of Chicago Press, 2003), 29.

development of congregational prayer life by (1) showing the relationship between song and prayer; (2) briefly exploring the Psalter to show that it is a school of prayer, one for all seasons; and (3) demonstrating that by using the Psalter in corporate and private worship we learn not only how to worship but also how to pray.

Song and Prayer

Although John Calvin (1509–1564) treats many topics in his *Institutes of the Christian Religion*, prayer receives more attention than nearly any other. His locus on prayer is perhaps one of the more sublime in his text for theological students. Calvin explains that prayer is "a communion of men with God by which, having entered the heavenly sanctuary, they appeal to him in person concerning his promises in order to experience, where necessity so demands, that what they believed was not vain, although he had promised it in word alone." Calvin continues, "So true is it that we dig up by prayer the treasures that were pointed out by the Lord's gospel, and which our faith has gazed upon."[2] Prayer is of the greatest importance, then, for receiving the blessings of God in the gospel of Christ and confirming the promises that He has made to us. One of the key points that Calvin raises in his locus on prayer is singing in prayer, a dimension of prayer with which some might be unfamiliar. Calvin explains that the chief use of the tongue in the church's public prayers is corporate song. When the church of God gathers together in corporate song and offers its prayers, it does so with "one common voice, as it were, with the same mouth, we all glorify God together, worshiping him with one spirit and the same faith."[3] To be sure, Calvin does not create *ex nihilo* the connection between prayer and corporate song.

Calvin bases his understanding of corporate song as prayer from a number of statements from the Scriptures. For example, Calvin cites the apostle Paul: "I will pray with the spirit, and I will pray with the understanding also: I will sing with the spirit, and I will sing with the understanding also" (1 Cor. 14:15). In his commentary on 1 Corinthians,

2. John Calvin, *Institutes of the Christian Religion*, ed. John T. McNeill, trans. Ford Lewis Battles (Louisville, Ky.: Westminster John Knox, 1960), 3.20.2.
3. *Inst.* 3.20.31.

Calvin further explains the nature of Paul's statement: "When he says, 'I shall sing the Psalms,' or I shall sing, he is speaking specifically instead of generally. For, since the Psalms had as their themes the praises of God, he uses 'singing psalms' (ψάλλειν) for blessing or giving thanks to God. For in our prayers we either ask something from God, or acknowledge the blessing He has bestowed upon us."[4] Calvin sees Paul's statement as equating prayer and singing in worship. He also believes these song-prayers are informed by the Psalms. Another passage to which Calvin appeals is Colossians 3:16: "Let the word of Christ dwell in you richly in all wisdom; teaching and admonishing one another in psalms and hymns and spiritual songs, singing with grace in your hearts to the Lord." In Calvin's treatment of prayer, he not only saw corporate song as a dimension of corporate prayer, but also as a means to edify the church.[5]

Presently, many see music in worship as entertainment, something to satisfy the individual. Calvin, on the other hand, saw it as a corporate expression of prayer, offering thanksgiving and praise to God through Christ, informed by the Psalms, and for the mutual edification of the corporate body, not merely the individual. Calvin was not alone in his judgment, as other theologians such as William Ames (1576–1633), an early Puritan, came to a similar conclusion. Ames writes, "The lifting up of the heart to God is required along with the thing sung and following it—this is also the goal of the meditation. We are, therefore, said to sing in our hearts to the Lord (Col. 3:16). Sung psalms are a kind of prayer."[6] If we see corporate song as an expression of prayer, in what way does the Psalter inform our prayer lives?

Exploring the Psalter

So often one of the greatest needs in the life of the individual Christian is knowing how or what to pray in a given situation or circumstance. Whether they find themselves in a time of joy or sorrow, people are often

4. Calvin, 1 Corinthians, CNTC, ed. David W. Torrance and T. F. Torrance, trans. John W. Fraser (1960; Grand Rapids: Eerdmans, 1996), 292–93.

5. Inst. 3.20.32.

6. William Ames, The Marrow of Theology, trans. John Dykstra Eusden (Grand Rapids: Baker, 1997), 262–63.

at a loss for words. This problem is further exacerbated if a person is asked to pray publicly. Even a rather chatty person can be reduced to silence if he is asked to pray. Perhaps one of the reasons behind this, though certainly not the only one, is that people are often told that prayer is a conversation between the believer and God. Who needs to learn how to have a conversation? Is this not something that people intuitively know? Yet going to a dinner party or fellowship of some sort and engaging a person in meaningful and informative conversation can be quite difficult. In other words, people can quickly discover that there is an art to fine conversation. The same can certainly be said of prayer. Dietrich Bonhoeffer (1906–1945) explains that people think it odd "to learn how to pray." He writes, "This is a dangerous error, which is certainly very widespread among Christians today, to imagine that it is natural for the heart to pray." He explains, "We then confuse wishing, hoping, sighing, lamenting, rejoicing—all of which the heart can certainly do on its own—with praying. But in doing so we confuse earth and heaven, human beings and God."[7] Christ's disciples certainly felt inadequate and therefore asked Him to teach them how to pray. Christ gave His disciples what we now popularly call the Lord's Prayer (Matt. 6:9–13). However, the Lord's Prayer is not the only place in the Scriptures where we can learn how to pray.

Bonhoeffer explains that the church has to learn how to pray, but how is this to be done? Children learn to speak because their parents speak to them, and so they learn the language of their parents—they repeat phrases, words, and expressions. God has spoken to His children primarily through His Word, and so as His children, we learn to speak to God by repeating His own words back to Him. In doing so, we learn how to pray. In such Scripture-filled prayers, we learn how to speak to God using His words, dialect, and manner of speech, not the false, confused language of our sin-burdened hearts or of the idolatrous world around us. If we want to pray in all assurance and joy, then the Word of God must be our foundation in prayer as well as in our song-prayers. Through Jesus Christ and the Word, we learn how to pray and even how to sing. But Bonhoeffer singles out one book that is most suited for learning how to pray: "Now

---

7. Dietrich Bonhoeffer, *Prayerbook of the Bible*, in *Dietrich Bonhoeffer Works*, ed. Geffrey B. Kelly, trans. James H. Burtness (Minneapolis: Fortress, 1996), 155.

there is in the Holy Scriptures one book that differs from all other books of the Bible in that it contains only prayers. That book is the Psalms."[8] For this reason, Bonhoeffer titled his work *Prayerbook of the Bible*. Given the connection between prayer and song, however, the Psalms could also be called, the Prayer-Songbook of the Bible. In what way does the Psalter enrich, promote, and inform the prayer life of the church?

All too often people use Paul's famous statement as a crutch in their prayer lives: "For we know not what we should pray for as we ought: but the Spirit itself maketh intercession for us with groanings which cannot be uttered" (Rom. 8:26). Think of Paul's statement in the context of his rabbinical training—he was one who was intimately familiar with the Scriptures of the Old Testament. So when Paul writes that there are times when we know not how to pray, he is not addressing situations where our own slothfulness and lack of attention to the Scriptures starve and impoverish our prayer lives. Through a steady diet of the Psalms, we can learn how to pray. Bonhoeffer identifies a number of key themes that run throughout the many different kinds of psalms that are instructive for our prayer lives.

Creation

Meditating upon and singing psalms about the creation can certainly tune our hearts not only to sing praises about God's work of creation, but also fill our prayer lives with a wealth of things for which we can praise our Creator. So often our prayers are filled with long lists of personal needs. God certainly wants us to tell Him of our needs, but when we stumble and find it difficult to praise God for who He is and what He has done, creation psalms can certainly remedy this weakness. Bonhoeffer notes that Psalm 8 praises the name of God and His gracious act of creating man (male and female) as the crowning glory of His work of creation. Likewise, Psalm 19 extols the wonders of the creation but then leads to a reflection upon the revelation of God's law and calls us to repentance.[9] However, if we praise God and reflect upon His wonderful work as Creator, we will inevitably be drawn to His outpouring of mercy in redemption. Who can pray about the

---

8. Bonhoeffer, *Prayerbook*, 156.
9. Ibid., 163.

glories with which man was crowned, of which the psalmist writes, "What is man, that thou art mindful of him? and the son of man, that thou visitest him?" (Ps. 8:4), without being reminded of man's fall into sin?

But in such a prayer, if we follow the Psalter and the One to whom it ultimately points, then with King David, we are inexorably led to the grand revelation of his greater son, Jesus Christ. With good reason, therefore, when Paul reflects upon Psalm 8, he connects this psalm with the resurrection and ascension of Christ, of whom he writes, "For he hath put all things under his feet" (1 Cor. 15:27), echoing Psalm 8:6b. In other words, according to Paul's inerrant, infallible, and authoritative commentary on Psalm 8, it is not only a psalm about the creation of man but ultimately about Christ, the Son of Man, who restores order to God's creation.[10] We must remember when we read, pray, or sing the psalms, that they are primarily about Christ. Bonhoeffer notes in this respect: "If we want to read and to pray the prayers of the Bible, and especially the Psalms, we must not, therefore, first ask what they have to do with us, but what they have to do with Jesus Christ. We must ask how we can understand the Psalms as God's Word, and only then can we pray them with Jesus Christ."[11]

The Suffering Messiah

The suffering Messiah is the subject of a number of psalms, most notably Psalms 22 and 69. Christ utters Psalm 22 during His suffering upon the cross: "And at the ninth hour Jesus cried with a loud voice, saying, Eloi, Eloi, lama sabachthani? which is, being interpreted, My God, my God, why hast thou forsaken me?" (Mark 15:34; cf. Ps. 22:1). Jesus was not merely pulling this phrase out of the psalm; rather, He had the entire psalm in mind. This has not gone unnoticed, and Psalm 22 has come to be called the fifth gospel account of the crucifixion. When we read of David's suffering as a messiah, one anointed by God to be king over Israel, we know that he was pointing forward to *the* Messiah. Think, for example, of what David writes in verses 17 and 18, "I may tell all my bones: they look and stare upon me. They part my garments among them, and cast lots

---

10. See Patrick Henry Reardon, *Christ in the Psalms* (Ben Lomond, Calif.: Conciliar Press, 2000), 15–16; also G. K. Beale and D. A. Carson, eds., *Commentary on the New Testament Use of the Old Testament* (Grand Rapids: Baker, 2007), 745–46.

11. Bonhoeffer, *Prayerbook*, 157.

upon my vesture," and then reflect upon the Roman soldiers casting lots for Christ's clothing (John 19:24).

When we sing-pray a psalm such as this, we are driven out of our-selves, away from the introspective gaze upon our own souls, and our faith looks extraspectively to Christ, His suffering, and His work on our behalf. But such prayer in song not only drives us to the crucified Messiah but also gives us hope in our own persecutions, great or small, for the sake of the name of Christ. Bonhoeffer observes, "We can pray this psalm only in community with Jesus Christ as those who have participated in the suffering of Christ. We pray this psalm not out of our random personal suffering, but out of the suffering of Christ that has also come upon us. But we always hear Jesus Christ praying with us and through him that Old Testament king. Repeating this prayer, without ever being able to measure or experience it in its entire depth, we walk with Christ praying before the throne of God."[12]

Such a psalm can be a great source of encouragement in the face of persecution from unbelieving family, co-workers, or even from others in places where there is great physical violence and hostility directed toward the church of Christ. Indeed, the psalm ends on a note of hope: "I will declare thy name unto my brethren: in the midst of the congregation will I praise thee" (Ps. 22:22). The author of Hebrews connects this verse with the finished work of Christ (Heb. 2:11–13).[13] As we sing-pray psalms like this, we are not only giving thanks for the work of Christ, but also praying for our deliverance from persecution in a God-honoring way.

Suffering

Intense personal suffering is something with which many in the church are intimately familiar. But the problem with many contemporary forms of worship music is that there is no place given for an expression of such suffering. In a day when many Christians associate suffering with failure or as the just consequence of hidden and unrepentant sin, like Job's so-called friends, people are all too ready to dispense with depression and sadness in their prayer lives and especially in congregational song. Yet reflect upon

---

12. Ibid., 166.
13. Beale and Carson, *New Testament Use of the Old Testament*, 947–49.

the lives of the saints of the Old Testament—Abraham, Joseph, David, or Jeremiah. They are marked by great periods of trial and sadness. A quick read of the Psalter will most certainly leave us with the impression that there were many days of despair for the author. Much of contemporary culture will tell us to take a vacation, pop a pill, or make a new purchase to alleviate ourselves of whatever ails us.[14] Then we are told to clap and sing away our sadness in church. But what happens when the music goes silent and we are back at home, still burdened by our trial, depression, or grief?

Here is where the prayer book of the Bible is so instructive to our prayer lives. The Psalter, notes Bonhoeffer, knows of all sorts of grief and sorrow: serious illness, imprisonment, deep isolation from God, threats, persecution, and any other type of peril one can find on earth (Psalms 13, 31, 35, 41, 44, 54, 55, 56, 61, 74, 79, 86, 88, 102, 105, and many others).[15] The Psalter knows nothing of trite answers but instead offers shelter beneath the mighty wings of God in Christ. As we sing-pray such psalms, whether as individuals or even corporately as a church, we cry out to God using His own words, telling Him that we are desperately in need of His grace and mercy in Christ. We admit we are unable to carry the burden, and we cast it upon Christ. As Bonhoeffer writes, "That is the goal of all the psalms of lament. They pray about the one who took upon himself our sickness and bore our infirmities, Jesus Christ. They proclaim Jesus Christ as the only help in suffering, for in Christ is God with us."[16] In our prayer-songs, we learn how to give expression to our laments as well as how to seek shelter in God's mercy in Christ. The Psalms shape our hopes, our expectations, and our character, as God uses His Word to conform us to the image of His Son. Perhaps we don't know how to pray in times of sorrow and lament because we have not sat in the Psalter's school of prayer. Perhaps we don't know how to sing in times of sorrow because we have not learned how to sing the blues in a godly, Christ-centered way. The world knows how to sing only the blues—such sorrow is worldly. The Psalter teaches us to sing-pray the blues in the hope of redemption and deliverance—in the hope of Christ.

14. Carl R. Trueman, *The Wages of Spin: Critical Writings on Historic and Contemporary Evangelicalism* (Fearn: Mentor, 2004), 159.

15. Bonhoeffer, *Prayerbook*, 169.

16. Ibid., 170.

Building Our Prayer Lives

We have surveyed only a few of the main themes that are found in the Psalter, but hopefully this brief exploration shows us how we can enrich our prayer lives through singing the Psalms. However, there are a few other things that we should observe that can be helpful in building our prayer lives through psalmody, both corporately and individually.

Careful Attention to the Words of Prayer
Pastors and elders should make a concerted effort to explain what congregational singing is. Most every church sings in worship, but few actually understand why they sing. If pastors made an effort to show biblically how singing functions in the life of the church, more people would understand that it is an expression of corporate prayer. As the congregation comes to know that they pray when they sing, they might also pay greater attention to the actual words of what they are singing. One of the dangers in the use of music in worship is that people get carried away with the tune without focusing upon the words. This problem was identified a long time ago by St. Augustine (354–430). Augustine grew concerned when the music moved him more than the actual words of the song, so he was on guard against this. "Nevertheless," he writes, "when I remember the tears which I poured out at the time when I was first recovering my faith, and that now I am moved not by the change but by the words being sung, when they are sung with a clear voice and entirely appropriate modulation, then again I recognize the great utility of music in worship."[17] Knowing that we are in prayer as we sing can help remind us to focus upon the words, and in this case, the words of Scripture, the Psalms.

Singing in the Name of Christ
One of the more crucial elements of prayer is the recognition that we pray in the name of Christ because He is our mediator before the throne of God; He intercedes on our behalf in the heavenly Holy of Holies. As John writes in his first epistle: "And if any man sin, we have an advocate with the Father, Jesus Christ the righteous" (1 John 2:1). Likewise, Christ tells

---

17. Augustine, *Confessions*, trans. Henry Chadwick (Oxford: University Press, 1991), 10.33.50.

us: "Verily, verily, I say unto you, Whatsoever ye shall ask the Father in my name, he will give it you" (John 16:23). However, to sing in the name of Christ does not simply mean to end the song with the phrase, "in Jesus' name, amen." Rather, it is recognition that as we sing the psalms we pray to God through Christ in the power of the Holy Spirit. A vital element of this is to recognize that the Psalm that we pray-sing is ultimately about Christ. People are ready to identify some psalms as messianic because they so prominently feature the Messiah, such as Psalms 2, 16, 22, or 110. However, we should understand that every psalm is messianic.

Every psalm relates to the person and work of Christ in some sense.[18] Bonhoeffer has a helpful observation regarding how we can identify how Christ is legitimately present in the psalms:

> According to the witness of the Bible, David, as the anointed king of the chosen people of God, is a prototype of Jesus Christ. What befalls David occurs for the sake of the one who is in him and who is to proceed from him, namely Jesus Christ. David did not remain unaware of this, but 'being therefore a prophet, and knowing that God had sworn with an oath to him that he would set one of his descendants upon his throne, he foresaw and spoke of the resurrection of the Christ' (Acts 2:30f). David was a witness to Christ in his kingly office, in his life, and in his words.[19]

A helpful exercise for congregational prayer and song life is for the pastor to preach sermons from the Psalms, show where and how Christ is present, and then have the congregation sing-pray the psalm that he just preached. With such a practice, not only will the church grow in its understanding of redemptive history and the work of Christ, but also in its prayer life as it takes upon its lips and in its hearts the revelatory Word of God in Christ in song-prayer.

The Psalms in Private Worship

Another important dimension of psalmody for the prayer life of the congregation is the use of the Psalms in private worship. Public worship is the

---

18. On this point see the discussion in Richard P. Belcher, Jr., *The Messiah and the Psalms: Preaching Christ from All the Psalms* (Fearn: Mentor, 2006), 1–20.

19. Bonhoeffer, *Prayerbook*, 158–59.

fulcrum for the spiritual life of the church, but it should always be supplemented with a steady diet of private worship, reading and studying the Scriptures, and prayer. If one looks to the Psalter as part of that diet, then his prayer life can be greatly enriched. Through psalm singing, a person becomes better equipped to understand and even memorize large portions of Scripture. Bonhoeffer notes, "In the early church it was nothing unusual to know 'the entire David' by heart. In one eastern church this was a prerequisite for an ecclesiastical office. The church father Jerome says that in his time one could hear the Psalms being sung in the fields and gardens. The Psalter filled the life of early Christianity. But more important than all of this is that Jesus died on the cross with words from the Psalms on his lips."[20]

This observation demonstrates how psalmody in private worship can permeate our lives, so much so that we can carry the Word of God upon our lips and hearts in moments of joy, trial, sorrow, or persecution. Just as the Psalms were a source of comfort for David, Solomon, faithful Israelites, and even Christ Himself, they can be a wealth of blessing and comfort to us in our own day-to-day lives.

Conclusion: Pray-Singing the Psalms

In a time when churches seek to entertain and woo visitors to their churches with all sorts of music, greater attention needs to be given to the scriptural teaching that song in worship is a corporate prayer. In pray-singing the Psalms, we sing the Word of God, learn how to pray by speaking the words of our heavenly Father back to Him, and find a source of joy, consolation, and encouragement, as well as a food source for our sanctification and growth in grace. If we do not know how to pray, could it be that we know not because we sing not the Psalms? The words of Bonhoeffer seem like an appropriate way to end this chapter: "Whenever the Psalter is abandoned, an incomparable treasure is lost to the Christian church. With its recovery will come unexpected power."[21] Bonhoeffer's observation is true not only for our prayer life, but also for the song-life and worship of the church. Psalmody is a vital element in the prayer life of the church that must be recovered and practiced.

---

20. Ibid., 162.
21. Ibid.

Scripture Index

Scripture Index

137	111, 112
137:3	130, 133, 134
137:4	131
137:8–9	165
138–145	106
139	111
139:14	89
139:19–22	115
139:21–24	118
140	111
144	ix
144:9	ix, 89, 132
145–150	42
145:3	125, 126, 127
145:10	125
145:17	89
146–150	106
146:6	42
147:7–9	125
148:13	125
149	ix
149:1	ix, 140
150	ix, 14
150:6	106, 110

Proverbs

24:17–18	112
25:21–22	112

Isaiah

26:19	126, 127
30:29	133
35:10	126
38:9–20	130
38:10–20	100
38:20	99, 100
40:8	133
42:10	89
43:7	125
43:21	125
44:23	124

48:11	125
58:13–14	123
60:21	125

Jeremiah

7:31	122
17:14	125

Ezekiel

47	170

Daniel

4	119
6:10	5
10:21	124

Amos

8:3	130

Habakkuk

3:1–19	100, 130

Malachi

3:1	143

NEW TESTAMENT

Matthew

1:1	158
5:43–44	112
6:9–13	123
15:3	123
15:9	123
21:13	135
22:42–43	140
23	117
23:13–29	116
23:39	84

26:30	3, 29, 31, 84, 123, 136, 138, 140	20:19	123
28:18–20	135	20:26	123
28:19–20	123		
28:20	123	**Acts**	
		1:16	131, 140
Mark		1:20	113, 130, 140
1:39	135	2:22	141
12:36	131, 135	2:24–26	43
14:22–25	123	2:26	125
14:26	3, 84, 136, 138, 140	2:30f	182
		2:41–42	123
14:36	4	2:42	123
15:34	4, 178	2:44–45	2
		2:46	139
Luke		2:46–47	123, 126
1	139	3:1	6
1:46–55	89	4:23–31	109
1:67–79	89	4:24	42
2	139	4:24–30	139
4:16	135	4:25	42, 128, 131
18:1–8	117	4:25–26	42
20:42	130, 135, 139	4:27–28	43
24:27	135	4:29–31a	43
24:44	84, 131, 135, 140, 143, 147	4:31	139
		13:5	139
24:44–45	135	13:9–12	119
24:53	139	13:14	135, 139
		13:14–15	123
John		13:33	140
2	108	15:21	82, 123
2:12–22	83	16:25	85, 137
2:17	108	17:11	123
3	83	17:25	124
4	83	17:28	90
4:23–24	83, 123	20:7	123
5:39	141		
10:23	135	**Romans**	
16:23	182	1:20	125
19:24	179	3:10–14	140
19:28	4	3:18	140
		4:6–8	143

Contributors

Joel R. Beeke is president and professor of systematic theology and homiletics at Puritan Reformed Theological Seminary and a pastor of Heritage Netherlands Reformed Congregation in Grand Rapids, Michigan.

Robert Cathcart is the pastor of Friendship Presbyterian Church in Laurens, South Carolina.

J. V. Fesko is academic dean and associate professor of systematic theology at Westminster Seminary California and an ordained minister in the Orthodox Presbyterian Church.

W. Robert Godfrey is president of Westminster Seminary California and a longtime professor of church history whose major research interest is the Reformation.

D. G. Hart has served as director of the Institute for the Study of American Evangelicals at Wheaton College and is currently the director for partnered projects at the Intercollegiate Studies Institute.

Terry Johnson is the senior minister of Independent Presbyterian Church, Savannah, Georgia.

Michael LeFebvre is pastor of Christ Church Reformed Presbyterian in Brownsburg, Indiana.

David P. Murray is professor of Old Testament and practical theology at Puritan Reformed Theological Seminary in Grand Rapids, Michigan.

Hughes Oliphant Old is the John H. Leith Professor of Reformed Theology and dean of the Institute for Reformed Worship at Erskine Theological Seminary in Columbia, South Carolina.

Anthony T. Selvaggio is a teaching elder in the Reformed Presbyterian Church of North America and a member of the Rochester Reformed Presbyterian Church (Rochester, New York), where he contributes regularly to the preaching ministry. He is also a visiting professor at the Reformed Presbyterian Theological Seminary, Pittsburgh, Pennsylvania, and at the Ottawa Theological Hall, Ottawa, Canada.

Derek Thomas is the John E. Richards Professor of Systematic and Practical Theology at Reformed Theological Seminary, Jackson, Mississippi, and also serves as minster of teaching at First Presbyterian Church in Jackson.

Rowland Ward is the minister of Knox Presbyterian Church of Eastern Australia, near Melbourne.

Malcolm H. Watts is minister of Emmanuel Church, Salisbury, England, and is also a visiting lecturer at London Reformed Baptist Seminary and at Puritan Reformed Theological Seminary, Grand Rapids, Michigan.